China's Economic Growth

Also by Terry Cannon

AT RISK: Natural Hazards, People's Vulnerability and Disasters (*with Piers Blaikie, Ian Davis and Ben Wisner*)

THE GEOGRAPHY OF CONTEMPORARY CHINA: The Impact of Deng Xiaoping's Decade (*editor with Alan Jenkins*)

China's Economic Growth

The Impact on Regions, Migration and the Environment

Edited by

Terry Cannon
Reader in Development Studies
University of Greenwich
London

First published in Great Britain 2000 by
MACMILLAN PRESS LTD
Houndmills, Basingstoke, Hampshire RG21 6XS and London
Companies and representatives throughout the world

A catalogue record for this book is available from the British Library.

ISBN 0–333–71659–0 hardcover
ISBN 0–333–71660–4 paperback

First published in the United States of America 2000 by
ST. MARTIN'S PRESS, INC.,
Scholarly and Reference Division,
175 Fifth Avenue, New York, N.Y. 10010

ISBN 0–312–23217–9

Library of Congress Cataloging-in-Publication Data
China's economic growth : the impact on regions, migration and the environment /
edited by Terry Cannon.
    p.   cm.
Includes bibliographical references and index.
ISBN 0–312–23217–9 (cloth)
1. China—Economic conditions—1976– 2. China—Environmental conditions. 3.
Rural–urban migration—China. I. Cannon, Terry.

HC427.92 .C45145617   2000
338.951—dc21
                                                                99–089961

Editorial matter, selection and Chapter 1 © Terry Cannon 2000
Chapters 2–13 © Macmillan Press Ltd 2000

This book is printed on paper suitable for recycling and made from fully managed and sustained
forest sources.

10   9   8   7   6   5   4   3   2   1
09   08   07   06   05   04   03   02   01   00

Printed and bound in Great Britain by
Antony Rowe Ltd, Chippenham, Wiltshire

Contents

List of Figures

List of Plates

List of Maps

List of Tables

Preface

The majority of chapters in this volume were originally presented as papers at a major session (sponsored by the Developing Areas Research Group) of the annual conference of the Institute of British Geographers/ Royal Geographical Society (Glasgow, January 1996). Although there is always the danger in collecting conference papers that they are not going to form a very coherent whole, in fact I consider this book to be a good and well-integrated survey of some key geographical issues. The conference session itself was clearly focused on two main themes that are of crucial importance for most geographers – spatial processes (especially regionalisation, demography and migration) (Part I), and the environment (Parts II and III). And there is also another self-organising theme to many of the papers: most of those in Parts I and II concentrate on the impact of the economic reforms of the past twenty years, and how these have affected space and nature.

There was also a very pleasant surprise in convening the conference in the 'discovery' of a number of physical geographers working in various remote parts of China, most of whose work does not normally enter into the arena of China studies (Part III of the book). Their work is of such significance that it really deserves a volume of its own, and it is to be hoped that their research will become available in monographs or other forms soon. The access that they have to parts of the country that are normally not open to foreigners is of great significance for the extension of our knowledge of China. That their work is conducted largely separately from that of other 'China specialists' is something that we might hope is resolved by both sides of the divide that unfortunately operates between much physical and human geography.

One of the less positive things revealed by the conference is the dearth of people working on China in British geography. By contrast, the number of geographers in the Association of American Geographers (AAG) China Speciality Group is more than 120, and at the 1998 annual conference held in Boston there were over 40 papers presented on China. In part this reflects a reasonable number of people of Chinese origin in US academia, including a much larger presence of postgraduate students from the PRC and Taiwan, a significant proportion of whom remain in the US in teaching or research positions. But it also indicates the lack of interest in, or promotion of, the study of China generally in Britain. The number of specialists on China in all subject areas is far lower than other countries in Europe, and this suggests that the high figures for the USA are not simply a function of the larger population size. A survey of China specialists in Europe by the International Institute for Asian Studies (University of Leiden, The Netherlands) found that Britain had many fewer respondants than France (with an equivalent population) or even The Netherlands (with about a quarter of Britain's population). Given the undoubted crucial significance of China for the next century, this situation seems to be a sign of Britain's dangerous unpreparedness in terms of the knowledge base that seems essential. Perhaps this book will provide some of the resources that may encourage greater study of China at school and university level.

Given that the conference was in 1996, some of the chapters have been updated for this publication, which is appearing after considerable delay due mainly to illnesses and bereavement in my family. I appreciate the authors' patience in the long wait for the appearance of their work. Not all of the presenters at the conference were able to contribute to this book, and so I have included a few other chapters by people whose work I knew was highly relevant to the themes of the book.

TERRY CANNON

Note on Chinese Terms

Chinese words are transcribed in the pinyin system that is now widely used in foreign language writing about the People's Republic, and which is officially approved.

The currency is referred to as the yuan, which is its principal unit. The term *renminbi* is sometimes used as the name of the currency, meaning 'people's money'.

The spelling Yangtze River is used, though it is sometimes spelt Yangzi in official Chinese English-language materials. This is the same river as the Chang Jiang (or Changjiang), and the two names are sometimes used to refer to different reaches of the river.

The common term for unit of land area in China is *mu* (sometimes *mou*). There are about 15 *mu* in a hectare.

Notes on the Contributors

Andrew P. Barton was a postgraduate researcher at the University of Wolverhampton, and is completing his PhD thesis on the Yunnan Project. He currently works for FRCA, Reading.

Terry Cannon is Reader in Development Studies at the University of Greenwich. He has published widely on various aspects of post-Mao China, and was joint editor (with Alan Jenkins) of *The Geography of Contemporary China* (Routledge, 1990), a textbook on the impact of the economic reforms. His current research is on the regional consequences of the reforms and the interaction of spatial processes with political and economic actors. In addition, he works on social factors in disasters, and was co-author of *At Risk: Natural Hazards, People's Vulnerability and Disasters* with Piers Blaikie, Ian Davis and Ben Wisner (Routledge, 1994). Contact: School of Humanities, University of Greenwich, London SE18 6PF. Email: t.g.cannon@greenwich.ac.uk

Ian G. Cook is Professor of Human Geography, and Head of Geography and of Pacific Rim Studies at Liverpool John Moores University. His teaching and research interests in China focus on urban and regional issues, environmental tensions, and the steel industry. Recent publications include: *Fragmented Asia: Regional Integration and National Disintegration in Pacific Asia* (co-editor with M. Doel and R. Li, Avebury, 1996) and *Dynamic Asia: Business, Trade and Economic Development in Pacific Asia* (co-editor, with M. Doel, R. Li and Y. Wang, Ashgate, 1998), *China's Third Revolution, Tensions in the Transition to Post-Communist China* (with G. Murray, Curzon Press, forthcoming, 2000). His interest in Geographical Education is realised as a main author (with others) of *Geography in Focus* (Causeway Press, forthcoming, 1999). Contact: Human Geography Section, School of Social Sciences, Liverpool John Moores University, 15–21 Webster Street, Liverpool L3 2ET. Email: socicook@livjm.ac.uk

Delia Davin is Head of East Asian Studies Department at the University of Leeds. She lived in China for several years in the 1960s and 1970s, and has published extensively on Chinese society. Her most recent book is *Internal migration in Contemporary China* (Macmillan,

1999). Contact: Department of East Asian Studies, University of Leeds, Leeds LS2 9JT. Email: D.Davin@leeds.ac.uk

Richard Louis Edmonds is Senior Lecturer in the Geography Department of the School of Oriental and African Studies, University of London. He is author of *Patterns of China's Lost Harmony: A Survey of the Country's Environmental Degradation and Protection* (Routledge, 1994). He has published many chapters and papers on China, and is currently editor of *China Quarterly*. He is editor of *Managing the Chinese Environment* (Oxford University Press, 1999). Contact: Department of Geography, School of Oriental and African Studies, Thornhaugh Street, London WC1H 0XG. Email: RE2@soas.ac.uk

Mike Fullen is Reader in Soil Science in the School of Applied Sciences at the University of Wolverhampton and is UK Co-ordinator of the Yunnan Project. Contact: School of Applied Sciences, University of Wolverhampton, Wulfruna Street, Wolverhampton WV1 1SB. Email: M.Fullen@wlv.ac.uk

Lin Gan is Senior Research Fellow at the Centre for International Climate and Environmental Research, Oslo. His research interests include social science aspects of energy and environmental policy making and implementation in China and Asia, climate-change policy and institutional dynamics, international development assistance for the environment, and dynamics of energy and environmental technological change and dissemination in developing countries. Contact: Centre for International Climate and Environmental Research-Oslo P.O. Box 1129 Blindern, N-0317 Oslo, Norway. E-mail: lin@cicero.uio.no

David Higgitt is at the Geography Department of the University of Durham. As a geomorphologist his main research interest is in the development of techniques for the assessment of soil erosion and sedimentation. He joined an undergraduate expedition to the karst landscapes of Guangxi and Guizhou provinces, and has since been involved in a number of projects concerned with soil erosion assessment and land evaluation in China. This has included fieldwork in the Loess Plateau, the Three Gorges region, and Fujian and Jiangxi provinces. He has also led student expeditions to Guangxi on behalf of Brathay Exploration Group. Collaborating institutions in China have included Nanjing University, the Institute of Soil Science (Nanjing), the Institute of Mountain Disaster and Environment (Chengdu), the Institute of Loess and Quaternary Research (Xian) and Guilin College of Geology. Contact: Department of Geography, University of Durham, Science Laboratories, South Road, Durham DH1 3LE. Email: D.L.Higgitt@durham.ac.uk

Trevor J. Hocking is Professor of Applied Biology (specialising in crop science) and Associate Dean of Applied Sciences at The University of Wolverhampton.

Caroline Hoy is Lecturer in the Department of Geography at the University of Dundee in Scotland. Her research interests include fertility and migration behaviour, population policies, and wider development issues in China. Contact: Department of Geography, University of Dundee, Dundee DD1 4HN, Scotland. Email: c.s.hoy@dundee.ac.uk

Liu Liguang is Professor of Agronomy at Yunnan Agricultural University and the Chinese Co-ordinator of the Yunnan Project. Contact: Faculty of Agricultural Science and Technology, Yunnan Agricultural University, PO Box 650201, Yunnan Province, People's Republic of China.

Mahmoud Messkoub is Lecturer in Economics at the Leeds University Business School, Leeds University. His research interests include the economics of migration, the macroeconomic impact of population ageing and the social impact of structural adjustment programmes. Contact: Leeds University Business School, University of Leeds, ESS Building, Leeds LS2 9JT, England. Email: m.messkoub@leeds.ac.uk

David J. Mitchell is Senior Lecturer in Hydrology in the School of Applied Sciences at The University of Wolverhampton.

Richard Sanders is Senior Lecturer in international and development economics at University College, Northampton, and coordinator of the China Centre there. He has researched extensively in the Chinese countryside in recent years, his main research interests being rural environmental protection and sustainable agriculture. Contact: School of Business, University College Northampton, Park Campus, Broughton Green Road, Northampton NN2 7AL, England. Email: richard.sanders@northampton.ac.uk

Christopher J. Smith is Professor and Chair of the Department of Geography and Planning, and Professor of East Asian Studies, at the

University at Albany, State University of New York. He is an urban geographer who has specialised in studies of urban social problems, including health and healthcare delivery, homelessness, and mental illness. In more recent work he has been looking at some of the human consequences of China's transition out of socialism, with a particular emphasis on the social and cultural implications of modernisation in the largest cities, especially mass migration from the countryside. His recent publications include a number of articles dealing with migration and health care delivery issues in Chinese cities, as well as *China: People and Places in the Land of One Billion* (HarperCollins/Westview Press, 1999). Contact: Department of Geography and Planning, University at Albany, State University of New York, 1400 Washington Avenue, SS340, Albany, NY 12222, USA. Email: cjsmith@cas.albany.edu

Andrew Spencer was Lecturer in Geography at the National University of Singapore, and subsequently taught at the Transport Studies Group at the University of Westminster. More recently he has lectured in Transport Economics at City University Business School and also works as a freelance researcher and consultant. He has published several articles on transport planning and policy issues, particularly in relation to East Asia and other developing areas. Contact: 78 Limbury Road, Luton, Bedfordshire LU3 2PL, England. Email: a.spencer@pop.net.ntl.com

John G. Taylor is Professor of Politics at South Bank University. He is the author of several books, notably *From Modernisation to Modes of Production* (Macmillan, 1979), *The Sociology of Developing Societies: Southeast Asia* (Macmillan, 1988), and *Indonesia's Forgotten War: the Hidden History of East Timor* (Zed Books, 1991). During the early 1990s, he directed a project on environmental issues in Wuhan, funded by the UK Economic and Social Research Council. The present article presents some of the results of this research. Contact: Faculty of Health and Social Sciences, South Bank University, London SE1 0AA, England. Email: taylorjb@sbu.ac.uk

David Watts is Reader in Geography at the University of Hull. He is a biogeographer and was founder editor (now senior editor) of the *Journal of Biogeography*. His main research area is the Caribbean but he also has interests in Korea and China. Among his many publications are *Man's Impact on the Vegetation of Barbados, 1627–1800* (1966), *Principles of Biogeography* (1971), *The West Indies: Patterns of Development, Culture and Environmental Change Since 1492* (1987/1990). Contact:

School of Geography and Earth Resources, University of Hull, Hull HU6 7RX. Email: d.watts@geo.hull.ac.uk

Wu Bo Zhi is Dean of Agronomy at Yunnan Agricultural University.

Xia Zheng Yuan is a research scientist at Yuxi Experimental Station and completed his MSc thesis on the Yunnan Project.

Xie Qingshu is Lecturer in the Urban Economic Management, Department of Central China Normal University, Wuhan. He is the author of articles in Chinese on environmental policies in Wuhan, and on national environmental issues.

Zheng Yi is Associate Professor of Soil Science at Yunnan Agricultural University.

Zhou Yue is at the Yunnan Institute of Geogrpahy, and completed his PhD at the University of Hull in 1997. Contact: Yunnan Institute of Geography, 20 Xuefu Road, Kunming 650223, Yunnan, People's Republic of China. Email: yuezhou@public.km.yn.cn

1

Introduction – The Economic Reforms, Demographic Processes and Environmental Problems

Terry Cannon

China presents its own people and the rest of the world with a quite bewildering complexity, not only because of its size and variation, but also owing to the rapid pace of change. This book is an attempt at making some sense of a few key aspects of these complexities, through the research of a group of people (most of them geographers in Britain) working on various components of the demographic, regional and environmental systems.

For the most part what we see in the following chapters are a range of varied topics (as would be expected from the presentations at a conference), almost all of which seek to describe and explain an aspect of what has happened under the impact of the economic reforms of the past two decades. This post-1979 period has produced within this one country a series of economic and political shifts that amount to one of the most significant historical changes the world has ever seen. (When they will cease to be considered ongoing reforms and regarded as a new economic phase never seems to be considered.) During the space of just a few years in the early 1980s, practically all farmland was transferred from collective units under the People's Communes into family and individually controlled smallholdings. Coincident with this shift was the 'Open-Door' policy, which greatly increased foreign trade and encouraged a massive rise in inward investment. This also gave priority to economic growth in the coastal region, initially symbolised by the special economic zones (SEZs) and the other 'Open Cities' designated in the early and mid-1980s. These processes have been well described in the literature (see for instance Yang 1997; Cannon and Jenkins 1990) and now seem to belong in the past. But in fact the impacts and

2

Map 1.1 Location map of China and its provinces. Note that in 1997 Sichuan was divided and a new province of Chongqing created around that city in the eastern part.

consequences for migration, for regional and *local* development and for the environment are still being felt. It is these processes that are the subject of most of this book.

The changes in the rural sector, which also gave such a boost to local industry (especially township and village enterprises – TVEs), have changed forever the ways in which people use (and abuse) the land and all other natural resources, including water, forests and rangelands. They have also fundamentally altered the relationships of the people to the land in terms of control, ownership and rights of use. There are also new opportunities for the rural population to migrate to an extent quite impossible under Mao Zedong's leadership. But the risks people take, whether they migrate or not, are also much greater, since by and large they must now fend for themselves. There has been a devastating reduction of welfare and social safety nets in the countryside. In short, the rural economy is now in the midst of a deep social change in which there are many more individualised actors than before, together with many layers of 'local entrepreneurial states' that vie for control over land and other resources, labour, capital and government favours. The interactions of individuals and local governments and enterprises, and the actions of various levels of the state (which still controls a sizeable section of the economy), all combined with the impacts of foreign commercial interests, have created an economy that is unrecognisable in comparison with just twenty years ago.

The various ways in which this new economy operates in space and in relation to the environment have produced a corresponding new geography. Indeed, one way to interpret the impacts of the reforms is by evaluating those spatial and environmental changes. Tracking the impacts of the reforms in economic and environmental space allows us to identify some of the most important processes inherent in the reforms. It also allows us to evaluate some of their consequences, both positive and negative.

A comprehensive survey of all the issues is not possible in this volume, though it does include some of the key components. The chapters here illustrate the way the reforms have altered the behaviour of certain individuals, groups and institutions, and how this has been expressed in spatial terms. The text includes analysis of the changes in activities of key actors in the following terms:

- individuals and institutions, and how they are reacting to the new spatial opportunities and constraints (Chapters 3, 4 and 5 on migrants, attitudes to them, and their fertility behaviour);

- within enterprises of various types and levels, their fortunes in the reforms and their capacities to respond to and manipulate opportunities in the national and international systems (Chapters 6 and 8 on industry and government in Wuhan and Beijing, and in relation to foreign agencies);
- the actions of different levels of local government and their changing relations with various levels of the administrative hierarchy (Chapters 2, 4, 6 and 10 on regional development, migration, Wuhan, and ecological agriculture);
- how attempts to control negative impacts of economic growth on the environment are played out (Chapters 6, 8 and 10 on Wuhan, energy policies and farming);
- how environmental management issues have been altered through the reform period, either by the intensification of harmful activities by those seeking short-term gain, or by the changes in priority given to ameliorative policies, or their reduced chances of success under the new arrangements (Chapters 10, 11, 12 and 13 on village studies, and environmental damage in parts of the south and southwest);
- the way the drive for modernity and growth inherent in the reforms leads to contradictions such that environmentally beneficial practices are undermined (Chapter 9 on the importance of bicycles in city transport);
- how the Three Gorges Dam project (for flood control and electricity generation) has created political and environmental controversy and more than a million victims, despite its claim to be able to save lives and create cheap, clean energy (Chapter 7).

Background to the reforms

No one can have failed to notice that China in the 1990s is very different from what it was during the period up to twenty years ago. The Maoist era ran from 1958 (by which time the state-dominated economy was fully established) to 1978, two years after Mao Zedong's death. After 1979 significant changes became possible under a new leadership dominated by Deng Xiaoping, whose policies overthrew Maoist ideology.

The distinctiveness of the two periods is very important, not least since at a number of times between 1958 and 1989 there have been severe clashes related to the economic policies that underlay them. Economics is inherently political, and arguments in the Communist Party of China (CPC) over economic policies have led to conflicts and deaths within the CPC and among the population at large. Given the monopoly on power held by the CPC, there are no alternative places for such arguments to take place, and in effect this means that being on the defeated side has had much greater significance than having to spend some years on the opposition benches.

Yet unlike other authoritarian governments, including the 'crony capitalist' regimes or 'kleptocracies' found in parts of Asia and Africa, it is not easy to identify direct benefits that the rulers in China derive from their exercise of power. Perhaps very unusually in comparison with most of the world, arguments over economics and politics have had a curiously principled (but at times lethal) foundation. Leaders have genuinely argued over what they consider to be the best policies for the Chinese people, and not simply out of self-interest (in spite of the privileged lives that leaders have often enjoyed). In the process, the people themselves either have remained passive recipients of policy (revolution as something done to them, not by them) or have been involved as shock troops for various factions when some CPC leaders have invoked popular participation as a part of the ideological struggle (revolution as something that is 'permitted' by those above when they need mass support from below). At least that was the case for most of the Maoist period, and much of the first decade of the reforms. In the latter part of the reform process, independent and brave action by various groups of people in protest at exploitation, corruption and the lack of democracy has emerged in cities and countryside across China, and the CPC is facing some of the most determined (but disparate and uncoordinated) opposition it has ever seen.

What the reforms have unleashed is a different set of relationships between the CPC and the people, and between different levels of government. This is because the post-Maoist economy has produced not only much greater 'wealth' (over which there is more scope for dispute about its maldistribution and environmental costs) but also very different sets of economic actors. These new or transformed economic agents have at times been able to operate in the economic sphere at the expense of (or beyond the reach of) centralised power (both economic and political). Above all, the masses of people are no longer mere recipients of economic policies determined from above, which hitherto left them with very little room to manoeuvre and permitted very few options. They now have many more opportunities to act independently, within policy frameworks that allow for more private initiative.

The corollary, however, is that additional opportunities also involve greater risk-bearing by individuals, both on their own account and by being in effect abandoned by higher-level authorities that previously bore some responsibility for them. For instance, many of the enterprise units under government control, and local governments themselves, have been absolving themselves of accountability for collective welfare and social support mechanisms. Instead they seek to maximize internal benefits and reduce their own wider social responsibilities.

The themes of this book are concerned with two main areas in which the changed behaviour of various actors has affected the geography of the country. The reconfiguring of society and economy has given rise both to the emergence of changed behaviour of existing actors and the arrival on the scene of whole new sets of actors. The studies in this book allow us to analyse some of their geographical impacts. The new behaviour of old actors, and the emergence of new actors, has brought with it new interactions in space and different uses of nature and the environment. The resulting economic and environmental landscape is markedly different from the period before 1979. Until then the CPC exercised enormous influence over political, economic and environmental space, operating under the assumption that its control of space was legitimated by the needs of the revolution and its consolidation. That centralised control has been relinquished under the reforms, and regaining it is much more difficult than losing it.

Making sense of China

The world's most populous country (with more than 1.2 billion people in 1998), China still has a very high percentage of people on low incomes, and at least 60 per cent of them dependent on rural livelihoods. Yet it has nuclear weapons, is capable of launching satellites, and competes in the world market in manufacturing advanced electronic equipment. Since the reforms, China's cities have begun to resemble many of those in other developing countries, with emerging shanty towns, widespread begging and traffic chaos. Despite this, visitors often comment that it seems quite different from their impressions of much of Africa, Latin America and other parts of Asia, and that China has much less evident urban squalor and poverty.

Yet the impression that China is different is a feature of outsiders' reactions to the country since the early 1970s. Although this was partly a product of the government's own 'public relations' activities and information management, there are some very significant differences between China and other countries of the Third World (though of course there is a danger in lumping all less developed countries together in a category like this). China, rightly or wrongly, both deliberately and unwittingly, has conveyed an image of itself as a country that in key respects has been an economic success. In other words, although the

Chinese government has not been afraid of calling itself a Third World country, it seems to be different. What is interesting is that this perceived difference is independent of any particular set of policies or periods of economic change.

It is also difficult to relate China to any of the categories or groupings into which other countries are often put. Although in recent years some outsiders have tried to put China into the (in part mutually contradictory) boxes labelled 'Transition Economies', 'Newly Industrialising Countries' (NICs), 'East Asian Tigers', or 'Emerging Market Economies', there are key differences that make it rather an exception. These impositions of external 'wish-fulfilment' (the category is often tied to a theory of what has been the reason for the 'success' of that set of countries) relate to several factors. One in particular is the role of the state in regard to economic growth: China's is certainly an interventionist state, but with a crucial role for the *local state as well as the centre* that makes it difficult to link with other East Asian state-led models.

A further problem lies in the character of the markets that have emerged: there are many non-market phenomena that have promoted growth, and many economic actors whose behaviour differs considerably from the norm of profit-seeking enterprises (Cannon and Zhang 1996). More generally, the particular attributes of the transition in China are quite different from any other transition economy (in eastern Europe or Asia) – even if we could be certain about what the transition is supposedly *towards*. The way the reforms have affected the economic behaviour of various groups of people and other economic entities is crucial and significantly different from elsewhere. In fact, it is really difficult to speak of China as a transition economy, because the concept implies a process of change from a definitive set of economic characteristics (in particular central state planning and predominant state ownership) to a model liberalisation (with dominance for markets and private enterprise). In spite of the significance of markets and private enterprise, much of what is happening in the country departs from this caricature.

China has also long attracted outsiders as an example or model of what they have thought some or all of the rest of the world should do. Some saw China leading less-developed countries in the global conflicts engendered by the cold war. This role was suggested in part by the CPC's opposition to both superpowers during the Maoist years, and also significantly by its economic progress, which seemed to be superior to that of many other Third World countries. If economic progress between 1958 and 1978 could be ascribed to China remaining almost completely isolated from the world economy, and obeying neither Moscow nor Washington, then perhaps it was an alternative model of development others would find worthy of emulation?

In spite of this limited external approval, from 1979 there was a rush by the post-Mao leadership to overthrow the Maoist model of politics and economics, the very model that provided some outsiders with their positive image. Ironically, this has produced a new pattern of economic growth which suits the fantasies of those whose ideology is the diametrical opposite of the Maoists. In the new, entrepreneurial, market-oriented system established under the leadership of Deng Xiaoping, the real and supposed faults of egalitarianism have been cured, the inadequate production incentives have been replaced by individualistic rewards, and the wastefulness of political campaigns and spurious class-conflicts ended.

In the 1980s and 1990s, China has 'enjoyed' a period of rapid economic expansion in production and incomes. In general this has been enormously popular, at least until the late 1980s. The events of 1989, involving opposition to inflation, corruption and the lack of democracy, signalled the opening of various acute conflicts between the government and the people in both cities and countryside. In the 1990s these protests have been isolated and suppressed, despite being widespread and often violent. Yet they demonstrate that the economic reform model is now clearly capable of producing large numbers of losers and significant resentment at inequalities (Gittings 1996).

In respect of its economic growth, China has also been different from the rest of the world. For much of the 1980s and 1990s, its growth (at around 10 per cent per annum) has been much more rapid than that of practically every other country (and incidentally much faster than that of the first industrialised countries at the time of their industrial revolutions). This apparent success of the market, of entrepreneurship, and of the erosion of central planning, provides a model for many outsiders who argue that Third World problems arise from interventionist states, lack of markets and insufficient free enterprise. In other words, an entirely different set of people, espousing very different perspectives on what constitutes the best form of human progress, now hold up China as a model for development. This situation is compounded by the fact that China now exhibits significant differences from other countries that are still or were until recently ruled by communist governments. Unlike Russia and most of Eastern Europe, the economic reforms in China give the appearance of being successful. They also defy the belief that political reform must accompany changes in the economy. And unlike Vietnam, Cuba and North Korea, where communist or workers' party governments remain in power but the economies are in crisis, China has stayed communist-led and thrives (though China's critics in these other countries would argue that China's leaders have really abandoned communism).

Development and the links between economics and politics

This introduction tries to make some sense of this 'specialness' or exceptionalism of China, in the context of the distinctions between the Maoist and post-Mao periods, and in terms of the resulting differences in the configurations of economic and environmental space.

The positive developmentalism of Maoism was undermined by two factors. The first was the political structures that enforced it, through dictatorship over the people by a rigid party that acted in the name of the workers and peasants and invented its own view of what socialism should be. This also prevented feedback messages from the production units on how the economy was functioning, making it more difficult to modify policies. In a planned economy, where the success of political leaders is measured in terms of target fulfilment, there are many incentives to cook the books. The reporting of false successes to please superiors in the party power structure was commonplace. The worst case concerned exaggerated food production data in the Great Leap Forward of 1958–61, which exacerbated deaths in a famine that claimed between 13 and 30 million lives by masking the need for emergency action and relief. (Problems with official statistics remain serious. Within the past five years, and partly in the context of the controversy about the Lester Brown report on whether China can feed itself, the government announced that China in fact has around 25 per cent more arable land than it thought. While possibly good news for future food output, this also undermines confidence in the ability of the country to produce the relatively high yields per hectare that are also necessary for success.) (Brown 1995).

The second factor (and one connected to the first) was the rigidity of economic thinking, which limited the range of policies that could be tried even when it was evident that there were problems. The party ranks would close to exclude anyone (often with crushing consequences for the individuals or groups labelled 'capitalist-roaders' in such situations) who went against the orthodoxy. As a result, policies could not easily be changed to respond to problems, nor be altered in either the internal or the external sphere for fear that supporters of change would be accused. In such situations involving authoritarian party hierarchies, the role of an individual leader (to whom loyalty is the basis of survival for underlings) is highly significant, even though much Marxist writing suggests it is not. It was therefore two years after Mao's death before opposition within the CPC could make its mark and overthrow his imprint on the economy.

These points illustrate a theme vital for understanding China: the character of development (and of the economy in general) is so intrinsically connected with politics that it is impossible to separate discussion of the two spheres. This link of course exists in all countries. But in China it is expressed more forcefully, especially through the role and function of the state and the party that controls it. The state has been able to dominate much more of the economy – directly through ownership and control, and indirectly through its power structure as already indicated – than in most other countries. From 1958 until 1978, practically all the productive resources, in farming, forests, pasture, mining, industry and transport, were 'owned' by local, provincial or national representatives of the state. In almost every one of these production units, from the village level to the central ministries, their amateur (CPC) leaders or professional managers have been subjected to control by a CPC general secretary, appointed by the party to ensure compliance with party policy and ideology. This framework has had enormous consequences for the organisation of space, and the utilisation of the environment, and the fairly sudden shift from one system to the other after 1979 means that the processes of change are especially noticeable.

It is clear that both sets of policies (crudely, the Maoist and the Dengist) have benefits and problems inherent to them. In attempting to solve the difficulties of Maoism, the Dengist reformers have substituted a different set of problems. Making judgements about the relative merits of policies should take account of these new difficulties, as well as of the benefits. Each person's view of the balance of virtues and demerits is often related to an ideal or belief, and it is often very difficult to make an 'objective' evaluation of such a balance. This is compounded by the fact that very often we observe implementation of policies that are intended to bring about objectives some time into the future. So inevitably, a degree of faith is involved in their design and in anticipating their fruition. People differ in what they regard as the most important facets of human existence. But there are also primary disagreements about the means of achieving progress, and the relative merits of cooperation or individualism in the process. There may also be differences about how future benefits should be balanced with present-day consumption or sacrifice (crudely, the difference between spending, saving and investment, and how income is distributed to determine which social groups make sacrifices).

So some faith or belief is usually involved in the design and implementation of development policies, and they often involve an assumption about the character of human nature. In China the shift in policies since 1979 involves an almost complete policy reversal in the way 'human nature' is conceived. This has involved a shift from the idea that there is an inherent capacity to cooperate and realise the benefits of collectivism, to an explicit acceptance that self-seeking and profit- (or private-income-) maximising behaviour is not only proper for individuals but also efficient for the satisfaction of wider social needs. It is as well to be explicit about this, since such disagreements are at the root of much human conflict; they have perhaps been more explicitly contentious in China than in much of the world, and for outsiders China has therefore been a sort of laboratory for conflicting arguments about both ideology and human nature.

This volume is concerned with the configuration of economic and social space and the relationship of people to the environment. These must be understood in the context of this fundamental shift in attitudes to the balance between present and future. We need also to evaluate the change in people's behaviour, which has been modified to shift from self-effacement and collectivism ('shared poverty', but with a welfare safety net of sorts) to a system of self-satisfaction and individualism (with increased exposure to risks and uncertainties). This shift has profound consequences for where people live, how they circulate in geographical space, how different levels of government and enterprise behave, and how all these interact with the environment. The ability of people, local governments and enterprises to act in self-seeking ways has had immense significance for space and environment, so that the reform period is marked by the reconfiguration of these uses of space and environment in very different and/or more intensified ways than before.

Economic growth versus development

Economic growth involves crude measures of how the production of all goods and services in an economy is increased by two means. First is the utilisation of resources (such as labour, or nature) or capital (savings) that are underused (or able to be extracted from the environment); the second involves increasing the output (of a given quality) per unit of resource used in the production process. The first is, then, about bringing into play resources that are under-utilised (for various reasons), and can be called the utilisation problem; the second is about raising productivity and can be called the productivity problem. Each of these has implications for the distribution of income and assets, gender relations, environmental use and abuse, and regional variations.

We can consider economic growth to be a complex mix of these two utilisation and productivity components, and it is useful to try and understand the influences of the different factors involved in each. The 'mix' is heavily influenced by the level and types of technology available, the ideology that underlies the operation of the economy, and the degree of state intervention (and how effective it is). However, it has to be kept in mind that these issues are highly contentious, since for those who advocate growth above all else, the 'distortions' (unequalised distribution of income and assets, worsening gender relations, environmental damage and regional inequalities) that these problems represent are regarded as temporary, and/or reasonable costs to be expended for the wider gains. To remedy these problems, it is argued, would undermine overall growth at the expense of a larger proportion of the population.

Critics of such views argue that phenomena like inequality, uneven asset control, gender disparity and environmental damage cannot be considered temporary, and that the measuring of the costs is itself biased and a characteristic of the priorities inherent in the economic growth paradigm. They would argue that the negative consequences of growth strategies are measured differently according to who you are and where you live, and how you give weight to future needs. For instance, we need to understand in what ways women have to bear more or different kinds of burdens compared with men in the growth process, and the manner in which environmental resources are used to generate short-term growth as a substitute for other forms of growth and development.

These criticisms of the priority given to growth over development (a process which should involve the improvement of all peoples' lives) are well known in the development studies literature, and by many ordinary people engaged in popular protests against unequal development in many parts of the world. There are basically four reasons for this: first, just because an economy is growing does not mean that all its people share in the benefits of that growth; second, 'progress' in terms of economic growth normally entails the organisation of production such that there is considerable mismatch between what is produced and what is needed by the majority; third, gender inequality is often a significant component of the growth process; fourth, the negative impacts on the environment reduce human well-being (e.g. through health problems) and may jeopardise future generations' livelihoods through damage to resources.

These four sets of issues are often seen as the key differences distinguishing growth from development, and can be summarised as the distribution problem, the priorities problem, the gender problem and the sustainability problem. The first two emerged as critiques of Third World development theory and practice soon after World War II. The distribution issue involves not only how income is shared by the population, but also how assets and access to resources (including land and natural resources) are reorganised (and reallocated) during the growth process, and what impact this has on different groups in terms of their livelihoods. The distribution problem then overlaps with the issue of how priorities are defined, for whom growth is organised, how the structure of power operates, and for whose benefit. These issues have been of particular importance in China, where access to land and other resources for hundreds of millions of peasants and others have been radically altered during the reforms.

Concern about gender and environmental impacts, the third and fourth problems, did not emerge significantly in the world until the 1970s. (China in fact initiated its development under communism with a determination to avoid the distribution and priority problems, and with some concern for gender issues. As in other communist-led countries, environmental problems were not considered important before the last fifteen years). A fifth set of issues concerning the unequal regional distribution of growth has constituted a further area of controversy in some countries, and is of particular significance in China. Unequal regional patterns may result from the uneven distribution of economic activities across a country's territory, and the variations in the impact of growth on different places. This regional inequality problem is particularly significant in the critiques of uneven regional development that have been made within China (see Yang 1997).

In this volume, much of the discussion relates to the evaluation of growth in terms of the problems of priority, sustainability, gender, and regional inequality. To enter this type of analysis it seems that it is not so helpful to ask 'What is happening to the environment in China', or 'What are the regional consequences of the reforms'. Rather we need to know 'Why are environmental issues dealt with the way they are, who is involved in causation and amelioration, when and why did they get involved, and how and why is it different now from how it was in the past?' and 'Why and how is economic space being restructured, who are the new agents involved and how are they acting?'. It seems that most discussions of China's environmental problems and spatial restructuring give little attention to the significance of various actors' roles in the definition of problems, analysis of causality, designation of institutional responses, allocation of negative and positive outcomes of both the problems and proposed solutions.

One significant example of the problems arising from these gaps in the literature (which the contributions to this volume help to redress) is the almost complete neglect of the way environmental resources are reallocated and transferred between different sets of users, with clear losers and winners. Emphasis on 'environmental problems' distracts from the class, gender and 'ethnic' (involving China's 'national minorities') reallocation issues. Some light may be shed on this by making more explicit the different discourses operating in the category labelled 'environment'. Problem diagnosis and the associated remedies depend on the position of different actors and their differing modes of analysis of the environment and its problems. They will depend on the quality of science in investigation and analysis, but more significant are social and economic frameworks in which diagnosis and remedy are formulated. These include economic interest groups (national and international), classes of user and beneficiary (and sometimes losers, though these are often disempowered), institutions involved in doing the diagnosis or designing policies, and the state and its degree of openness to critical thought. Environmental critics in China run the danger of inclusion in the list of 'counter-revolutionaries', as announced by the Public Security Bureau in the mid-1990s. (MI5 in the UK announced that it would also include environmental protesters in its remit at around the same time!)

In other words, environmental diagnosis and the design of remedial policies involves examining the different ways the issues are perceived and their solutions proposed in terms of current user interests, potential user interests, the balance of power between different users and potential users, institutional capacities of various players, characteristics of the state. (Is it a player? Is it regulatory? Is it competent in its reach and action? Is it repressive?) How do different sources of explanation and related remedies tie in with diverse interests? The different analyses affect the way diagnosis is done, who engages in it, how empowered their analysis is, and what policy consequences arise – if any. It is interesting how since 1998, after the worst floods in China for more than a century, some members of the government have finally become willing to blame deforestation in the catchment of the various river systems. Hitherto, this viewpoint has been restricted to environmentalist critics of the impacts of the reforms, while government has been content to imply that the serious flooding of recent years is natural, thus distancing the problems from being the result of economic policies, and hence bringing the remedies within the sphere of operation of the state through some technical control mechanism like the Three Gorges Dam (with the additional potential benefit of attracting foreign aid).

The reforms and economic actors

In order to understand the way the economic reforms have reconfigured economic space and the environment, we need to know how to distinguish the various categories of actors who function in relation to that space and to environmental resources, and how this differs from what occured in the pre-reform period. In other words, we need to know what new actors have emerged as a result of the reforms (i.e. people and institutions whose behaviour has altered as a result of the change in economic framework resulting from the reforms). In addition we need to know how the 'old' actors fare in these new circumstances, and what changes (and difficulties) they face in pursuing previous (or new) patterns of behaviour. It is also helpful to distinguish 'passive' and 'active' actors: those who have to respond to impacts of the reforms with little choice or few bargaining weapons, as contrasted with those who have control over resources or the ability to use their power or privilege to stake significant claims.

The story of the reform decades can be traced through the emergence of such new groups, the eclipse of old actors, and the shifts in fortunes of those who were significant in the pre-reform period and have the opportunity to transform their actions. The capacity to be active or passive may have shifted over time, and depends in part on the qualifications of different individuals and institutions, their command over assets, their access to credit, their ability to 'mine' nature, and the property rights that can be exercised as the basis for such claims and access. The shifting fortunes of individuals and groups arise in part out of the competition for these assets or income, or the economic conflicts and contradictions that arise out of the pattern of behaviour established under the dominant economic framework.

Old and new actors, economic space and the environment

The Maoist political economy was in many respects more straight-forward than that of the subsequent reforms. In some ways the country had a classic dual economy, with an urban sector that was largely iso-lated from the vast majority of people living in the countryside. There were of course interchanges of materials between these two sectors. These consisted especially of the supply of manufactured goods from (mainly) urban enterprises to agriculture (especially producer goods like fertiliser, farm equipment, and some simple consumer goods) and of foodstuffs and industrial crops going to the manufacturing sector in the cities from the communes.

Under central planning, the administrative prices used in this ex-change did not relate to concepts of markets and supply and demand. There is contention (and confusion), which cannot be further discussed here, as to whether this dual economy involved an unequal exchange in which the rural population was exploited for the benefit of the urban sector. Suffice it to say that the urban population during the Maoist period consistently enjoyed higher living standards in terms of both incomes and welfare benefits. The income and welfare benefits (such as cheap housing, medical care and education) were derived mostly from wages in the state-owned enterprises sector (SOEs), which was (apart from remote mining operations) virtually congruent with the towns and cities (so that it is reasonable in this period to speak of the urban sector as if it were the industrial sector).

There was virtually no flow of labour between the two sectors, and rural residents were prevented from moving to even small towns in their area, let alone larger cities. Indeed, during some periods of the Maoist era, the flows were in the opposite direction, with both the compulsory return of migrants who entered cities in the 1950s and the rustication of urban youth during parts of the cultural revolution of 1966–76 (Kirkby 1985). The main rationale for this separation of town and countryside was the ideology of self-reliance, and the prop-erty rights system that allocated ownership and control of land and resources differently in the rural and urban sectors. Arable land was in theory under state ownership, but in practice it was under the control of the production brigades that were subsidiaries of the People's Communes. So long as obligations to fulfil state quotas on agricultural produce were fulfilled, the central authorities had little interest in the administration of rural affairs. In effect, rural self-reliance removed from the state any serious responsibility for peasants' welfare, and the property rights system enabled surplus to be extracted from them through quotas and the pricing system rather than through taxation.

Self-reliance in many senses can be regarded as a laudable objective for rural development. But it also imposed a heavy burden on resource-poor areas. They were in effect condemned to perpetual hunger and poverty if they were unable to produce adequate quantities of food, or of other surplus produce with which to earn money. And the restrictions on migration meant they were unable to shed labour to wage-earning opportunities elsewhere. Ironically, the early rural reforms of 1980 that established the Responsibility System (the redistribution of the collective's land into small parcels under the control of families, described in Chapter 10) were intended to assist such areas, but were soon applied everywhere. The situation of poorer areas has not changed much, except that they can now export labour.

By contrast, the SOEs were under direct state ownership (at either national or provincial level) partly in order to protect the state's own revenue: practically all central and provincial government budgetary expenditures were financed out of taxes and levies extracted from SOEs (whether they were 'profitable' or not). The significance of this is shown during the reforms by the central government's extreme reluctance either to grant greater autonomy to Shanghai or to allow its own special economic zone (SEZs). Shanghai provided a very significant share of total government revenues (around 10 percent), and to lose control of it would have been disastrous for the state. Meanwhile, Guangdong province, which surrounds Hong Kong, was able to initiate new investments and benefit from SEZs. Despite its rapid industrialisation, it had been insignificant for central government taxation, and this position did not substantially change until the late 1980s. It was also allowed considerable autonomy, as it was intended to perform a confidence-building role in respect of foreign and overseas Chinese capitalists.

In other words, variations in the economic performance and characteristics of different areas of the country in part depended on the way that different actors (in this case governments at provincial level and below) were able to respond to the new political economy of the reforms. How 'active' or 'passive' they could be is determined in part by the relationship of different levels of governments (a very significant set of actors) to the policy opportunities made available by the reforms. In effect, the capacity for local governments to be 'active' rather than 'passive' in economic terms has been one of the most significant shifts affecting actors' behaviour under the reforms. In the

Maoist system, the dominance of politics in determining peoples' and local authorities' actions meant that their status and vulnerability depended in large part on how well they performed in terms of current ideology. In a sense this meant that most actors were 'passive', and indeed one of the consequences of the Maoist system was to inculcate caution in the activities of many lower-level officials, who would prefer taking no action to the risk of doing the wrong thing. The reforms have not only increased the number and types of actors, but in part have done this by transforming previously passive actors into very active ones indeed.

Actors in economic space

Another key change in the way people and institutions respond in economic space is the degree to which they are 'atomised'. In the Maoist economy, peasant behaviour was confined to a narrow range of options, and the capacity of individuals to act independently was severely constrained by the institutional arrangements of the rural collectives (People's Communes). But from the early 1980s the Responsibility System meant that the rural population was atomised into millions of individuals or households who are now much more capable of being 'actors' in their own right. The Responsibility System meant that all the land (and most other production assets and equipment) was divided up and allocated to families. This started the process that broke the bond of peasants with the land, since only the labour necessary for farming needed to remain on this land. (Indeed, in cases where other opportunities were more rewarding, land has even been abandoned.) Thus was revealed the enormous surplus of labour not needed for agriculture alone that hitherto had been hidden by the sharing of work and incomes within the collectives. It is the mobility and opportunism of many millions of these individuals that has been mapped onto a new urban geography, as described in part in Chapters 2 to 5.

This newly atomised rural population has been restructured into new groups of actors whose behaviour has had profound effects in economic space, since for the first time in more than two decades tens of millions of people have become mobile. The main groups that can be identified from this process include:

- rural entrepreneurs in industry and services, many of whom were beneficiaries of the decollectivised assets (and often CPC leaders);
- migrant workers (with considerable gender differentiation – see Chapters 3, 4 and 5);

- those who remained in farming because they could succeed in the new market environment;
- those who were anchored to the soil through their lack of other options, including inadequate 'qualifications' for migration.

Key to understanding mobility behaviour is the removal of two previous restrictions on movement: the assignment of rights of residence, which specified that people were rural or urban (which effectively prevented any moves up the urban hierarchy); and the ration card, which could be used only in the unit to which people were assigned (their *hukou*). In the 1980s this 'fixing' of the rural population was undermined by the ending of the enforcement of the residence designation, and by the ability of migrants to find food and other essentials on the open market. It is these profound changes to the rural framework that released tens of millions of peasants onto the labour market, and lesser numbers into a wide range of entrepreneurial activities (both close to home and far away) that under Maoism would have been politically suicidal.

However, it is also important to note what happened to the institutions that had previously structured the rural system and acted as the economic and political interface with the state and higher-level local authorities. It is from this level of small towns and even villages that many manufacturing enterprises emerged in some areas of the country, especially in southern Jiangsu, northern Zhejiang, the Pearl River Delta, parts of Shandong, and in pockets of other coastal provinces such as Fujian. These township and village enterprises (TVEs) were able to thrive especially in parts of these provinces for reasons that vary significantly from place to place. In some areas (e.g. south Jiangsu and north Zhejiang) it was partly because of a tradition of commune-based rural industrialisation fostered during the Mao era. In the Pearl River Delta, it was the proximity of Hong Kong and the transfer from there of manufacturing jobs to towns that were within easy reach (for supervision and transport of materials and finished goods) and/or had kinship ties with Hong Kong capitalists.

The key point about these TVEs (and other new or refashioned enterprises at higher levels) is that although some of them could be considered private, the majority of them were effectively under the control of local government, or existed only within a framework of approval by those authorities. Discovering who actually 'owns' enterprises is notoriously difficult in China, and is partly a result of the legacy of danger attached to 'bourgeois' activities. But the main factor is that under the reforms, government officials in many areas transformed themselves into entrepreneurs or corporate managers. Their administrative and political functions enabled them to utilise the resources available within their boundary, including access to cheap credit from the banks (which continued to be state-owned). This phenomenon has given rise to the notion of the 'local developmental state' analogous with the concept of the developmental state often used in relation to the East Asian Newly Industrialising Countries (NICs). There are various versions of this type of analysis, which emphasis different characteristics of the localities. Jean Oi suggests the term 'local state corporatism' to indicate a convergence of political and economic power that serves local interests, with the local officials in effect managing enterprises (and opportunities) to maximise local benefits (Oi 1995).

In fact, the significance of local governments as new 'active' actors in economic space goes further up the hierarchy from villages to provinces themselves. For a variety of reasons, ranging from the abolition of the communes (for villages and townships) to the changes in financial relations between central government and the provinces and large cities, the reforms have enabled all levels of government below the centre to act so as to maximise local value-added, minimise revenue obligations to higher levels, and as far as possible to promote local economic activities. Crucial in this process has been the emphasis that the actors have placed on their own locality. It is place-specific development, with local leaders engaging in activites that grant as many benefits of growth as possible while accepting the least possible obligations or responsibilities. This form of economic behaviour derives from the property rights inherited from the Maoist system, a legacy that is absolutely crucial to understanding what is going on. Because local governments continue to *control* land and local resources even if the actual concept of *ownership* is muddled, it is certainly they and nobody else who could make claims on them. And because this legacy remained for existing enterprises, it was possible for them to retain that function to legitimate their control over *new* activities.

This localising inertia is also driven in part by the fact that success for party officials is now measured in terms of economic growth in their area, not in terms of politics or ideology. This means that success has a bounded local dimension, and is not such a political risk should there be a reversal of policies and renewed criticism of capitalist tendencies (a serious concern in the early days of the reforms). This localising of growth (or attempts at it, for it was not possible for it to succeed everywhere) also means that capital does not flow easily across the boundaries of different administrations, as this would mean it leaving official control and certainties behind.

Likewise, market-driven transfer of raw materials and finished products has not occurred in the way that would normally be expected in an economy that is supposedly in transition to capitalism. Instead, China's economic growth could be described as 'bounded localised development' (BLD) in which the administrative powers and functions available to each level of government under the Maoist system were manipulated and used to maximise local benefits within the boundary of each local administration under the new macro-political-economic framework. This administrative system consisted of a nested hierarchy of authorities, with each level owing allegiance (and economic obligations) to the next highest level. But with increased autonomy in this hierarchy, localities have sought to defend their own enterprises and resources. It is not surprising that the reform economy has been characterised by many forms of local protectionism alongside the development of market forces (Cannon and Zhang 1996; Yang 1997).

In addition to the atomised individuals, these 'institutional' players are the most important new or activated participants in the reform economy and territory, especially as entrepreneurs. Four main types of entrepreneurial actors can be identified whose actions can be understood within the BLD model (i.e. whose activities are mainly locally based, and are derived from inherited administrative powers, with more concern for maximising economic activity – turnover or value-added – than maximising profit). These are:

- SOEs administered by provincial government;
- provincial and city-level independent (new) enterprises;
- township and village enterprises (TVEs);
- private enterprises.

In addition to these, it is clearly also essential to know the position of both foreign capital and the central government. The centre was responsible for a large share of the industrial sector administered through the SOEs. Foreign direct investment (FDI) into the economy is a fairly new (post-1979) and very significant player under the reforms, but it is important to note that in almost every case foreign capital is tied into a joint venture, either with central SOEs or with one of the four categories of *local* actor.

Reformers, in awe of market, found it difficult to conceive a new role for the state in which it was not commanding the economy, but 'merely' providing the macroeconomic framework and regulation. The position of the central government is quite different from before the reforms. Under central planning it was the most significant of all economic actors, and operated in a relationship with lower-level authorities that amounted to negotiation and conflict over assets, investments and revenue extraction, based on both partnership and rivalry.

Under the reforms some of the factional struggle in the CPC has been between the Dengist reformers and those who would recentralise the economy in order to regain control over revenue. The reformers, having realised that ending central planning means giving power to lower-level authorities, have basically had to forgo much of the state's control over revenue in order to allow the other reforms to succeed. While this was a voluntary submission of power, necessary in order that the CPC maintain its legitimacy as the creator of the circumstances for economic growth, the corollary has been the diminution of the central government's own authority. Thereby the CPC has deprived itself of its capacity to manage economic affairs at the national level. Factionalism and opposition to the reforms within the CPC at the centre has therefore tended to focus on *some* of the economic consequences (especially the diminished capacity of the state in revenue terms) (Wang Shaoguang 1994) and some of the political consequences (especially 'moral pollution' by capitalism).

Below the national level, the congruence of political power and the acquisition of new economic power (in terms of revenue and control over new enterprises) has meant that local authorities enjoy a high degree of autonomy. Loyalty to the party has become more of an obligation to support economic growth in the relevant locality than of adhering to central government needs. There is another part of the bargain though, since the legitimacy at the local level is dependent on the capacity of the CPC to maintain rule at the national level. Those holding power locally derive their right to do so (and the crucial 'property rights' that allow them to control new as well as old enterprises) from the continuity of CPC authority at the centre. So there is a mutual need to shore up this hierarchy. In the words of Ye Xuanping, one-time governor of Guangdong, 'Beijing pretends to rule, we pretend to be ruled' (Wilson 1996, p. 300), a convenience that could be applied more widely.

Bounded localised development (BLD) is the consequence of quasi-government entrepreneurial entities using their inherited powers within their specified boundaries to create localised development. As a result, local administrations have emerged – at all levels of the hierarchy – as active actors whose administrative functions have enabled them to extend responsibility to new areas of industrial and commercial activity. Territorial identity and the boundaries that legitimate new economic activities have remained highly significant in a period when the transition to commercialisation would normally be expected to see a diminished role for government and the rise of clearly identifiable private ownership. Although local governments may not want 'loss-making' enterprises, they do want to keep control of profitable ones and to have the opportunity to start and keep the *new* ones. So there is little incentive to break the link between the functions of government and of enterprise, and this could be considered one of the factors that have led to the reluctance to make many SOEs bankrupt in the period up to the mid-1990s (after which, mass layoffs of workers in state-run enterprises, even at provincial level, became much more common). Actor behaviour is encouraged to seek forms of control that allows existing personnel and administrations to remain as beneficiaries.

Even the concept of loss-making is often difficult to unravel, as local authorities may maintain a collection of enterprises in a sort of holding company (ccompare Oi 1995) in which individual accounts are blurred. If local governments accede to the idea of privatisation (of successes) and bankruptcy (of failures), then they run the risk of losing control of everything. This would mean missing out on private benefits (for local leaders) and a diminished status in government. Although some individuals may make more money out of a privatised company if they control it, they also have to deal with risks, and the responsibilities of what happens if it all goes wrong. Actors who emerge from local authorities can remain in control of enterprises, so that they enjoy the benefits while bearing very little of the possible risks. Bounded localised development is in effect an unusual type of territorially defined economy peculiar to China under the reforms. It could even be named 'topocracy', or 'locality-derived power' (this term is used in a different context and continent by Reilly 1995, p. 259).

Topocracy, or BLD, has also led to another significant territorial issue. Since localised development can (sometimes) lead to protectionism and the inward-looking pursuit of commercial opportunities, it can also lead to a two-way process of administrative 'capture' and 'secession'. In order to maximise their own potential, higher-level authorities try to absorb and take greater command over subordinate administrative units. This is so that the higher-level units can try to increase their power, territory and access to resources. In the 1980s it was a means for larger towns and cities to enhance their control over food and staples. This led to the phenomenon of towns and cities claiming large areas of rural counties in their hinterland (with resulting confusion about the real percentage of urban population) (Kirkby 1985). One of the key economic advantages for local authorities in this 'capturing' process is increased access to revenues within their administrative boundary. Under the reforms, local authorities acquired much greater autonomy in determining what these could be used for and what proportion they were allowed to retain at the local level. This provided a significant incentive for higher-level authorities to capture lower levels where these were considered capable of generating resources.

However, this also worked in the other direction too, as a sort of secession. In order to enhance their revenue base and increase control over other resources, some local authorities have an incentive to devolve from higher levels, and establish themselves as a separate entity with correspondingly greater powers. Alternatively they may try to get promoted to a higher administrative level, something that is especially attractive if it places them within the threshold that grants particular powers available only at that level and above. Important examples of such 'threshold powers' are the rights to retain higher proportions of foreign exchange earnings, and the right to arrange foreign direct investment up to particular limits. In this way, a local authority can engineer matters so that they can enjoy benefits that otherwise were controlled by their superiors. That localised development is 'bounded' also means that where the boundaries are is highly significant, since these territorial markers are also the basis of so much of the economic activity and political legitimacy of the topocrats. So there are strong incentives to move the boundaries, or make new ones that grant greater power to a locality.

One of the most recent and significant examples of this is the separation of Chongqing from the province of Sichuan in 1997. This large city took with it an extensive chunk of the east of the province, and now has metropolitan (province-level) status on a par with Shanghai, Beijing and Tianjin. In return for its promotion, Chongqing is expected to have to take on the problems of the resettlement of the million and more people expelled from the reservoir area of the Three Gorges dam (see Chapter 7). In 1988 a similar province-level separation occurred when Hainan Island was established as a province in its own right, hived off from Guangdong. At the same time it was also granted SEZ status, making it by far the largest in the country. Similarly in the 1980s around thirty large cities like Wuhan were permitted to become 'separately planned cities', which allowed them more financial autonomy and reduced their subordination to provincial governments that had sought to milk them of revenues (these tensions are well illustrated in Chapter 6).

Topocracy involves several key factors that help to retain a distinct preference for local investment and restrict interactions between localities. These include the power of the CPC at the local level to continue its control over much of the *new* economic activity going on with the reforms, because of their inheritance of property rights through the *old* system of state ownership. Because the power of the local authority is strongly related to the revenue it can raise, rather than just the profits its enterprises earns, some localities may seek not to maximise profit but to maximise revenue or value-added. This is a further significant deviation from the supposed triumph of markets that is often cited as the main factor in China's rapid growth. Bounded localised development has also arisen from the need for trust and discipline that can arise from local control and investment under CPC auspices, which may be put at risk when economic activities operate at a greater distance and loyalties are uncertain.

It is important to assess at what stage China will see this system being *eroded* and the undermining of local control becoming significant. It will depend on changing conditions at the national policy level, and the impact of the aggregate development (and lack of it) through this localised model at other spatial levels. Some actors may be able to escape the restrictions inherent in BLD. Some local entrepreneurs will feel the need to escape from local controls, including those who are at a disadvantage compared with others who get better support from local cadres. The emergence of markets for equities, with stocks and shares, will reduce the need for locally based investment and can encourage flows of capital from outside localities and undermine the significance of boundaries. These will also enable local capital to move out of the locality to seek higher profits elsewhere. Some local authorities engaged in this practice soon after the SEZs were established, by sending funds through Hong Kong to invest in factories in the SEZs. In addition, there is likely to be a decline in significance of the CPC as the legitimating source of property rights, as the control over the enterprises spawned by the reforms become *de facto* new forms of property rights. The need for 'owners' to be wary of personal involvement in capitalist activities has already disappeared, although being accused of corruption is potentially dangerous or even fatal.

In these changes we see that marketisation is not only changing the way that goods and services are produced and exchanged, but is also a process that will alter relations between places and regions: if it works it will have considerable impact on localisation. Along with the spread of markets and free competition there is considerable large-scale corporate development (involving SOEs), with mergers and an increase in size of some production enterprises. But there will not be an even or complete transition to markets in economic space, and the success of big business may provoke resentment and resistance in some places. Although the decline in the political need to avoid economic risks will make it less necessary to link local administrations to local production, different places will find it easier than others to give up the benefits of BLD. What is likely to emerge, then, in the next phase is a spatial patchwork of production that contains tensions not only between competitors in the market but also between more and less successful places, some of which will continue to be defended by local authorities.

Actors in environmental space

If we overlay these changing patterns of economic behaviour onto the various categories of the environment, we can begin to incorporate the changes in economic space with environmental space by interpreting the impacts of actors' behaviour. For the purposes of this discussion I will deal with the environment in terms of its provision of productive resources, and its being used as a sink for waste. In short, the way that new actors have emerged, or become active rather than passive, has:

- altered and intensified the way that environmental resources are used for production (in farming, forests, rangelands, and mining), resulting in the rapid degradation and toxification of land, soils, air, and surface and substrate water, with the quality of life and sustainability in general being harmed (e.g. through increased noise pollution, loss of biodiversity, and perhaps even increased incidence of flooding and drought);
- induced or increased the competition for some resources between different types of users, such that resources derived from nature have become a field of conflict between economic actors;
- increased the emissions and effluent discharges from industry in consequence of rapid economic growth and the rise in numbers of enterprises, especially TVEs which had no experience of environmental controls;
- increased the burden on environmental protection agencies (EPAs), at the same time as their budgets from central and local government have been constrained and reduced;.

In short, the reforms have greatly increased the number and types of polluters, raised the demands made on environmental resources, and made it increasingly difficult for the authorities to implement and enforce regulations. There is evidence of widespread concern about environmental problems among the general public and some levels of government officials, and there is wide-ranging and in many respects adequate legislation. But the desire to regulate and reduce the causes of problems is severely constrained by the overriding emphasis on economic growth above all else. This is compounded by the fact that local authorities are (as we have seen above) both major actors in the new economic system as well as being in control of the EPAs: they are in conflict over these contradictory objectives. Given the difficulty (and dangers) for ordinary citizens in organising independent non-government environmental organisations, there is little scope for adequate checks and balances through civil society.

This is not to say that environmental problems are entirely new and never existed under Maoism. If the Mao period was less environmentally costly, this was more by good fortune than design. The previous system was not inherently any more environmentally friendly: there was just much less industry and fewer sources of pollution. There is little evidence that there was any conscious environmentalism at that time (but the same was true in the West). In general the dominant discourse was of Nature being made subservient to the superiority of human needs and capabilities. Under the collectives, some attempts to extend agriculture into inappropriate areas created considerable environmental damage. Also, 'Maoist' political campaigns sometimes involved activities that were environmentally damaging, most notably with the tree-felling to provide charcoal for the amateur iron production of the Great Leap Forward (1958–61). The one significant counterexample is the campaign against 'desertification' (especially in the widening belt of semi-arid land stretching from Xinjiang in the northwest to the edge of the Gobi north of Beijing). However even this fell within the 'dominate Nature' paradigm, and seemed to involve a reluctance to accept human causation as part of the problem.

This history of environmentalism in China remains significant. What we observe now is the result of a transition from a discourse in which Nature had to be dominated by Socialist Man, to a reform economy in which economic growth is paramount such that Nature is irrelevant or ignorable (and acts merely as a sink for waste or to be mined for productive resources with no concern for the future). This runs parallel to the change in ideology and conceptions of human behaviour outlined above. In Maoist times, economic actors were collectives and subservient to the centre. It is possible that the rise in awareness of environmental problems that emerged in the West could have been superimposed on that system. The collectives were capable of adopting an environmentalist approach under centralised direction, given the lack of competitive drive between collectivised actors that would otherwise undermine attempts to control pollution.

Environmentalism emerged in the West to impinge even on the most rabid market-driven economic actors (aided by the potential for civil society to permit heterodox thinking and political campaigning, but also the ability of businesses to escape controls at home by exporting their dirty processes to the Third World). Yet in China a pro-capitalist set of reforms got under way which transformed many institutional actors into localised polluters and miners of the environment. This happened in a context where the central authorities sanctioned the rush for economic growth above all else, and provided the basis (through the continued domination by the CPC) to prevent any emergence of civil society, let alone environmentalist protesters, that could monitor the proper implementation of environmental laws and regulation. Thus the commercial exigencies of growth at (almost) any cost is meshed with topocracy and localised development in a nexus that makes the environmental problems of the country extremely difficult to remedy (Jahiel 1997). There are many thousands of localities willing to accept revenue-generating activities with little concern for their environmental impacts, and with reduced institutional capacity to implement the legislation. With an effective, repressive state at all levels of the hierarchy, which is able to suppress disquiet and prevent the emergence of effective independent checks and balances, the prospects are not very good.

There is evidence, however, that many officials are now willing to recognise the extensive financial damage that pollution causes, not only to health but also to other areas of production (including crops). The National Environmental Protection Agency (NEPA) has itself argued for a significant increase in capital spending on emission controls. If this was increased (from around 0.5 percent of GNP to about 1.5 per cent) it could to reduce the negative impacts of pollution on total output from 10 to around 5 percent of GNP (Vermeer 1995). But such arguments, which look an incredible bargain on paper, have to be implemented across all sectors and require localities to take action that may be judged to have an immediate negative impact on growth, with no certainty of future benefits, or with those benefits accruing to other enterprises or localities. The NEPA has in any case largely failed to secure such investment levels at national level. It is possible that with greater World Bank support for environmental remedies that more progress may be made (see World Bank 1997). But the political and fiscal capacity of the central government to deal with the myriad of local actors is severely constrained (Vermeer 1998, p.962). Those actors and localities have interests that are both more narrow and short-term than those that would properly serve environmental protection.

References

Brown, L. R. (1995) *Who Will Feed China? Wake-up Call for a Small planet*: W. W. Norton/Worldwatch Institute.

Cannon, Terry and Alan Jenkins (1990) *The Geography of Contemporary China: the Impact of Deng Xiaoping's Decade* (London: Routledge).

Cannon, Terry and Le-yin Zhang (1996) in Cook *et al.* (eds.)

Cook, Ian, Marcus Doel and Rex Li (eds) (1996) *Fragmented Asia: Regional Integration and National disintegration in Pacific Asia* (Aldershot: Avebury).

Gittings, John (1996) *China – From Cannibalism to Karaoke* (London: Simon & Schuster).

Jahiel, Abigail R. (1997) 'The Contradictory Impact of reform on Environmental Protection in China', *China Quarterly*, 149 (March).

Kirkby, R. (1995) *Urbanisation in China: Town and Country in a Developing Economy, 1949–2000 AD* (London: Croom Helm).

Oi, Jean C. (1995) 'The role of the Local State in China's Transitional Economy', *China Quarterly* 144 (December) 1132–49.

Reilly, Charles (1995) *New Paths to Democratic Development in Latin America* (New York: Lynne Rienner).

Vermeer, E. (1995) 'An Inventory of Losses Due to Environmental Pollution: problems in the Sustainability of China's Economic Growth', *China Information*, 10(1) (Summer) 19–50.

Vermeer, E. (1998) 'Industrial Pollution in China and Remedial Policies', *China Quarterly*, 156 (December) 986–1016.

Wang Shaoguang (1994) 'Central-Local Fiscal Politics in China', in Jia Hao and Lin Zhimin.

Wilson (1996) *China the Big Tiger: A Nation Awakes* (London: Little, Brown).

World Bank (1997) *Clear Water, Blue Skies* (Washington DC).

Yang, Dali (1997) *Beyond Beijing: Liberalization and the Regions in China* (London: Routledge).

Part I

Demographic Processes and the Economic Reforms

2

Pressures of Development on China's Cities and Regions

Ian G. Cook

This chapter reviews the rapid pace of development in recent years, and examines some of the tensions this is causing in China's cities and regions. In cities, these include the environmental impacts of rapid urbanisation, social polarisation and disintegration, the absorption of China's huge rural labour surplus, and the impact of 'Westernization' on urban society. At the regional level, rapid urbanisation enhances regional disparities and tensions between the generally more wealthy coastal region and the poorer interior. The implications of such issues for governance and stability are considered and alternative urban and regional futures for the country are raised.

The rapid pace of development

The speed of change in China in recent decades is now well known. The changes are primarily economic, rather than political, and are having a massive impact on society and culture, geography and the environment. The key features of the policies that have brought such rapid change include:

- the Open Door policy and related Four-Modernisations Policy, which have sought to open China up to the global economy in order to transform and update China's industrial and technological capacity (Yabuki 1995);
- the role of foreign trade (Lardy 1992) and foreign direct investment (FDI) (Cook and Wang 1997) in the process of transformation, as new external and internal linkages are developed, assisting in the channelling of financial resources into China;

- the role of overseas Chinese networks (OCNs) in stimulating these linkages and combining their financial and managerial skills with China's labour and natural resource base (Khong 1996);
- internal structural adjustments such as those to the Rural Responsibility System in the early 1980s (Sen 1990)
- the reduction of restrictions on joint ventures with foreign companies in 1986, 1988 and 1990 (Lardy 1994).

All of these have combined to create a multifaceted process of economic transformation.

The tremendous economic strides China has been making include, for example, the rise in the value of its trade from US$38.14 billion in 1980 at the beginning of the reforms to US$69.60 billion in 1985, US$115.41 billion in 1990 and a massive US$165.61 billion by 1993 (Lardy 1994, p. 2). Similarly, FDI rose from a relatively low base of US$0.64 billion in 1983 (as the first faltering steps were taken by both Chinese and foreigners to stimulate investment), to US$2.31 billion in 1987 (after further liberalisation), reaching US$11.01 billion in 1992 as 'China Fever' hit the markets, and up to a huge US$33.77 billion in 1994 (Cook and Wang 1997). China became the number one 'hot spot' for FDI in the 1990s, as investment poured in from not only Hong Kong and Taiwan, but also South Korea and Japan and many other countries. The result of these and other aspects of structural change was that the Chinese economy has become one of the largest in the world. By 1992, for example, China was ninth in the world in terms of Gross National Product (GNP), with a total of US$442.3 billion (after the USA, Japan, Germany, France, Italy, the UK, Canada and Spain; see Yabuki 1995, p. 81). Some experts also suggest that this GNP data underestimates the strength of the Chinese economy in terms of purchasing power, and that the Chinese economy could be ranked third, behind only the US and Japan (Lardy 1994, p. 3).

Despite such dramatic evidence (and more could readily be provided), these economic successes have not been bought cheaply, and are not without cost. Many Western observers in particular are concerned that political adjustments have not matched those in the economy. Some consider China is an example of a BAIR (a bureaucratic authoritarian industrialising regime; see Simone and Feraru 1995, p. 163), or a country dominated by 'neoauthoritarianism' (Baum 1992). The latter term describes a repressive situation in which economic liberalism is increasingly in contradiction with political illiberalism, giving rise to questions of human rights and democratisation, as well as inbuilt instabilities within the political economy of China. Such instabilities are considered to endanger the future of China itself. In addition, if such problems promoted an increasingly militaristic and hardline regime seeking to right past wrongs or to deflect internal dissent via external action, then the future of China's relations with its neighbours may be at risk, and through such crises the international system itself. Then there is the issue of the incomplete nature of the economic reforms:

> It is important to emphasize that Chinese reforms have been far from an unqualified success. There are many areas where they seem to have failed. For example, the attempts at reforming the state-owned enterprises have not made much progress towards transforming them into market-oriented firms, responsible for their profits and losses. Many of them are loss-making. (Hussain 1994, p. 19)

Given that state-owned enterprises (SOEs) are still a major element in the economy, such losses are a significant drain on the country's financial resources. Official estimates of the subsidies they received were US$6 billion in 1995 (*Business Beijing* 1995b), and the attempt to 'smash the iron rice bowl' of SOEs' reliance on state subsidies remains unfinished.

It is the unevenness of the economic reforms, both in time and space, which is so perturbing. Over time they proceed, as Hussain notes, in stop–go cycles, and these normally follow periods of intense debate within the Communist Party of China (CPC). In space, as I show next, it is very much the cities and certain provinces which are benefiting most from the reforms, while other parts of the country are lagging behind. And although the country has one of the largest economies in the world, this does not amount to much on a per capita basis. Yabuki notes that China is 103rd in per capita GNP (Yabuki 1995, p. 82), and although a purchasing power parity calculation would raise this figure, China as a whole has a long way to go in its development trajectory. China is a relatively rich country, therefore, but it still contains many poor people. The economic growth has been phenomenal, and China is to be congratulated on the successes so far achieved; the pressures of development remain great, however, and it is to their urban aspects that I now turn.

Urban pressures of development

Urban pressures are considered here in relation to the pace of construction, the environmental impact of expansion, the broad social, economic and political concomitants, and lastly the ambience of the city. These issues relate to research pertaining to the West Pacific Rim in general, and to China's large cities in particular (Cook 1993; Cook 1995; Cook and Li 1996).

The pace of construction: building, building: the concretisation of the Earth

Edgar Snow, the great American commentator on China, used the title 'Building, Building' for one of his chapters on Shanghai in the classic *Red China Today*. In it he briefly described revisiting the city in 1960, and the contrasts with the pre-revolutionary era, especially the construction of the satellite towns around the city itself. The 'building, building' of the late 1950s pales into insignificance with the scale and speed of contemporary construction, in Beijing, in Pudong (Shanghai), in Shenzhen and Guangzhou (Canton), and most other cities. A massive investment is being made in new high-rise commercial office blocks, hotels, trade centres, shopping centres and residential blocks, as well as related port facilities, freeways and, occasionally, mass transit systems. Cities reverberate to the sound of piledrivers, and the dust from construction work is everywhere. The conversion of raw-material resources into the gleaming concrete, steel and plate glass spires of modernity is on a huge scale. It is sucking up a high proportion of China's own finances, as well as the international finance that is pursuing the potentially lucrative property markets underpinning these developments.

Consider, for example, the current and planned growth of Pudong (the development zone on the east of Shanghai), which resembles a cross between London's Docklands and Hong Kong. A total investment of 40 billion yuan was planned up to 1996 (since increased to 70 billion, with perhaps 200 billion being required to year 2000) in commercial, high-tech, port, science park, residential and other facilities in developments that dwarf those on the Bund waterfront on the other side of the Huang Po River (DTI 1992; Li Jianeng 1993; Yabuki 1995). Shanghai itself is hardly lacking in new developments, including a cluster of high-rise hotel and commercial buildings west towards the airport, and a smaller-scale cluster around the huge new railway station slightly to the north of the city centre. With these, plus other hotels, retail and commercial projects within the central area itself, there are hundreds of high-rise structures none of which existed before the 1980s. The rate of building has been such that it is estimated that Shanghai as a whole has over a million square metres of vacant office space. Even by 1992 (only two years after it was initiated) there were worries about Pudong becoming 'overbuilt' (Sender 1992). Some estimates suggest that at the national level there is a surplus of 50 million square feet of office space (*China Mail*, 1996). If Shanghai was considered the Paris of the East before World War II, then Pudong is 'La Defénse' (Sudjic 1992), with all the pluses and minuses that such an alternative, 'eccentric' location entails. It is interesting to note recent reports that the local authorities are now encouraging foreign banks, for example, to reoccupy buildings in the partly renovated Bund area, perhaps some extent to balance the growth on the east side of the river.

What of the impact of such a scale and rapidity of urban growth? On the credit side, cities are often exciting, glamorous and futuristic places in which opportunities abound – for self-development free from the restrictive cultural norms of the countryside; for educational, research and commercial possibilities emanating from the diverse interactions and possibilities opened up in the urban situation; and for economic growth to be generated via the complex, multi-layered networking at different levels that urban high-tech connection facilitates. It is noticeable that China is pursuing economic growth largely through an urbanisation strategy, despite the development of TVEs (township and village enterprises). Thus the first special economic zones (SEZs), which began as small villages or towns, are now large urban entities, although Shenzhen dwarfs the others with a population of at least 2 and possibly 3 million. The Chinese authorities, in common with many urbanists, believe that there is a law of urbanisation relative to industrialisation, and that China is under-urbanised by at least 22 per cent (Yan Mingfu 1995, p. 4).

In terms of the current scale of urbanisation, State Statistical Bureau figures suggest that by the end of 1994 the urban population was 28.6 per cent of the total population (*China Statistical Yearbook*, 1995, p. 59). This compared with 26.4 per cent in 1990, 23.7 per cent in 1985 and 19.4 per cent in 1980.[1] Also in 1994, the bureau recognised 622 'cities' throughout the country. Of these, coastal provinces rank highest, with 51 in Guangdong alone, followed by 46 in Shandong, and 39 in Jiangsu (ibid., p. 3). In 1993, 32 of these were 'million cities' (with a million or more registered population). Most of these play a key role in economic growth at the local, regional and (in some cases such as Beijing or Shanghai), the national or even international level.[2] The return of Hong Kong in 1997 has added another key international player to this urban lineup. The official expectation is that by the year 2000 the urbanisation level will reach 34 per cent nationally (with 724 cities), and by 2010 more than 42 per cent (with 1003 cities) (ibid., p. 5). Kam Wing Chan, however, projects two scenarios of 4 per cent and 5 per cent annual growth, respectively (Kam Wing Chan, 1994, pp. 152–3). On his data, therefore, urbanisation in 2000 would be 35.6 per cent or 39.2 per cent, and 48.2 per cent or 58.3 per cent in 2010. The numbers involved would be enormous, at up to 838.4 million people in 2010 in a 'worst-case' situation. If these predictions are accurate 'What is going to happen in China in the coming two decades is thus truly momentous – the urban percentage will almost double and the size of the urban population *added will be about that of the current US urban population*' [my emphasis] (Kam Wing Chan 1994, p. 153). There is potentially a high price for this urban expansion within the city itself, and also the nation and the international community. For example, local neighbourhoods are overwhelmed by high-rise developments in Beijing, Guangzhou and other cities of China. The atmospheric and ancient back-street hutongs of Beijing, despite a few successful attempts at redevelopment (Gaubatz 1995), are mostly being engulfed or destroyed by the inexorable growth of mid-rise or high-rise blocks. In 1991 it was stated that 'in the last decade a total of over 2000 residential quarters, each with a floor space of more than 50,000 square metres, have been built', and this climbed to 4000 by the mid-1990s (Zou Deci, 1995, p. 29). This policy of new build is often justified by the perceived poor provision of public utilities in the old low-level residential areas. For me, in spite of the urban pressures on China, such a policy has uncomfortable echoes of the justification for British inner-city developments of the 1960s.

Environmental impacts: ecological tramplings – local, national, global

The expansion of the urban area is also using up productive farmland around most cities (see Smil 1993, p. 141). William Rees has presented the concept of the *ecological footprint* of cities to describe their impact on natural resources and ecosystems, described in Hardoy *et al.* 1992). I have chosen to modify this to ecological tramplings, given the deleterious impacts that many cities have upon their enveloping ecosystems at the local, national and even global scales (Cook 1993). Thus, at the local level, most of China's large cities suffer from some form of environmental pollution, whether from traffic noise, vehicle exhaust, industrial atmospheric pollution, the degradation of valuable agricultural land surrounding these centres or the problems of sewage and waste disposal.

Such local issues as these (and many more examples could be given – see Burnett, 1992; Dong Liming, 1985; Hardoy *et al.* 1992; Yan Zhongming 1985; Yeung 1990) were once regarded as just that – local issues. But it is increasingly recognised that local urban issues have a much wider impact, owing to their severity and scale. Nationally it is the urban dwellers who are most responsible for high energy use, food consumption, industrial and traffic pollution, resource depletion and other ecological tramplings, as they are encouraged to pursue high levels of consumption, production and exchange. For example, 80 per cent of urban surface water is reckoned to be polluted, mainly by ammonium salts and nitrogen compounds. Similarly, 80 per cent of air pollution is attributed to industry. Much of this is a result of coal burning, discussed below. Increasing vehicular traffic is contributing to a growing smog problem and pollution from particulates, carbon monoxide, hydrocarbons and nitrogen oxides, among others, into the atmosphere. The authorities are taking considerable steps to control pollution sources, and are having some successes (for example in tackling smog problems). But the pace of industrialisation and growth in traffic usually outstrips their efforts. In addition, there seems to be an increase in noxious industries, as other places (especially Taiwan and Hong Kong) export their own pollution problems to the less-regulated mainland China.

At the national level in China, the total volume of industrial liquid waste in 1990 was 28.6 billion tonnes. By 1991 only 32 per cent of this was treated. Similarly in 1991 only 29 per cent of the 320 million tonnes of industrial solid waste was recycled. The year 2000 target for treatment and recycling is 82 per cent and 37 per cent respectively, while 'Around a quarter of urban sewage will be treated by the year 2000' (Qu Geping 1992, p. 64). 'Night soil' collection (a centuries-old practice for the transfer of human excrement to farms surrounding cities) is diminishing fast. The pace of economic development means that the content of the average household dustbin is likely to contain far more non-biodegradable material than ten years ago, especially in the cities. Only 2.3 per cent of urban refuse is treated and despite the building of some incinerators, it is once again difficult to keep pace with the problem. Edmonds quotes one prediction that 'China's urban rubbish will have annual growth rates of 8 to 10 per cent between 1980 and 2000' (Edmonds 1994, p. 170). Edmonds also notes that by 1991 control of solid wastes was costing over 672 million yuan annually, accounting for 11 per cent of spending on pollution control. But it is local authorities rather than central government that will be

increasingly expected to come up with these funds, which they are unlikely to be able or willing to do (ibid., p. 171). (Chapter 6 discusses this problem in relation to Wuhan in more detail.)

Coal is still the main source of power, accounting for 78 per cent of total energy consumption in 1994 (*China Statistical Yearbook 1995*, p. 199). But Edmonds notes that fuel conversion efficiency (the amount of energy obtained from fuel compared with its potential) is low at 28 per cent (compared with 40 to 55 per cent in North America and 60 per cent in Japan). The burning of coal also results in enormous losses from metal corrosion, estimated as $US11,000 million for 1988). One report notes:

> In Chongqing, for example, where the locally mined coal has a very high sulphur content, 820 000 tonnes of sulphur dioxide are emitted into the atmosphere every year. And because the city is sheltered from the wind by the surrounding mountains, most of this sulphur dioxide comes straight back down in rain so acid that it can dissolve steel. In 1990, Chongqing spent US$250,000 just to replace lamp-posts and buses that had been eaten away. (Catton 1992, 21)

Yet a switch to hydroelectric power (HEP) involves major controversies, as with the Sanxia (Three Gorges) Dam on the Yangtze (discussed in detail in Chapter 7). Nuclear power is becoming an important alternative, but is seen as expensive in comparison with the massive reserves of cheap domestic coal. It is estimated that coal use will have doubled between 1980 and 2000, further contributing to problems of global warming.

The authorities are aware of these and other issues, but given the dominance of the drive for growth, there is always tension over the need for controls. In 1996, for example, the Traffic Management Bureau in Beijing introduced drastic measures to cut road traffic by almost half. The plan was to restrict vehicle engines (except in taxis) to one litre or less, and for licence plate restrictions for travel on certain dates. Intense lobbying began immediately against these measures, so their long-term application may be in doubt. The 'Beijing Master Plan' proposes to increase the length of the city's small subway system to 90 km, adding another ten lines to the current two by 2010. So there is some evidence of a willingness to tackle these problems (*China Monitor* Special Report 1994; *Business Beijing* 1996). Nevertheless, 'The prime objective of the [Beijing Master Plan] will be to accelerate Beijing's economic development' (*China Monitor* Special Report, 1994, p. 12), therefore such measures will be taken only if they are seen to complement, or at least not to undermine, the economic targets which are set.

Social, economic and political issues

A wide range of interrelated social, economic and political issues are associated with the urbanisation process in China. I have chosen to categorise these as follows: pressures towards social polarisation and disintegration; problems of mass migration, homelessness and labour absorption; gender issues; the role of urbanisation in modernisation and cultural imperialism.

Pressures towards social polarisation and disintegration

Cities render disparities of wealth, status, housing provision and the like highly visible, and can threaten social cohesion because of this manifestation of unequal access to goods, services, wealth, employment opportunities and other features of contemporary life. As well as policing cities, the state can also deflect social unrest by a wide range of sophisticated controls. But the scale and nature of urban change is such that new expectations and aspirations for a 'better' life are continually being created.

Social polarisation reflects the massive increase in wealth for a small minority, a significant increase in wealth for a larger number, coupled with the exclusion of a substantial minority (majority?) from the wealth creation process. This is combined with increased materialism, and the erosion of cultural norms of social cohesiveness (whether emanating from Confucianism, various religions and cultural practices, or the impact of socialism and egalitarianism). Other factors have enhanced the impact of polarisation, such as the new allocation mechanisms for property, housing and labour markets which rely on non-traditional procedures, and the strong emphasis on individualism and 'privatised' consumption patterns that are socially divisive. The already high population densities in urban areas also give rise to stress, despite the supposed ability of the much-vaunted Chinese family to cope with such pressures. My view, based on frequent research visits to Chinese cities over a number of years, is that such intra-urban disparities are on the increase. For example, beggars are to be found outside the affluence of the World Trade Centre in Beijing, and poor-quality residential accommodation encountered behind the sophisticated hotels of the capital. Detached houses are being sold in exclusive estates in different cities around the country at prices of 1, 2 or even 3 million yuan, in a country where the official average annual wage in Beijing was 6523 yuan, 7405 yuan in Shanghai, and 7117 in Guangdong province (*China Statistical Yearbook* 1995, p. 114).

Problems of mass migration, homelessness and labour absorption

The impact of migration on large, medium and small cities has imposed tremendous pressures on the infrastructure, especially on mass housing provision. Where mass public housing is provided it seems to be generally of low quality and to pose long-term problems of upkeep and maintenance, social integration, lack of 'defensible space' and inflexibility of unit size for changing family circumstances. As a result it resembles some of the worst features of mass housing provision provided for Western cities in the 1960s.

Then there is the problem of those without housing at all. Estimates were given in the *China Daily* in summer 1992 of 1.2 million people in Beijing without official registration cards, and up to 60 million nationally in other cities. Known in China as the 'floating population', many are homeless, while others are squatters who may at least have their own roof over their heads and a degree of security within squatter settlements. By the end of 1993 there were probably 100 million unofficial migrants, although the World Bank estimated the number as 120 million (Balls 1993) and it may now have risen to 130 million. It is often the large cities which attract these migrants, who tend to be most visible in and around the railway stations and tourist areas. As the 'restructuring' process operates in the rural areas (Kirkby 1994), and as urban–rural disparities continue to increase (Cook and Li 1996) then the flood of migrants is likely to increase even further unless measures are taken to restrict movement and offer greater opportunities in their home location. Further, there is already evidence of considerable prejudice and discrimination against these migrants by the indigenous population, an issue discussed in detail in Chapter 4 (see also Solinger 1995).

For the 100 million people who became surplus to agricultural requirements in the changes of the 1980s, the labour absorption problem is enormous. Most have been employed in the small townships as well as the cities:

During 1979–89 the newly employed in China's cities and towns ran into 85.071 million, 30 per cent of which [were] in units of collective ownership and 8 per cent working on their own ... In 1990 another 4 million people got jobs in the cities and towns ... The development of township industries in the rural areas has opened up new outlets for the rural surplus labor ... The output value of the country's township industries increased 12.5 per cent in 1990, outstripping by far the 7.6 per cent industrial growth speed of the country and playing a positive role in absorbing the surplus rural work force. However, the managerial level of some enterprises in certain cities and towns is still very low, and there is a waste of labour power due to overstaff [sic]. Besides, with the rising of productivity in agriculture, there will be more and more surplus labor in the countryside. *These problems are yet to be solved.* (Shi Min 1991, 80; emphasis added)

It is difficult to see how labour can continue to be absorbed into basic low-tech production as at present, given that the main drive of capitalistic development is to shed labour, and progress to high-tech activities. Some relief is likely in the medium term as service industries expand further, but in the longer term large levels of investment will be required in education and training, as is the case in other countries in both East and West.

Gender issues

Women traditionally had a low place in Chinese culture, owing in part to the male-dominant ethic of Confucianism, which emphasised duty and obedience through the male line and insisted on patrilocal residence. The 1950 marriage law and its successor the 1980 marriage law emphasised the importance of equality in relations between husband and wife as regards, for example, freedom to work, study, or divorce, and banned traditional marriage-brokers and dowries (Wolf 1985). In practice, however, although women have achieved much in post-revolutionary China, much still remains to be done (Andors 1983; Wolf 1985). Thus, for example:

Women workers in the urban sector were not viewed differently from other women in society – they too had to reconcile their 'female' roles with their 'productive' roles in the industrial work force. Even though many articles advocated job protection or the adjustment of work schedules, *it was still primarily the woman's responsibility to integrate the two roles.* (Andors 1983, 81; emphasis added)

Similarly, Wolf in her interviews in Beijing and Shaoxing found that most of her female respondents enjoyed their occupations and did not

wish to return to the domestic sphere. However, 'throughout the interviews there was a theme of constant weariness which was largely the
result of women's 'second shift' in their domestic duties' (Wolf 1985,
p. 81), while wages for women were on average 71.7 per cent of men's
(better than Britain, but far worse than Sweden), and this for a sample
selected by Wolf by the authorities. Further, Wolf found throughout
her sample that there were expectations that women would carry
domestic responsibilities and that men would make better leaders
among both male and female respondents. Since that research, Croll
suggests, there has been 'a more open acknowledgement of the discrepancy between the rhetoric of equality and women's experience of
inequality during the years of Revolution' (Croll 1995, p. 13). Croll
refers to a 1994 All China Federation of Trade Unions report in 1994
which demonstrated the appalling conditions in which women work
in a survey of 914 foreign-funded enterprises (Croll 1995, p. 14). My
own observations suggest that women are still much more likely to be
employed in more menial occupations than are men. They are also
now surrounded by the beginnings of western-style advertising which
presents them as sex symbols, with all the extra pressures to which that
will give rise. The authorities hoped that the Fourth World Conference
on Women (held in Beijing in September 1995) would focus on the
positive side of women's situation in China. The vice-director of the
official All China Women's Federation stated that the Conference 'had
propelled developments in women's causes all over the country' (Liu
Yingiang 1996), and it is to be hoped that the examples provided in
her article prove to be more than mere window-dressing.

Role of urbanisation in modernisation and cultural imperialism

Processes of global transformation operate through and from cities,
escalating and concentrating the pace of change via the complex high-
tech interactions and linkages that annihilate old spaces and structures
and continually create the new structures, images, icons and products
of modernity – and postmodernity. And so, at the mundane level,
'Wheat replaces rice and corn as a major staple of Third World Cities
and radio, television, cinema and pop music supplant the traditional
entertainments of oral history, theatre and folk music' (Armstrong and
McGee 1985, p. 5). At a more dramatic level,

> Cities are, stated simply, the crucial elements in accumulation at all
> levels, regional, national and international, providing both the
> institutional framework and the *locus operandi* for transnationals,

local oligopoly capital and the modernising national state ... cities also play the role of diffusers of the lifestyles, customs, tastes, fashions and consumer habits of modern industrial society ... we see Third World urban systems not only as theatres of accumulation, but also as centres from which are diffused the culture and values of westernisation. (ibid, p. 41)

This is evident in a number of ways. For example, there are the highly visible multi-storey international hotels and business centres in cities such as Guangzhou and Shanghai. Sophisticated ring roads count BMWs, Nissans and Mercedes together with joint venture Volkswagens and Beijing Jeeps, among their traffic. Kentucky Fried Chicken, Pizza Hut and McDonald's takeaways dominate shopping districts, while satellite dishes large and small sprout on roofs and buildings. Department stores (some Japanese-owned) offer a growing range of domestic and foreign goods. (Retail sales were expected to rise by 20 in 1996.) Then there are the karaoke bars, laser discos, and bright lights, especially prominent the further south one travels. Many of these changes appear to the outside observer to be westernisation, but it is also 'Japanization' or even 'Tokyoization', given the local influence of Tokyo itself (Hanes 1993).

New products, ideas, exemplars cascade down the urban hierarchy and into the countryside. The foreign influence is not just economic but is also social and cultural. I suggest that McGee's concept of *Kotadesasi* (McGee and Greenberg 1992), employed to describe the intense interaction between town/city and countryside, should be explored also at the cultural level, for example to help explain rural-to-urban migration, which is due to more than the attraction of the bright lights of the city or the push of rural poverty and tradition. It is also important to consider the cultural dominance of the urban, in which material goods, materialist lifestyles, and the positive features of city life overwhelm the presumed dreariness and drudgery of the rural alternative.

The ambience of the city: the past, the present and the urbanisation of nostalgia

In the face of this relentless onslaught of change, there is a small but significant return to the past, a 'back to the future' tendency. Perhaps this is to fulfil a psychological need to localise identity within these essentially globalising processes of change, and a way of dealing with the problems to which they give rise. China, of course, has a rich and varied tradition of urbanisation going back several millennia (Wheatley 1971), and many ideas for alternative futures. Urbanisation is not a recent phenomenon in China, even though the massive expansion of cities has been recent. The return to the past is in part to preserve artefacts, sites and symbols as islands of the past in a sea of modernity resulting from this 'massive expansion'. In Shanghai, for example, 'past and present are indistinguishably mingled' (Pan Ling 1982, pp. 2–3). Hybrid urban forms that attempt to fuse indigenous and foreign styles are increasingly evident in various cities, with Chinese roofs and other features, for instance, appearing on high-rise offices or hotels.

The past may also be tapped as a source of ideas, even 'enlightenment', as Shen illustrates in an interesting review of ancient city planning in China (Shen Yahong 1992). He illustrates the strengths of ancient practice in terms of its unified nature, its 'macroconcept' of the role of the city as the regional centre of the countryside, and its ecological consciousness. To this I may add that many ancient traditions were ecologically sound. Daoist concepts, for example, emphasised the harmonious relationship between 'Man' and Nature, contrasting with the largely 'control' conceptualisation of the Judaeo-Christian traditions. The intensive agriculture that developed to support and stimulate the large population of China was based on good practices of the minimising and recycling of waste, in whatever form. The modern era, however, brought the more interventionist traditions of the West to China, and Maoism shared the Marxist materialist view that the earth could be controlled via human intervention. Human development would know no bounds once the feudal shackles were broken, and this ideological perspective informed the Great Leap Forward and the later Cultural Revolution.

Shen Yahong argues that the overemphasis on experience and techniques led to a neglect of theory and hence, eventually, to stagnation. From this analysis he developed 'seven historical insights', which include the need to develop 'a theoretical system of modern urban planning with an advanced world level and with Chinese characteristics' (ibid., p. 73); to draw on the experience of the 'excellent' ancient traditions; and also to include ecological theory. The indigenous tradition, therefore, must be reinterpreted for the needs of the future. Many parts of China's large cities are, to Western eyes at least, dull, unimaginative and unattractive, with little attempt to preserve and conserve some of the positive legacies of the past in the face of rapid economic development. The return to ancient traditions would, in my opinion, enhance the ambience of the city through the retention and redevelopment of those urban features and forms that are unique to China, enabling China's cities to be Chinese cities, rather than just 'cities', and fusing the best of the past and the present.

Regional pressures of development

Regional contrasts: ever-increasing disparities

The urban pressures just discussed have crucial connections with those at the regional level. In regional disparities in China, for example, 'when the urban dimension of development is added there is an even greater divergence between the highly urbanized coastal zone and the poorly urbanized interior as urban economic growth continues apace' (Cook and Li 1996, pp. 203–4). Despite occasional attempts to ameliorate the differential spatial impact of development, China still contains poor provinces that share some or all of the following characteristics: landlocked; a high proportion of ethnic minorities; low levels of urbanisation, industrialisation, and GNP per capita; and low proportion of exports per capita. Map 2.1, for example, shows the high levels of GNP per capita in 1994 in the three municipalities of Shanghai, Beijing and Tianjin, plus such coastal provinces as Guangdong, Liaoning, Heilongjiang, Shandong and those in the Shanghai delta, Zhejiang and Jiangsu. The use of mean GNP per capita masks the starkness of the spatial contrasts, in my view, and Map 2.2, which illustrates utilised FDI in the 'China Fever' year of 1994, portrays what I regard as a sharper and more realistic distinction between most of the coastal provinces, compared with the interior. Similarly, the data provided for 1995 in Table 2.1 further support this viewpoint.

Table 2.1 shows that of the nine provinces with utilised foreign direct investment (FDI) of $1 billion or more, *are all coastal*. Conversely, for those with utilised FDI of $300 million or less, *all are interior provinces*. To me, there is little doubt of the dependence on state intervention of those poorer provinces in the interior. Cannon and Zhang summarise the policy debates concerning the need to balance growth to a greater extent, and refer to a policy document that 'suggested that the state should further develop its regional compensation policy, improve its existing policy of "aid to poor areas", strengthen policies for minority nationalities, and continue fiscal subsidies to compensate regional interests' (Cannon and Zhang 1996, p.88). Officially, for example, there are 80 million people regarded as being in poverty, and the true number may be nearer 100 million, many of them resident in the poorer provinces or the migrants who move from those provinces.

48

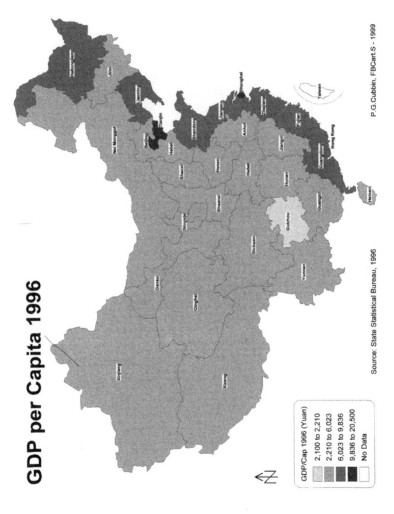

GDP per Capita 1996

GDP/Cap 1996 (Yuan)
- 2,100 to 2,210
- 2,210 to 6,023
- 6,023 to 9,836
- 9,836 to 20,500
- No Data

Source: State Statistical Bureau, 1996

P.G.Cubbin, FBCart.S - 1999

Map 2.1 Per capita GNP by province, 1994.

49

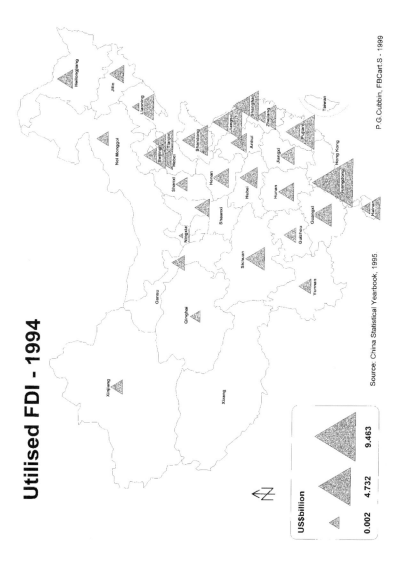

Utilised FDI - 1994

US$billion

0.002   4.732   9.463

Source: China Statistical Yearbook, 1995

P.G.Cubbin, FBCart.S - 1999

Map 2.2 Utilised foreign direct investment by province, 1994.

Table 2.1   Utilised foreign direct investment by province, 1994

Province	Utilised FDI (US $ billion.)
Guangdong*	9.46
Jiangsu*	3.76
Fujian*	3.71
Shandong*	2.55
Shanghai*	2.47
Liaoning*	1.44
Beijing*	1.37
Zhejiang*	1.14
Tianjin*	1.02
Sichuan	0.92
Hainan*	0.92
Guangxi*	0.84
Hubei	0.60
Hebei*	0.52
Henan	0.39
Anhui	0.37
Heilongjiang	0.35
Hunan	0.33
Jiangxi	0.26
Jilin	0.24
Shaanxi	0.24
Gansu	0.09
Yunnan	0.07
Guizhou	0.06
Xinjiang	0.05
Inner Mongolia	ˋ0.04
Shanxi	0.01
Ningxia	0
Qinghai	no data
Tibet	no data

* Coastal province.
Source: *China Statistical Yearbook 1995*, p. 557.

Implications of regionalism: one China; many Chinas

Although the government of the Communist Party has consistently sought to exercise strong control over the country, it has at times done so by decentralist rather than centralist policies. The Dengist reform policies, for example, have had a strongly decentralist element, as control has been devolved to the provincial governments. This is often with a veneer of deference to the centre, in which 'the centre pretends to rule and the provinces pretend to be ruled' (Cannon and Zhang 1996, p. 85). New regionalisms have developed that owe much to the heady mix of increased local autonomy, rapid economic growth and a proliferation of new external linkages to the global economy. The cities have a key role in this process, one which is occurring throughout Pacific Asia and elsewhere (see Cook, Doel and Li 1996 for other examples). It is these new regionalisms that largely give rise to the 'China Deconstructs' scenario (Goodman and Segal 1994), which in turn is largely fuelled by growing Western concerns about the rising economic and military might of China.

Three scenarios for the future of China are discussed briefly here: no substantial change; China shrinks; and China expands (see Cook and Li 1996 for detailed analysis). No substantial change would require a relatively smooth post-Deng transition of power, and Hong Kong to be assimilated without conflict. Problems of the sort described previously would continue, and 'Social inequality and corruption within the CCP [that is, the CPC] and government might remain serious' (Cook and Li 1996, p. 211). But continued economic growth and consumerism, plus the power of the PLA if needs be, would counter internal tensions, and an element of regional autonomy would be tolerated. Western concerns over human rights and copyright infringements would be muted by business opportunities. 'China would remain as a unitary state and the Communist regime would continue in control; the borders of the PRC would remain sacrosanct' (ibid., p. 211). But in the second scenario, the erosion of sovereignty by the combined pressures of globalisation, new regionalism and ethnic dissent, would lead to fragmentation. In this possibility,

> Rich regions like Guangdong and Fujian might attempt to break away from the centre to form a South China state with Hong Kong and Taiwan in order to maintain their economic prosperity, while poor regions would become poorer with the possibility of social unrest and even civil war. (ibid., p. 213)

Some western observers might be quite sanguine about such a scenario, viewing it as a means of restricting the potential threat of China. Rex Li and I, however, regard it as a 'nightmare scenario' in that the potential upheaval could lead to enormous loss of life, and serious consequences for the international community, especially in Pacific Asia.

The final scenario we considered was that of an expanding China, in which not only Hong Kong but also Taiwan were successfully assimilated into a new 'Greater China'. The dispute over the Taiwanese elections in March 1996 may have delayed such a possibility, but it remains plausible. The outcomes would be less predictable, depending upon whether

China chose to reassert militarily its claims in the South China Seas (Khong 1996 p. 178). This would increase arms expenditure in Pacific Asia (there are already signs of this occurring), and this scenario, too, could be dangerous, 'potentially destabilizing the entire international system' (Cook and Li 1996, p. 215). The unpalatibility of the potential outcomes are, therefore, what makes the study of regionalism so crucial to the contemporary New World Order.

Conclusion

Cities and regions are complex and multifaceted phenomena, and require study from different angles and disciplines, to develop policy for dealing with economy, society, spatial features and governance (Cook 1995). The best of Western concepts should be combined with traditional Chinese concepts of balance and harmony to help in the development of policy. Thus, there is a need to balance and harmonise, for example, macro-level with micro-level policies, central guidance and direction with local participation and involvement, modernisation and change with preservation and stability, global with local needs and action and activity with reflection and passivity. In so doing, we must seek to resolve contradictions, for example, between economic growth and environmental costs, and balance the yang with the yin, working to create new solutions for old and new problems alike (see also Khong 1996, p. 179).

Whichever of the scenarios unfolds, the urban and regional pressures summarised above will severely limit the room for manoeuvre of the regime(s) in power. It seems to me that, unless the government develops and facilitates a series of effective responses at city and regional level to the pressures of urbanisation, industrialisation and general economic growth, the entire fabric of Chinese society may be unstitched. It remains, however, for us in the West not merely to wring our hands or to preach catastrophe, but instead to become involved and assist in the amelioration of some at least of these enormous pressures of development. In an ever-shrinking world, although the problems are China's to resolve, their potential global impact means that they are not theirs alone but ours also.

Notes

1. Definitions of what is urban are extremely complex in China. Kirkby (1985) provided a seminal explanation of changing definitions, and this has been more recently updated in an analysis by Kam Wing Chan (1994).

2. Yang Minfu, Vice-Minister of Civil Affairs, has suggested that 'Shanghai, Beijing Guangzhou and Tianjin all have the possibility to be developed into internationalised metropolises' (Yang Minfu, 1995, p. 6).

References

Andors, P. (1983) *The Unfinished Liberation of Chinese Women 1949–1980* (Brighton: Wheatsheaf).
Armstrong, W. and McGee, T. (1985) *Theatres of Accumulation* (London: Methuen).
Balls, E. (1993) 'Migrant Labour Moves to Cities', *Financial Times*, 18 November.
Baum, R. (1992) 'Political Stability in Post-Deng China', *Asian Survey*, 32 (June) 491–505.
Burnett, A. (1992) *The Western Pacific: Challenge of Sustainable Growth* (Aldershot: Edward Elgar).
Business Beijing (1995a) 'China Drafts Long-Term Plan', 8 (November) 12–13.
Business Beijing (1995b) 'Reviving the Public Sector', 8 (November) 14–16.
Business Beijing (1996) 'Back and Beyond: Beijing in '95 and '96', 9 (January) 16–18.
Business Beijing (1996) 'Beijing Facts: The Invisible Artery', 9 (January) 22–3.
Cannon, T. and Zhang, Leyin (1996) 'Inter-region Tension and China's Reforms', in I. G., Doel, M., and Li, R. (eds.) *Fragmented Asia: Regional Integration and National Disintegration in Pacific Asia*, (Aldershot: Avebury) 75–101.
China Mail (1996) 'An Overstock of Commodity Property in China', Vol. 9, No. 1, January- February 1996, p. 76.
Catton, D. (1992) *Tears of the Dragon: China's environmental crisis*, Channel 4 Television, London (booklet to accompany the Central Television series).
China Monitor Special Report (1994) 'Beijing's 20 Year Master Plan', *China Monitor*, (2) 12–14.
China Statistical Yearbook (1995) State Statistical Bureau, People's Republic of China, English ed, (Beijing: China Statistical Publishing House).
Cook, I. G. (1993) 'Urban Issues in the West Pacific Rim', paper presented to the British Pacific Rim Research Group, Liverpool John Moores University, May.
Cook, I. G. (1995) 'Reflections on Pressures of Development in China's Large Cities', paper presented to the Symposium on International Urbanization in China, Shunde City, Guangdong Province, 28 August–1 September 1995.
Cook, I. G. and Li, R. (1996) 'The Rise of Regionalism and the Future of China', in Cook, I. G., Doel, M., and Li, R. (eds) *Fragmented Asia: Regional Integration and National Disintegration in Pacific Asia* (Aldershot: Avebury).
Cook, I. G. and Wang, Y. (1997) 'Foreign Direct Investment in China: Patterns, Processes, Prospects'.
Cook, I. G., Doel, M. A., Li, R. and Wang, Y. (eds.) *Business, Trade and Economic Development in Pacific Asia* (Aldershot: Avebury).
Croll, E. (1995) 'Women in China: Experience and Action', *China Review*, 1 (Summer) 12–15.
Department of Trade and Industry (1992) *Provincial Profiles: Shanghai* (London) 1992.
Dong Liming (1985) 'Beijing: The Development of a Socialist Capital', ch. 2 in Sit, V. F. S. (ed.) *Chinese Cities: The Growth of the Metropolis Since 1949* (Oxford University Press).

Edmonds, R. L. (1994) 'China's Environment: Problems and Prospects', ch. 9 in Dwyer, D. (ed.) *China: The Next Decades* (Harlow: Longman).

Gaubatz, P. R. (1995) 'Urban Transformation in Post-Mao China: Impacts of the Reform Era on China's Urban Form', ch. 2 in Davis, D. S., Kraus, R., Naughton, B. and Perry, E. J. (eds) *Urban Spaces in Contemporary China: The Potential for Autonomy and Community in Post-Mao China* (Cambridge: Woodrow Wilson Center Press and Cambridge University Press).

Goodman, D. S. G. and Segal, G. (eds.) (1994) *China Deconstructs: Politics, Trade and Regionalism* (London: Routledge).

Hanes, J. E. (1993) 'From Megalopolis to Megaroporisu', *Journal of Urban History*, 19 (2) pp. 56–94.

Hardoy, J. E., Mitlin, D. and Satterthwaite, D. (1992) *Environmental Problems in Third World Cities* (London: Earthscan).

Hussain, A. (1994) 'The Chinese Economic Reforms: An Assessment', ch. 2 in Dwyer, D. (ed.) *China: The Next Decades* (Harlow: Longman).

Kam Wing Chan (1994) *Cities with Invisible Walls: Reinterpreting Urbanization in Post–1949 China* (Oxford University Press).

Khong, Cho-Oon (1996) 'Pacific Asia as a Region: A View From Business', in Cook, I. G., Doel, M., and Li, R. (eds.) *Fragmented Asia: Regional Integration and National Disintegration in Pacific Asia* (Aldershot: Avebury) 167–80.

Kirkby, R. (1985) *Urbanisation in China: Town and Country in a Developing Economy, 1949–2000 AD* (London: Croom Helm).

Kirkby, R. J. R. (1994) 'Dilemmas of Urbanization: Review and Prospects', ch. 8 in Dwyer, D. (ed.), *China: The Next Decades* (Harlow: Longman).

Lardy, N. R. (1992) *Foreign Trade and Economic Reform in China, 1978–1990* (Cambridge University Press).

Lardy, N. R. (1994) *China in the World Economy* (Washington, DC: Institute for International Economics).

Li Jianeng (1993) 'The Planning and Development of Shanghai: The Pudong Initiative', paper presented to the China Day, Department of Civic Design, University of Liverpool, 29 January 1993.

Liu Yingiang (1996) 'Women Expanding Their Role in Society', *China Daily*, 28 February.

McGee, T. G. and Greenberg, C. (1992) 'The Emergence of Extended Metropolitan Regions in ASEAN', *ASEAN Economic Bulletin*, 1, 6.

Pan Ling (1982) *In Search of Old Shanghai* (Hong Kong: Joint Publishing Company).

Qu Geping (1992) 'Technology to Tackle Pollution Problems', *China City Planning Review*, 8, (1) 64.

Sen, N. C. (1990) *Rural Economy and Development in China* (Beijing: Foreign Languages Press).

Sender, H. (1992) 'Eastern Promise: Hongkong Developers Flock to Shanghai', *Far Eastern Economic Review*, 17 September 72.

Shen Yahong (1992) 'Enlightenment From the Development of Ancient City Planning in China in the Ancient Times', *China City Planning Review*, 8 (1) 65–75.

Shi Min (1991) 'China's Human Resource Development in the 1990s', *Asia-Pacific Studies*, 1, 78–85.

Simone, V. and Feraru, A. T. (1995) *The Asian Pacific: Political and Economic Development in a Global Context* (White Plains, New York: Longman).

Smil, V. (1993) *China's Environmental Crisis: An Inquiry Into the Limits of National Development*, (Armonk, NY: Sharpe).

Solinger, D. J. (1995) 'The Floating Population in the Cities: Chances for Assimilation?', ch. 5 in Davis, D. S., Kraus, R., Naughton, B. and Perry, E. J. (eds.) *Urban Spaces in Contemporary China: The Potential for Autonomy and Community in Post-Mao China* (Woodrow Wilson Center Press and Cambridge University Press).

Sudjic, D. (1992) 'Birth of the Brave New City', *Guardian*, 1 February 1992, pp. 2–3.

Wheatley, P. (1971) *The Pivot of the Four Quarters: A Preliminary Enquiry into the Origins and Character of the Ancient Chinese City* (Edinburgh University Press).

Wolf, M. (1985) *Revolution Postponed: Women in Contemporary China* (London: Methuen).

Yabuki, S. (1995) *China's New Political Economy: The Giant Awakes* (Oxford: Westview Press).

Yan Mingfu (1995) 'Modern Civilisation and China's Urbanization Toward the 21st Century', paper presented to the Symposium on International Urbanization in China, Shunde City, Guangdong Province, 28 August–1 September 1995.

Yan Zhongming (1985) 'Shanghai: The Growth and Shifting Emphasis of China's Largest City', ch. 3 in Sit, V. F. S. (ed.) *Chinese Cities: The Growth of the Metropolis Since 1949* (Oxford University Press).

Yeung, Yue-Man (1990) *Changing Cities of Pacific Asia: A Scholarly Interpretation* Hong Kong: Chinese University Press).

Zou Deci (1995) 'The Introduction of Urban Development in China', *China City Planning Review*, 11 (1) (March) 25–32.

3
Patterns of Migration under the Reforms

Mahmoud Messkoub and Delia Davin

In the 1950s the Chinese government evolved what was perhaps the strictest set of controls over population movement ever exercised within a modern state. A legal transfer of residence within China, especially if it involved a move from a rural to an urban area, could involve greater bureaucratic difficulty than migration across national boundaries elsewhere in the world. In the 1960s and 1970s, migration in China occurred mainly as a result of policy decisions and government direction rather than individual responses to the workings of the market.

Since the economic reforms of the late 1970s, the number of people involved in permanent and temporary migration has greatly increased. Some of the increase is the deliberate result of policy. State enterprises and state labour supply companies (employment agencies) have actively recruited labour from the countryside for new industrial expansion, peasants whose land has been taken over for industrial development are often given non-agricultural jobs, and the restriction on rural migration to small and middle-sized towns has been eased. However the state still attempts to restrict migration into large cities. It is hampered in its ability to do so by the fact that market reforms have deprived it of many of its old means of monitoring and control, and by the strong demand for cheap labour created by the rapid growth of the big city economies.

Millions of rural people have entered the big cities and live in them on a semi-permanent basis, working as contract labourers or traders. Many have temporary urban residence while others come and go from their places of origin so often that they do not need it, or stay illegally in the cities. The least successful are the so-called blind migrants who are highly visible as they mill around railway stations and other public places in search of employment and sleep rough at night. Lapses in public order and raised crime rates are constantly attributed to the presence of this 'floating population', a fact that has given rise to much debate about the desirability of a stricter exclusion system and how this might function (see Chapter 4). Migration is thus a sensitive and much-discussed issue in China at present. Despite the recommendation of some economists that inter-regional flows of labour are desirable, and will increase economic efficiency, migration is predominantly viewed in rather a negative way, and a moral panic about its effects is prominent in media coverage of migration (Davin 1996a). However, official sources do sometimes recognise the potential contribution of migration to the supply of urban produce markets, the development of small towns and the relief of the surplus labour problem in the countryside. Furthermore, the poorer regions also see migration as a means of alleviating poverty.

Control of migration before the reforms

The main means of control of population movement in China is the household registration (*hukou*) system developed in the 1950s (Christiansen 1990). Derived partly from the *baojia* (the registration system of imperial China designed to maintain social control), it also incorporated elements of the labour registration system of the USSR that functioned to control the movement of labour.[1] Temporary regulations regarding urban residential registration issued in 1951 applied only to urban dwellers and were designed essentially to tighten labour discipline (Dutton 1992, p. 207). Later regulations of 1955 and 1958 strengthened the system and extended it to rural areas. The rigid distinction maintained from then on between the agricultural and the non-agricultural population produced what has been called 'a caste-like system of social stratification' designed to keep the peasants on the land and minimise the non-agricultural population (Potter and Potter 1990). Members of households with an agricultural registration were generally unable to establish residence in urban areas or to take up non-agricultural employment. Non-agricultural employment conferred great privilege, for it meant rights to grain and other foodstuffs at heavily subsidised prices, as well as access to superior education, health and welfare systems. The urban population was thus costly for the state to maintain, hence the determined effort to keep its numbers down.

Important further distinctions exist within the non-agricultural population. The most difficult registration to obtain is that for one of the great municipalities of Beijing, Shanghai and Tianjin. Next come the provincial capitals, then the district cities, the county towns and finally the townships. For urban people, a transfer down this hierarchical ladder, or one to an urban place at the same level, is relatively easy, whereas a transfer up the ladder has been extremely difficult. For peasants,until recently it was very difficult to obtain any sort of non-agricultural *hukou*, nor was a move from one rural area to another easy. Few agricultural brigades wanted new members who would increase the number of people to be fed from their fixed area of land. Women marrying across administrative borders were the only peasants to transfer their *hukou* in significant numbers (Lavely 1991, pp. 289–91).

In the past, the extraordinarily effective control that the household registration system gave the state over population mobility was reinforced by its close links with the rationing system. Peasants received grain through the collective unit in which they worked. They could not purchase it elsewhere. Indeed, peasants who went to do a few days' contract work away from home often had to carry their food grain with them. Urban dwellers received grain coupons valid only for the city in which they lived. These were required not only for the purchase of grain in the shops, but also for grain- and flour-based dishes in restaurants and canteens. Cadres who had to travel on official business were issued with national grain coupons, valid anywhere in China, but these had to be accounted for, and unused coupons were supposed to be surrendered at the end of each trip. Even today urban residents can purchase some foodstuffs at the lower state price on production of their *hukou* book, but as almost anything can now be bought in the free market, food is no longer a problem for migrants to the city. However, without valid registration, regular employment is still difficult to obtain, and children cannot be enrolled in kindergarten or school.[2] Visitors from outside a locality must register at the local public security bureau, where a special section is charged with maintaining the *hukou* system. They are granted 'temporary household registration'. When drives against illegal migration are undertaken, public security personnel may raid homes searching for unregistered people.

Children's household registration follows that of their mother. This rule is at first surprising as it runs contrary to patrilineal tradition under which children belong to their father's family. It is surely intended to limit the growth of the urban population. The majority of those emigrating from rural to urban areas are men, but their wives have no automatic right to follow them and indeed separations of many years are common. This system makes it possible for towns that are short of labour to recruit workers who will live in dormitory accommodation without the need to invest in housing, schools and other types of infrastructure for their dependants.

Rural-to-urban and urban-to-rural migration: the 1950s to the 1970s

Despite the severe restrictions on migration before the 1980s, migration was considerable. Unfortunately, it is only possible to quantify it very approximately. As government policy sometimes resulted in the relocation of millions of urbanites to the countryside, China's migration history is unusual in that there were large flows both into and out of the urban areas. When the PRC was established, urbanisation was seen as a necessary and desirable corollary to recovery and industrialisation. Although attempts to control the flow into the cities began in the early 1950s, the pronounced urban bias of the first five-year plan (1953–7) ensured that the flow would continue. There was official recruitment of the peasants to supply labour for expanding industries while rural people were drawn to the cities by the hope of economic betterment. Estimates suggest that urban population grew by 20 million from 1949 to 1953, of which 70 per cent was attributable to migration rather than to natural growth. Migration was less important from 1953 to 1957, but still accounted for 42 per cent of urban population growth (Sit 1985, p. 13).

The major expansion of industry attempted in the 1958–61 Great Leap Forward (GLF) stimulated higher rural-to-urban migration and this was sustained as peasants sought refuge from the concurrent famine. This phase of high rural-to-urban migration was ended by a clampdown. Implementation of the household registration and the associated rationing system, which had begun in the mid-1950s, became much stricter, peasants were expelled from the cities, and millions of citizens formerly registered as urban dwellers were relocated to the villages in an attempt to reduce urban unemployment, which had soared with the collapse of the GLF. In the years before the outbreak of the Cultural Revolution in 1966, the urban population actually declined. The Cultural Revolution itself brought new intensity to the rustication policy. Millions of young people, the Red Guards, intellectuals and political dissidents were sent to resettle in the countryside. Ironically, however, this movement coincided with an inflow of peasants to the cities as millions were taken on as contract workers, and others took advantage of the chaos to enter the cities without authorisation. Any attempt to assess the net flow in this period is complicated by the fact that some of the rusticated urbanites retained their urban registration, while many peasant migrants were still registered in their villages (Scharping 1987, pp. 101–4). After 1976, with the death of Mao, the end of the Cultural Revolution policies, and the introduction of the economic reforms, a strong rural-to-urban flow developed. At the same time strict birth control policies affected natural growth rate of population in urban areas. 80 per cent of urban population growth in the period 1978–81 is attributable to in- migration (Goldstein and Goldstein 1990, p. 67).

Causes of migration before the reform

In China as elsewhere, migrants are motivated by a variety of considerations. Perhaps the clearest division between different types of migration is between organised migration (of which there have been many in China) where people moved as a result of state policy, and individual migration where motivation is personal. The latter can be further subdivided into those who obtained authorisation and those who did not.

Organised migrations began in the 1950s, when peasants were officially recruited into cities to join the urban labour force. In the late 1960s and the 1970s this type of migration largely gave way to the recruitment of contract workers who could be more easily returned to the countryside if demand for labour fell. Another type of relocation of labour was the transfer of skilled labour from the comparatively advanced coastal region to inland cities. Migration to both the cities and the countryside of the frontier areas of Xinjiang, Ningxia, Qinghai, Inner Mongolia, Heilongjiang, Hainan and Yunnan was also officially promoted, usually with enhanced salaries (similar to the policy used in the Soviet Union to encourage moves to Siberia). Migrants included peasants from heavily populated provinces, demobbed soldiers, unemployed people from the cities and those in political trouble.

Irrigation and other development projects have sometimes necessitated large-scale migration. By the mid-1980s, 5.04 million people had been moved to make way for reservoir construction (Yan Hao 1991, p. 226). Most of them were given farmland in less densely populated regions. In recent years much farmland has been lost to urban and industrial development. In such cases the population may be reclassified as non-agricultural without any movement taking place. For example, when all the arable land of Beixincun village (in Changping county north of Beijing) was taken over for the construction of a golf-course, the peasants were compensated by being granted non-agricultural registration and jobs (Zhao 1992, p. 123).

Students in tertiary education are granted 'collective household registration' in the city where they study. Graduates were until recently always assigned employment by the state, which, except in the Cultural Revolution period when many were rusticated, was normally in the urban areas. Now, they may, if they choose, decline a state assignment and seek employment for themselves. Educational migration has probably made only a limited impact on the urban population total, since numbers in higher education have never been very large and only a small minority of students originate from the countryside.

In the past, what might be called 'political' migration produced a substantial urban-to-rural movement. From the early 1960s urban school-leavers for whom no job could be found were urged, and later directed, to relocate in the rural areas. In 1970 this flow was swelled as Red Guards were directed to go to the countryside for re-education. Urbanites who became victims in the many political campaigns that characterised the 1950s and 1960s were also rusticated, the lucky to some village with which they had family connections, the unlucky to labour reform camps in poor, remote areas where conditions could be very grim indeed. Very large numbers were politically disgraced during the Cultural Revolution, and the flow to the villages was increased as all intellectuals were declared to be in need of political reform through labour, and were sent in huge numbers to the countryside on a rotation system.

People involved in non-state-directed or 'spontaneous' migration tend to be motivated either by the hope of economic gain or by family considerations. The rigid control of migration has meant that it was difficult for people to move in search of work or a better life. Such economic migration never completely ceased, but there is little doubt that the population growth of many of the fastest-developing cities through migration was suppressed by the strictness of the policy. Migration to achieve family reunion has also been severely limited. Spouses have frequently waited years before being allowed to transfer in order to live in the same town, and many families, separated by events during the Cultural Revolution, spent years obtaining permission to move back together. Bringing an aged parent into the city to join a son or daughter with urban status has sometimes been less difficult than transferring a spouse, perhaps partly because old people neither leave a job nor require one in the place they move to, but also because the authorities are easier on migrants whose reproductive years are over. The authorities also seem to tolerate prolonged visits by the elderly parents of city-based offspring.

Clearly in the period before the economic reforms, state-sponsored migration was the major form of migration. Many individuals involved in this process were not willing migrants, and made their move under great pressure or straight coercion. When they got the opportunity they tended to return to their places of origin, and indeed any study of population movement in the 1970s and 1980s must take account of the movement of such exiles. Spontaneous migration in the pre-reform period was difficult, and such people lived a rather marginal life unless and until they could get household registration. They were unlikely to be able to manage at all without friends or relatives, and this restricted the distance travelled by migrants and the destinations chosen, probably to an even greater extent than is normal in the migration process.

Contract workers occupied a place somewhere between state-sponsored and spontaneous migrants. Their movement was authorised, their food supply organised, and they did not have to fear sudden expulsion in a sweep to clear illegal migrants. On the other hand their position was by no means secure. A decline in the demand for labour would mean dismissal and return to their villages. Moreover, if a higher authority decided there were too many contract workers in a city, their work unit might simply be ordered to get rid of them.

The economics of pre-reform migration policy

The pre-reform migration policy can best be analysed in the context of the accumulation regime in China. We can observe two distinct phases in the pre-reform migration policy: 1949 to the late 1950s, and 1960s to the late 1970s. The first period was characterised by a 'hands-off' policy – migration was not an issue for the state. The primary concern in this period was one of accumulation and growth under a Soviet-type rapid industrialisation model that manifested itself in the first five-year plan. Investment had a high priority in this period and consequently fixed capital formation rose from 7.7 million yuan in 1952 to 19.5 yuan in 1957. Corresponding figures for the gross capital formation as a proportion of GDP are 17.8 per cent and 21 per cent. These figures are certainly very impressive by any standard, but it is important to note that the jump in investment took place in the earlier part of the 1950s.

The state budget provided the finance for this investment drive. In the early 1950s, 50 per cent or more of the state revenue came from agricultural and industrial taxes, with the rest coming from the profits and depreciation allowances of state enterprises and other sources such as miscellaneous taxes and custom receipts. Over the years, however, the share of state enterprise profits rose and reached the figure of 62 per cent in 1959 (Riskin 1987, pp. 71–5).

It is this drive for rapid accumulation, financed by the retained profit of the state enterprises that, in our view, lies at the heart of the migration policy of the government. The cost of labour to state enterprises was not limited to wage payments. Workers in the state sector were entitled to a range of heavily subsidised benefits that were mostly paid for by the enterprise. These included services like health, sick pay, maternity leave, housing, childcare and education. There were also other types of subsidies, such as those on food and transport, which were paid for out of the state budget. The cost of these subsidies increased with a growing rural–urban migration, which in turn was induced by the existence of a rural–urban wage gap and the availability of urban-based and work-related services.[3] Rural-urban migration also contributed to a growing urban unemployment problem.

In the face of rising wage costs and urban unemployment the government responded by changing its recruitment policy from permanent to temporary (contract) employment. This not only offered flexibility to the state employers, but also ensured that wage costs were kept down. At the same time, stricter control was imposed on movement of population. In short, the state used the migration and employment policies to control urban unemployment, maintain the high level of retained profit of the state enterprises and control state subsidies.

The Chinese experience provides an interesting case of accumulation and growth in a labour surplus economy, which can be examined in the context of the Lewis model (see Figure 3.1). This regime of accumulation changed with the reforms after 1979, which brought private accumulation, slowly but surely, into the Chinese economic arena. This private accumulation now takes place in both rural and urban areas, with direct and far-reaching consequences for population mobility.

Migration and the economic reforms

Many changes with an impact on migration occurred in the 1980s. The rural reforms created a large pool of surplus labourers in the countryside to whom the economic opportunities in towns and cities looked tempting. The rapid growth of the urban economy has created a huge demand for labour, especially in construction and the service sector. Higher incomes and the raising of restrictions on private enterprise

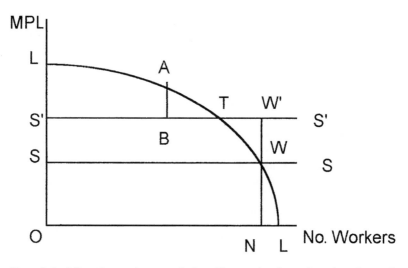

Figure 3.1   Migration and accumulation. The graph relates the urban demand for and supply of labour to the generation of surplus in the that sector. On the horizontal axis we have the number of workers and on the vertical axis the marginal productivity of labour (MPL). (All of Lewis's assumptions from his paper of 1954 are maintained in this analysis.) The intersection between the LL curve (the MPL schedule or the labour demand curve) and SS (the labour supply curve) gives the level of employment. Given that the wage rate (paid to the workers) is OS, the wage bill is equal to OSWN. If there were no other costs to the employer but the wage bill, the surplus (the difference between the total output, OLWN, and the wage bill) would be equal to SLW. However, as noted above, the employers' labour costs were not limited to wages paid to the workers. Thus the labour supply schedule shifts to S'S', increasing the wage bill of employers to OS'W'N and reducing the surplus to S'LAB (note that BAT = WTW'), which obviously limits the scope for raising the level of investment. By restricting the movement of population and by changing its employment policy, the Chinese government was able to arrest the erosion of surplus, and hence maintain the high level of capital accumulation in the urban industrial sector.

have produced particularly fast growth in the informal sector, and incomers to the large cities have been quick to take advantage of the opportunities offered by this development.

Although there are still restrictions on movement through the *hukou* system, they have been considerably relaxed. The first important legal measure was enacted in 1984 when the State Council allowed people with a rural *hukou* to move freely to the 60,000 towns (*zhen*) below the county level if they could supply their own grain rations. New regulations in 1985 introduced procedures for obtaining temporary urban *hukou* for those who stayed over three months in a city. State labour supply companies for the recruitment of labour have been set up in the special economic zones, but much migration is now spontaneous rather than state-sponsored. Although many migrants travel only short distances, migration involving travel across one or several provincial boundaries is now common. Surveys have revealed that significant proportions of the population of all China's major cities are migrants. For example in the boom city of Guangzhou, according to survey data, of those living in residents' households in 1987, 33 per cent were migrants (Cheng 1992, pp. 60–9). Clearly many migrants must have been living in other types of accommodation, and the total migrant population may therefore have formed an even higher proportion of the population.

The primary demographic concern in China is population growth and fertility. Far more attention has been lavished on this area than on population movement. The comparative neglect of migration has led to a dearth of data until recently. The 1982 census did not even include questions on migration, although it is possible to use its results to make some educated guesses about the direction of inter-provincial migration in the period 1952–82 by looking at the provincial population growth rates (Banister 1987, pp. 301–12). Data from the household registration system is not a satisfactory source for the study of migration because people living in the urban areas who are registered elsewhere are not considered to be permanent residents, and are not included in enumerations. Conscious of the need for more information about migration, various migration surveys were conducted in the 1980s. The most important of these was a sample survey of 74 cities and towns carried out by the Chinese Academy of Social Sciences (CASS, 1988). It is a useful source for the study of migration in the early period of the economic reforms, and is discussed in Goldstein and Goldstein (1991) and Ma *et al.* (1997).

The 1990 census was the first to include a question on migration, which asked for each person's place of residence in July 1985. The resulting census tables provide data on intra- and inter-provincial migration, indicating place of origin as city, town or countryside.[4] It also provides information on sex ratios among migrants and on the reasons for migration. Even the census data tends to understate migration, because of the way data were collected. Enumerators in a given place were told to count: (1) persons who lived and had their household registration in that place; (2) persons who had lived in that place for more than one year although their household registration was elsewhere; (3) persons who, although they had lived in that place for less than one year had been away from the place of their household registration for more than a year; (4) persons living in that place awaiting permanent household registration; (5) persons now working or studying abroad who were therefore temporarily without household registration, but whose registration had been in that place. The many millions of temporary migrants who spend less than a year away from their place of origin, or who come and go from their places of origin to take up contract or seasonal work, will have been registered in their places of origin even if they were absent from them at the time of the census. This means that what the Chinese call the 'floating population' is not captured as migrant population in the census. The data also does cover those who have migrated and obtained official registration elsewhere, and those who have been continuously absent from their place of registration for a year. This group, whom we might call long-term rather than seasonal migrants, is clearly worthy of study. The next section of this chapter presents migration data from the 1990 census and offers a discussion of it.

Migration trends 1985–90: census data

An overview of national trends

According to the 1990 census (based on a primarily *de facto* enumeration), 34 million people had changed their residence since 1985 (3.4 per cent of total population). The average annual flow of migrants was therefore 6.8 million between 1985 and 1990. It is important to note that these figures may well underestimate the actual flows, since repeated moves and return migration within the review period are not accounted. There is also the strong possibility of under-reporting as a legal change of residence still requires official approval.

Tables 3.1 and 3.2 summarise the salient features of the internal migration over the review period. From Table 3.1 we can calculate that:

- The predominant migration flows are within provinces – 23 million (68 per cent of total) migrants moved to other places in the same province, as compared with 11 million (32 per cent of total) moving from one province to another.
- The main destinations of both inter- and intra-provincial migrants were urban areas (cities and towns). 57 per cent of migrants settled in urban areas of the same province, while 26 per cent moved to

urban areas of other provinces, with the remaining 17 per cent moving into rural areas (counties).

- As for the origin of migrants, 62 per cent came from rural areas, with little difference in the numbers moving within or between provinces.
- Rural-to-urban migration dominates, amounting to 78 per cent of all migrants (the remaining 22 per cent going from one rural location to another).
- 78 per cent of all migrants residing in rural areas originated in other rural areas.

In Table 3.2 we have the gender breakdown of the migrants for each category of movement.

- 43 per cent of all migrants are women and 57 per cent men (the figures are similar for inter- and intra-provincial migration).
- Women comprise 41 per cent of migrants residing in cities, 43 per cent in towns, and 51 per cent in counties.
- As for the origin of migrants, of 14,735,000 total female migrants, 67 per cent originated in rural areas compared with 59 per cent of male migrants; similar figures hold for the origin of inter- and intra-provincial migration.
- The majority of rural-to-urban migrants are men – 57 per cent, with similar sex patterns holding for inter- and intra-provincial migration. population;
- Women outnumber men in rural-to-rural migration at both inter- and intra-provincial levels: 53 and 60 per cent respectively (see also Davin 1996b on the impact of migration on women who remain)

Regrettably we cannot compare these figures with earlier migration figures, which are almost entirely based on household registration system. There was significant state-directed movement of population in all directions, e.g. rural to urban, urban to rural, south to north. However, we can offer some limited comparison of the more recent rural-to-urban migration with estimates of rural-urban migration in the past. As a rough estimate the net flow of rural out-migration between 1949 and 1982 could be put at 2 million per annum, an indirect measure based on urbanisation figures in Goldstein and Goldstein (1991). In the period 1985–90 the net rural out-migration was 16.7 million, which translates into a per annum figure of 3.3 million, 67 per cent higher than the estimate for me period 1949–82. The actual increase, in all probability, is higher, given that the census misses many short-term and illegal migrants.

Table 3.1 Internal migration in China by origin (residence in 1985) and destination (residence in 1990)

Destination 1990	Origin 1985							
	Total		Urban: City		Urban: Town		Rural: County	
	Number (000)	%	Number (000)	%	Number (000)	%	Number (000)	%
Other provinces								
Total	11 085		2 812	44	1 549	24	6 724	32
%	100		25		14		61	
City	6 500		2 046	32	911	14	3 543	17
%	100		31		14		55	
Town	2 401		493	8	455	7	1 453	7
%	100		21		19		60	
County	2 184		273	4	183	3	1 728	8
%	100		13		8		79	
Same province								
Total	23 014		3 576	56	4 852	76	14 586	68
%	100		16		21		63	
City	14 746		2 376	37	3 248	51	9 122	43
%	100		16		22		62	
Town	4 553		764	12	1 180	18	2 609	12
%	100		17		26		57	
County	3 715		436	7	424	7	2 855	13
%	100		12		11		77	

Table 3.1 Cont.

Destination 1990	Origin 1985						
	Total	Urban:				Rural:	
		City		Town		County	
		Number (000)	%	Number (000)	%	Number (000)	%
National Total	34 109	6 388	100	6 401	100	21 310	100
%	100	19		19		62	
City	21 246	4 422	69	4 159	65	12 665	59
%	100	21		20		59	
Town	6 954	1 257	20	1 635	26	4 062	19
%	100	18		24		58	
County	5 899	709	11	607	9	4 583	22
%	100	12		10		78	

Source: Our calculations based on the 1990 census, vol. IV, Table 11.1.

Table 3.2 Female migration as a percentage of internal migration by origin (residence in 1985) and destination (residence 1990)

	Origin 1985							
	Total		Urban:				Rural:	
			City		Town		County	
Destination 1990	All	Female	Number (000)	Female	Number (000)	Female	Number (000)	Female
Other provinces								
Total	11 085	4 274	2 812	881	1 549	510	6 724	2 883
%		39		31		33		43
City	6 500	2 255	2 046	684	911	271	3 543	1 300
%		35		33		30		37
Town	2 401	977	493	144	455	169	1 453	664
%		41		29		37		46
County	2 184	1 042	273	53	183	70	1 728	919
%		48		19		38		53
Same province								
Total	23 014	10 461	3 576	1 279	4 852	2 179	14 586	7 003
%		45		36		45		48
City	14 746	6 461	2 376	952	3 248	1 486	9 122	4 023
%		44		40		46		44
Town	4 553	2 017	764	228	1 180	523	2 609	1 266
%		44		30		44		49
County	3 715	1 983	436	99	424	170	2 855	1 714
%		53		23		40		60

Table 3.2 Cont.

	Origin 1985							
	Total		Urban:				Rural:	
			City		Town		County	
Destination 1990	All	Female	Number (000)	Female	Number (000)	Female	Number (000)	Female
National								
Total	34 109	14 735	6 388	2 160	6 401	2 689	21 310	9 886
%		43		34		42		46
City	21 246	8 716	4 422	1 636	4 159	1 757	12 665	5 323
%		41		37		42		42
Town	6 954	2 994	1 257	372	1 635	692	4 062	1 930
%		43		30		42		48
County	5 899	3 025	709	152	607	240	4 583	2 633
%		51		21		40		57

Source: Our calculations based on the 1990 census, vol. IV, Table 11.1.

The earlier migrations were primarily directed by the state, and related accumulation policies. These shifted from the promotion of heavy industrialisation in the 1950s (with its associated liberal migration policy) to one of greater emphasis on agriculture and rural development in the 1960s and 1970s. The migrations of the 1980s, on the other hand, are more influenced by the market forces unleashed by the economic reforms after 1979. These reforms have accentuated the differentiation of the rural population (into more unequal groups) and have opened up new opportunities in the fast-developing areas of the south and east (including the economically important municipalities of Beijing and Shanghai). An important consequence of the reforms has been the growth in private sector activities. In 1990 the private sector accounted for 9 per cent of the industrial output and 27 per cent of the retail sales, a phenomenal increase over the 1980s figures of, respectively, 1 per cent and 4 per cent (ODI 1993). In the new regime of development in which 'some people get rich before others', the flow of migration is going to be directed less by the state than by an accumulation regime dictated by market forces. Migration has played an important role in allowing households to take advantage of the growing opportunities in urban areas.

Regional trends

In Table 3.3, column II presents intra-provincial migration, column III inter-provincial out migration and column IV inter-provincial in-migration by province for the period 1985–90. We have calculated net migration from out- and in-migration and it is shown in column V. As we would expect, Guangdong has been the biggest gainer, with 1.26 million migrants from other provinces, while it has lost only 250,000. Adjacent to Hong Kong, Guangdong has benefited most from China's 'open-door' policy. In 1990 it received about one-third of all direct foreign investment in China and the proportion was higher still in 1990 (SSB 1991b). In terms of fixed assets per person, gross GNP and industrial output per person, Guangdong also scores very high, as it does on the physical quality of life index (Leeming 1993, pp. 169, 162, 160, Rong and Wang 1991, p. 208). The great municipalities of Beijing, Shanghai and Tianjin also had high levels of in-migration with low out-migration. These again are very rapidly developing areas with high scores for all the measures of development.

For Shanghai this represented a reversal of the trend in the first three decades of the People's Republic, during which time 1.3 million Shanghai people took up jobs in the hinterland and the border areas.

Table 3.3 Net migration (residence in 1990) by province

Province	Population in 1982 I	Intra-provincial migration II	Inter-provincial out-migration III	Inter-provincial in-migration IV	Net provincial migration IV − III = V
Beijing	9 230 687	84 336	132 148	681 356	549 208
Tianjin	7 764 141	35 423	72 193	245 274	173 081
Hebei	53 005 875	812 532	645 704	520 698	−125 006
Shanxi	25 291 389	627 347	218 481	307 232	88 751
Inner Mongolia	19 274 279	578 138	303 129	254 410	−48 719
Liaoning	35 721 693	872 395	305 996	553 096	247 100
Jilin	22 560 053	611 199	355 532	237 510	−118 022
Heilongjiang	32 665 546	1 055 517	607 485	367 576	−239 909
Shanghai	11 859 748	173 150	132 562	670 612	538 050
Jiangsu	60 521 114	1 188 589	620 487	792 651	172 164
Zhejiang	38 884 603	799 618	632 323	337 720	−294 603
Anhui	49 665 724	869 545	533 388	338 346	−195 042
Fujian	25 931 106	722 698	238 489	252 617	14 128
Jinangxi	33 184 827	734 087	293 772	225 460	−68 312
Shandong	74 419 054	1 190 017	534 842	610 397	75 555
Henan	74 422 739	1 238 943	589 626	478 286	−111 340
Hubei	47 804 150	1 088 391	346 274	431 745	85 471
Hunan	54 008 851	1 297 956	528 614	272 326	−256 288
Guangdong[a]	53 369 998	2 671 746	249 794	1 259 939	1 010 145
Guangxi	36 420 960	888 402	588 889	142 891	−445 998
Hainan[a]	5 929 922	142 873	105 977	150 449	44 472

Table 3.3 Cont.

Province	Population in 1982 I	Intra-provincial migration II	Inter-provincial out-migration III	Inter-provincial in-migration IV	Net provincial migration IV – III = V
Sichuan	99 713 310	2 344 256	1 317 049	473 482	–843 567
Guizhou	28 552 997	464 694	312 787	190 892	–121 895
Yunnan	32 553 817	732 225	277 432	254 334	–23 098
Tibet	1 892 393	no data	54 582	no data	not calculable
Shaanxi	28 904 423	706 163	371 340	314 877	–56 463
Gansu	19 569 261	449 530	280 816	199 480	–81 336
Qinghai	3 895 706	150 900	101 141	115 861	14 720
Ningxia	3 895 578	122 752	56 609	91 997	35 388
Xinjiang	13 081 681	360 912	277 412	341 759	64 347
Total	1 003 937 078	23 014 334	11 084 873	11 113 273	28 400[b]

[a] In 1982 Guangdong province included Hainan, which became a seperate province in 1988. We have assumed that the distribution of population between these two provinces in the 1990 census was the same for 1982.

[b] The net migration figure should equal zero in the absence of international migration and other omissions that are not taken into account in our calculations. However, the error of 28 400 is a very small proportion (0.03 per cent) of the total migration figure.

Source: Our calculations based on 1990 census , vol. IV, table 11.1, and the 1982 census.

Indeed Shanghai appears to have been the only province to have experienced a long-term net loss through out-migration (Banister 1987, pp. 301–2). Like other cities, Shanghai experienced out-migration in certain periods of these three decades because of the government's policy of rustication of the urban youth and unemployed or surplus labour. But there was another special factor in the city's net loss. Shanghai was the most advanced city in China in 1949, with a population that enjoyed and has continued to enjoy comparatively high levels of education. The city has therefore been the source of much of the skilled and technical labour required for the government's programme of promoting industry in the hinterland. Beijing, as the national capital, had a very different migration history, with a reported out-migration of 4.33 million in 1950–1980 being more than compensated for by an in-migration of 5.37 million (Banister 1987, p. 339). The large gains made in the 1980s by both these cities (and to a lesser extent by Tianjin, the third municipality) reflect the strength of the pull generated by their fast-growing economies. In addition, although the government still declares its intention to limit the growth of large cities, it is less strict in implementing this policy than in the past. Of the areas where net migration was large, it was of course far more significant as a proportion of total population in the three great municipalities with their comparatively small populations than in the populous provinces (see Table 3.3).

The remaining big gainers of migrants in Table 3.3, Liaoning and Jiangsu provinces, are also characterised by higher out-migration. Whereas out-migration was less than 25 per cent of in-migration for Beijing and Shanghai, for Liaoning it was 55 per cent and Jiangsu 78 per cent. Like the other gainers, these two provinces score well on fixed assets, GNP and industrial output per capita, and on the physical quality of life, with Liaoning scoring better than Jiangsu on this last measure (Leeming 1993, pp. 169, 162, 160; Rong and Wang 1991, p. 208). It is easy to see why they attract incomers, but what explains the high out-migration from these provinces? First, their comparatively high levels of industrialisation and urbanisation and good standards of education will have tended to create a relatively mobile population with marketable skills. Second, Jiangsu borders on the population magnet of Shanghai, while Liaoning is within reach of the municipalities of Beijing and Tianjin. A breakdown of the Liaoning out-migrants shows that while they have gone all over China, the largest numbers went to the other provinces of the north-east, Jilin and Heilongjiang, and to Shandong, the province from which many settlers in the north-east came over the past century (1990 Census). Significant numbers also moved to the sparsely populated and poorly developed Inner Mongolia, to Hebei province in the Beijing–Tianjin area, to Beijing and Tianjin themselves and to Jiangsu. Of the areas which received large numbers of Liaoning migrants, only Beijing and Tianjin had higher levels of GNP per capita than Liaoning itself. We may deduce that while some migrants sought economic advantage or a superior lifestyle in the great municipalities, others were drawn to less-developed provinces such as Heilongjiang, Hebei or Sichuan, or to developing areas such as Inner Mongolia, where their skills were in demand or other opportunities more easily secured.

Of Jiangsu's 1.8 million migrants, 1.2 million moved within the province while over 620,000 left it. Of these, by far the most significant number, 214,000, went to Shanghai, over 33 000 went to Beijing, and over 24,000 to Guangdong (1990 Census). Jiangsu is a highly commercialised province so it is probable that many migrants were involved in trading. The neighbouring provinces of Anhui, Zhejiang and Shandong received 62,000, 38,000 and 33,000 Jiangsu migrants respectively, and an outer circle of neighbours of these neighbouring provinces received significant though lower numbers. Of the border regions, Xinjiang was the main destination for Jiangsu's migrants, receiving over 20,000 of them.

When we consider provinces which experienced a net loss through migration, the case of Sichuan is so outstanding among the high net losers that it would seem to merit a discussion of its own. With well over a 100 million people, Sichuan is the most populous province of China and has a larger population than many of the world's major states.[5] Out-migrants from Sichuan numbered 1.317 million in 1985–90, against only 526,000 in-migrants, producing a net loss of 844,000. Its location, in the interior and cut off from the coast by mountains, has prevented Sichuan from sharing fully in the commercial and industrial boom of the reform years. It is a rich province agriculturally, with a surplus of grain produced on the fertile Chengdu plain, but some of the province's mountainous areas are poor. 25 per cent of its counties have been classified as wholly or partly in poverty (Kuchler 1990, p. 129). It is in the bottom group of provinces for per capita fixed assets, GNP and industrial output, and is low on the physical quality of life index (Leeming 1993, pp. 169,162, 160; Rong and Wang 1991, p. 208).

Out-migrants from Sichuan chose a wide range of destinations. Over 127,000, went to the neighbouring province of Yunnan. Among other neighbours, Guizhou and Hubei received around 100,000 each, while

Hunan and Shaanxi received over 70,000 Sichuan migrants between them. However, many Sichuanese went further afield. Their most popular destination was Guangdong, which attracted almost 154,000, while over 118,000 went to Xinjiang, and 96,000 to Jiangsu. Beijing, Fujian, Henan and Shandong also attracted significant numbers. Proximity obviously contributes to the migrants' choice of destination, so that large numbers moved to Guizhou, although it is a considerably poorer province (Leeming 1993, p. 162). Quite distant provinces such as Guangdong and Fujian are made attractive by their booming economies. Jiangsu and Anhui are comparatively accessible to Sichuanese, despite the distances involved, because they can make the journey by boat down the Yangzi river.[6]

In most cases migrants from Sichuan who went to cities and towns outnumbered those going to the countryside, but the ratio varies considerably. Sichuanese migration to rural areas of other provinces was predominantly from rural areas. In many such cases women greatly outnumbered men among the migrants, in sharp contrast to other types of migration where men predominate. For example 31 227 women left rural Sichuan for the countryside of Jiangsu as against only 3035 men, and 16,281 women were involved in rural-to-rural migration to Shandong against only 731 men. In other cases the sexes are more evenly represented; for example 1177 men went to the countryside of Guangdong compared with 1013 women.

Women are recruited to work in village enterprises, sometimes across great distances, so shortage of rural labour may also be a pull factor, as with male migration. Marriage in China is overwhelmingly patrilocal, and it is also possible that where women significantly outnumber men in rural-to-rural migration that a marriage migration chain is in existence.[7] The data give some support for this as a factor, at least in the case of Sichuan. The tabulation of the distribution of migration by cause and province show that Sichuan had exceptionally high levels of inter-provincial migration for the purpose of marriage, with those marrying out considerably outnumbering those marrying in (1990 Census and SSB 1991a).

Most of the other provinces that have lost population through migration, – Inner Mongolia, Heilongjiang, Jilin and Gansu in the north, and Yunnan, Guizhou and Guangxi in the south – are comparatively sparsely populated areas. They were recipients of government-directed migration in the first thirty years of the People's Republic, and many of those people have tried to return. These are border provinces, or (in the case of Jilin and Guizhou) share many of the characteristics of border regions. However, in other ways they are far from homogeneous. Heilongjiang has above-average fixed assets per capita, while Inner Mongolia and Jilin have between average and 60 per cent of average, and Gansu, Yunnan, Guizhou and Guangxi all have below 60 per cent of average (Leeming 1993, p. 169). Alone of these provinces Heilongjiang has a relatively high per capita GNP and level of industrial output per person (Leeming 1993, pp. 162, 160). Most of these provinces are in the bottom two groups on the quality of life index. But Heilongjiang, Jilin and Guangxi all turn out to be exceptions, being placed in the second highest group, higher for example than the province of Jiangsu, which, it will be remembered, was a net gainer from migration (Rong and Wang 1991, p. 208). Two other significant losers, Hebei, and Anhui, although much less remote than the provinces discussed earlier, are nonetheless relatively disadvantaged. In terms of fixed assets per capita, Hebei is below average and Anhui more than 60 per cent below. They also rate relatively low for GNP per capita and in the case of Anhui for rural land per capita. Both are immediately adjacent to wealthier provinces to which they lose population.

The final loser we consider, the province of Zhejiang, poses a greater puzzle. It is not disadvantaged according to any of our measures, yet 632,000 of its population migrated out. Even with a considerable in-migration of 338,000 this left it with a net loss of 295,000. Part of the explanation here must lie in the province's proximity to Shanghai, which received over 100,000 Zhejiang migrants. However over 52,000 went northwards to Jiangsu and 46,000 crossed into Fujian to the south, although these two provinces had lower per capita GNP and lower levels of urbanisation than Zhejiang. It may be that limits to agricultural growth are coming into play in this densely populated province where agriculture is already extremely intensive.

Given the 30 provincial-level administrative divisions, inter-provincial migration is inevitably a complex subject. However, certain clear trends can be observed from the 1990 census data. There was an overall movement from the poor, less developed and less heavily populated provinces of the hinterland to the fast-developing, more urbanised provinces of the coastal region, where the quality of life is better. This reversed the trend of earlier years when the more remote and sparsely populated provinces such as Heilongjiang, Qinghai, Ningxia and Xinjiang tended to receive the greatest in-migration (Banister 1987, pp. 304–5).

The data for 1985–90 indicate that comparatively poor provinces within the richer regions draw migrants from even poorer regions, but also lose population to richer neighbouring provinces. Despite all the efforts of the government to control entry to the three municipalities they exert a very strong pull on migrants, as does the wealthy province of Guangdong. However, not all migration fits these general patterns. Xinjiang, Qinghai and Ningxia, all remote inland provinces, have all made slight gains through migration. Heilongjiang is remote yet a comparatively rich, developed and urbanised province and might be expected to hold or even gain population through migration. In fact it lost quite heavily, as did its neighbour Jilin. Of the three north-eastern provinces only Liaoning (one of the richest provinces in China) gained.

Causes of migration as recorded by the census

Where a person had been resident elsewhere in 1985, the census enumerator had to record the reason for the move under one of nine categories:

1. People of 15 and over who have moved to that place because of a work transfer.
2. People of 15 or over recruited or allocated to work in that place at the time of graduation (from secondary or tertiary education).
3. People of 15 or over who live in that place in order to carry out work, business, trade or commerce.
4. People of 6 or over who have come to that place to enrol in a school, or for a course or class run by a work unit in that place.
5. People who have moved to that place to live with relatives or friends.
6. Cadres, employees and workers who have left their posts to retire and have come to this place. Includes peasants from those rural districts that have set up pension systems.
7. Accompanying family members who have moved with a cadre, employee or worker who has been transferred.
8. People of 15 and over who have moved to their spouse's place of residence because of marriage.
9. Those who have migrated for reasons other than those listed above.

Of the first three categories, all work-related, we have tended to regard the first two as mainly involving state employees and the third as being closely linked to private economic activity. Tables 3.4 and 3.5 show the importance of each of the nine categories for inter-provincial migration, and intra-provincial migration by type of place of origin (city, town and county).

Table 3.4 Percentage distribution of causes of inter-provincial migration by destination of migrants (residence in 1990) and sex

Causes	Total			City			Town			County		
	Total	Male	Female	Total	Male	Female	Total	Male	Female	Total	Male	Female
Job transfer	15	20	8	34	39	25	25	31	15	5	8	2
Job assignment	5	6	2	14	16	10	3	3	1	1	1	0
Work/business	29	37	19	6	7	5	17	21	13	42	56	25
Study	8	10	6	15	14	16	14	16	10	4	7	2
Relative	10	8	13	6	3	10	10	8	14	12	11	14
Retirement	1	2	1	4	5	2	2	3	1	0	1	0
Move with family	11	7	16	14	9	25	16	10	24	8	6	11
Marriage	14	2	30	2	1	6	8	1	18	20	3	40
Others	6	7	5	4	5	3	6	7	5	7	8	6
	100	100	100	100	100	100	100	100	100	100	100	100

Source: Our calculations based on 1990 census, vol. IV, table 11.6.

Table 3.5 Percentage distribution of causes of intra-provincial migration by destination of migrants (residence in 1990) and sex

Causes	Total			City			Town			County		
	Total	Male	Female	Total	Male	Female	Total	Male	Female	Total	Male	Female
Job transfer	10	13	7	24	26	20	19	23	14	4	6	2
Job assignment	7	9	5	22	24	19	8	9	6	3	4	2
Work/business	23	29	16	5	6	4	14	16	11	30	41	20
Study	14	16	12	17	14	21	20	21	19	11	14	8
Relative	10	7	12	5	3	8	8	6	10	11	9	14
Retirement	2	3	0	5	7	1	2	3	1	1	1	0
Move with family	10	8	13	10	6	16	14	10	18	9	7	11
Marriage	14	2	28	3	1	6	8	1	15	19	3	35
Others	10	14	7	10	12	5	9	12	6	11	15	7
	100	100	100	100	100	100	100	100	100	100	100	100

Source: Our calculations based on 1990 Census, vol. IV, table 11.6.

If we begin by considering the relative importance of the work and business category, we find that it is the most important cause nationally, accounting for 29 per cent of all movement between provinces. It is much more important for migrants from the countryside, accounting for 42 per cent of inter-provincial and 30 per cent of intra-provincial migrants. The equivalent figures for migrants originating in the cities are 6 per cent and 5 per cent. It is also much more important as a 'male cause' than as a 'female' cause: 37 per cent of male inter-provincial migration and 29 per cent of male intra-provincial migration was attributed to work and business, as opposed to 19 per cent and 16 per cent for females. It was the cause of 57 per cent of in-migration to Guangdong and 30 per cent to Fujian but only 16 per cent to Beijing. As this cause probably covers most private economic activity, its pre-eminence in boom areas is predictable. Its lesser relative importance as a cause of movement to the capital can be explained by the importance of education and, to a lesser extent, transfer and assignment (both categories of officially directed movement) that takes place into Beijing. Particular caution is probably in order in all consideration of the work or business cause. It is likely that the majority of short-term and illegal migrants to the cities fit this description, and the census enumeration of these people is likely to have been incomplete.

Work transfer (item 1) was cited in 15 per cent of inter-provincial migrations, second in importance only to the work and business (item 3) factor. For Xinjiang, Gansu and Ningxia Jilin and Tianjin it was actually more important than work and business, presumably reflecting the interest of the state in developing these areas and the relative importance of the state sector in them. The much less important job assignment category (item 2), which also represents state-directed movement, shows a similar scatter. Job assignment is more important than work and business as a cause of in-migration for Shanghai, Tianjin and Xinjiang, reflecting the continued dominance of the state sector in these areas, and perhaps also the success of the state in continuing to limit free-enterprise-inspired settlement in the municipalities.

Job transfer and job assignment are important causes of migration for city people and, to a lesser extent, for those from towns. They are not important causes of migration from the countryside. (This distribution reflects the state's greater involvement in the economy of the urban areas.) They are also less important as causes of female migration than of male migration. This gender difference is no doubt partly the result of women's lesser involvement in the state sector, but probably also reflects a cultural inclination for officialdom to post women close to their families and thus to their places of origin where possible. Marriage migration at 14 per cent is the third major category in inter-provincial migration and the second in intra-provincial migration. This pattern holds good for most of the provinces, though here too there are intriguing variations. For Sichuan, marriage migration at 24 per cent of all in-migration is the most important category, while it is only 6 per cent and sixth most important in Xinjiang. Its relatively low ranking for Shanghai (7 per cent) and Beijing (10 per cent) is probably due to a mix of factors. Young people in big cities usually wish to marry other urbanites whom they chose for themselves or meet before a marriage is agreed to. This tends to reduce the number of long-distance marriages. Moreover, the spouses of city residents who are not themselves registered as urban residents do not acquire the right to urban registration through marriage. Some apply for and obtain it, though this process may take years, while others simply resign themselves to living apart from their spouses. The general awareness of the difficulties involved in marrying an outsider probably deters many urban residents from doing so.

The most striking point about marriage migration is its gendered nature. Tables 3.6 and 3.7 show that 91 per cent of all migration for marriage within provinces and 92 per cent between provinces was by women. Females dominate marriage migration, whether the place of origin is county, town or city. However, men do make up almost a fifth of the marriage migrants from cities, as opposed to less than a tenth in the countryside. Tables 3.4 and 3.5 show that marriage was the most important cause of both intra- and inter-provincial migration for females nationally. This is also true for female migrants from the countryside, but other causes have greater importance for female migrants from urban areas.

Migrating to education facilities is an important factor within provinces (14 per cent) and accounts for 8 per cent of all inter-provincial migration. It is more important as a cause of male migration, accounting for 16 per cent of male intra-provincial migration and 10 per cent of male migration between provinces. The equivalent figures for female migration were 12 per cent and 6 per cent. If we take all education migrants involved in inter-provincial migration, 71 per cent were male. But males were less dominant among migrants of city origin (64 per cent), while they constituted 81 per cent of those going into education from rural areas. Males also dominated educational migration within provinces but to a significantly lesser extent, at 61 per cent of the whole

Table 3.6 Causes of migration within a province by sex and origin (residence in 1985) of migrants (percentage shares in each category)

	Origin							
	Total		Urban				Rural	
			City		Town		County	
Cause	Male	Female	Male	Female	Male	Female	Male	Female
Job transfer	69	39	71	29	66	34	72	28
Job assignment	69	31	69	31	64	36	72	28
Work/business	67	33	71	29	64	36	67	33
Study/training	61	39	55	45	58	42	64	36
To relative/friends	41	59	40	60	40	60	41	59
Retired and resigned	86	14	90	10	79	21	87	13
Moved with family	40	60	41	59	40	60	39	61
Marriage	9	91	19	81	9	91	9	91
Other	70	30	83	17	73	27	67	33

Source: Our calculations based on 1990 census, vol. IV, table 11.6.

Table 3.7 Causes of migration between provinces by sex and origin (residence in 1985) of migrants (percentage shares in each category)

	Origin							
	Total		Urban:				Rural	
			City		Town		County	
Cause	Male	Female	Male	Female	Male	Female	Male	Female
Job transfer	78	22	76	24	76	24	85	15
Job assignment	78	22	78	22	77	23	82	18
Work/business	72	28	76	24	71	29	72	28
Study/training	71	29	64	36	72	28	81	19
To relative/friends	47	53	42	58	46	54	48	52
Retired and resigned	81	19	82	18	79	21	81	19
Moved with family	39	61	42	58	40	60	37	63
Marriage	8	92	18	82	10	90	8	92
Other	66	34	79	21	70	30	61	39

Source: Our calculations based on 1990 census, vol. IV, table 11.6.

group (55 per cent of those from cities and 64 per cent of those from the countryside).

Tianjin, Shanghai and Beijing, all great centres of education, attracted large numbers of educational migrants. Places like Xinjiang, Ningxia, Inner Mongolia and Qinghai, drew very few. Education rated low as a cause in the Guangdong figures, where other pull factors are very strong. Conversely, educational migration was the second most important cause of in-migration to Jilin, an educationally-advanced province that may lack other attractions.

We had supposed that moving to be with relations or friends might be used as a cover for getting into places like Shanghai and Beijing for which residence is hard to obtain. But the figures do not really confirm this, as they come out around the national average for this category, and only in Tianjin are the numbers significantly higher. This is an important category throughout the north-east, as it is for the less desirable areas such as Inner Mongolia, Ningxia and Xinjiang. This may reflect the existence of migration chains with their origins in the policies of Maoist China. Many young urbanites were resettled in these developing areas in the 1960s and 70s. Their relatives in the next generation can rely on them for help if they seek to make good in these provinces where there are shortages of skilled labour. Dependent migration stands at 11 per cent nationally but is much lower for the municipalities, where dependants would not automatically be allowed to follow the breadwinner. The low level of this factor generally (compared with work transfer and the other work-related categories) probably reflects the fact that family and marital separation for work-related reasons is commonplace in China.

The retirement category is small for all provinces. Nobody seems to retire to Xinjiang, Ningxia, Qinghai, Inner Mongolia or Heilongjiang. The larger than average proportion retiring to Shanghai perhaps reflects its high rate of out- migration in the past.

We turn now to the causes of out-migration for which we have to rely on the 10 per cent sample as they were not tabulated in the publication of the full census. Job transfer and job assignment are relatively important reasons for leaving Beijing, Tianjin and Shanghai, while very few people leave these places for work and business. This probably reflects the fact that the state transfers people out of these places, whereas few people choose to leave them. Graduates from the municipalities will in many cases have come in from other provinces for study and will accept that they may be being assigned elsewhere. Large numbers leave Zhejiang, Jiangsu and Anhui for work and business, which must reflect the high level of involvement by people from the dynamic parts of these provinces in trade outside. The Fujian data seem to resemble this, and this category also explains a high proportion of migration from Sichuan, Guangxi, Hunan and Henan, although here many migrants are probably labourers rather than traders. Provinces of the north-west such as Xinjiang, Qinghai and Ningxia, and the poor south-western provinces of Yunnan and Guizhou, provide few migrants in this category.

Marriage migration seems to have provided an important means of leaving the province for the women of Yunnan and Guizhou, where marriage migration accounted for fully half total out-migration. Marriage out-migration from Guangxi and Sichuan was also an important phenomenon. Yunnan, Guizhou and Guangxi are poor provinces, not seen as desirable destinations, and for all these provinces except Sichuan, marriage as a cause of in-migration was below the national average. By contrast with the south-west, marriage does not seem to be used as a way of leaving the poor provinces of north-west China. Marriage migration from these provinces is low. Marriage migration out of the municipalities is also below average, as is dependent migration, no doubt because those with residence rights in the great cities would be reluctant to relinquish them. The only exception to this rule indicated in the table is in the retirement column. Retirement is of more than average importance as a cause of out-migration for both Shanghai and Beijing, perhaps because both cities contain large numbers of outsiders, some of whom may prefer to retire to their places of origin, where they retain family or other contacts and the cost of living is lower.

Conclusion

The experience of migration in China is unique among developing countries for the extensive control that the state has exercised over the distribution of population across regions. In their pursuit of industrialisation and the restructuring of the economy, the planners viewed labour as an important asset. The accumulation regime that came into operation after the revolution was based on the state ownership of the means of production, and was designed to channel resources into the development of industry, agriculture and infrastructure.

In the early 1950s the planners followed a rather lax migration policy, on the assumption that so long as labour is productive it does not matter where it is located. But the concern with feeding and maintaining a large and growing urban population led to a change of policy that imposed barriers on movement of people. One of the most important restrictions was the food ration system, in particular with respect to grain, which was linked to the household registration. As we have seen, from the mid-1950s until the advent of the economic reforms these two systems worked together to restrict urban population growth. However, one should note that it was less difficult to move into towns than cities.

Since 1979 the reforms have produced a major change in government attitudes, and in its ability to control movement. Obtaining temporary permit to change residence been made easier. But, and more importantly, the emergence of a nation-wide food market has stripped the government of one of its most effective measures. In the 1980s the rural reforms created a large pool of surplus labourers in the countryside to whom the economic opportunities in the cities looked tempting. The rapid growth of the urban economy has created a huge demand for labour, especially in construction and the service sector. Higher real incomes and the lifting of restrictions on private enterprises have produced particularly fast growth in the informal sector, and incomers to the large cities have been quick to take advantage of the opportunities offered by this development. Consequently the 1980s witnessed substantial increases in the annual volume of migration, which according to our conservative estimates is at least 40 per cent above the annual flows in the preceding three decades.

By all accounts this trend is going to continue, and the challenge facing the government is how to direct the massive movement of population as the economy becomes more integrated. The evidence suggests that officials view urban in-migration as more of a 'public order' problem than an economic phenomenon, hence the regular and arbitrary rounding up of migrants in big cities. However, the existence of a clearly defined policy with regard to the development of small and medium-sized towns and cities should help the government to regulate rather than restricting the flow of migration, which in any case cannot be effective under current economic conditions.

Notes

1. For a detailed comparison of the systems see Dutton 1992, ch. 6.
2. Agence France Press reported (16 August 1997) that a scheme has been announced that may be the start of improved rights for the migrants. 400 towns have been chosen to try out a policy of granting urban status and allow access to education and health care for migrants and their families.

3. While opinions vary as to its extent in the 1950s, there is general agreement on the existence of a gap between rural and urban incomes which varied between 15 to 100 per cent depending on the method and location of study. It is also important to note that urban wages were rising much faster than rural wages over the same period (Riskin 1987, p. 62).
4. Most of the information we use on the Census is drawn from Guowuyuan Renkou Pucha Bangongshi (1993) *Zhongguo 1990 nian renkou pucha ziliao* (Tabulation of the 1990 population census of the People's Republic of China) (Beijing: Tongji Chubanshe) vols I–IV. In the text we refer to these volumes as 1990 Census.
5. These figures refer of course to the province before its division in 1997 (see Chapters 1 and 7).
6. The source here is the 10 per cent sample survey (SSB 1991a, pp. 616–21), because the full four volume tabulation of the census results used elsewhere in the article does not provide information on the causes of out-migration by province.
7. For studies of marriage migration in China, see Lavely, 1991; Han Min and Eades 1995; Ji Ping *et al.*, 1985.

References

Banister, J. (1987) *China's Changing Population* (Stanford University Press).
Cheng Chaoze (1992) 'Bashi niandai Zhongguo dalu renkou liudong wenti', *Zhongguo dalu yanjiu*, 7.
Chinese Academy of Social Sciences (CASS) (1988) *Migration to 74 Cities and Towns Sampling Survey* Beijing: (Cass Population Research Institute).
Christiansen, F. (1990) 'Social Division and Peasant Mobility in Mainland China: The Implications of the Hu-k'ou System', *Issues and Studies*, 26 (4) 23–42.
Davin, D. (1996a) 'Affreux, sales et mechants: les migrants dans les medias chinois', *Perspectives chinois*, 38, 6–12.
Davin, D. (1996b) 'Migration and rural women in China: a look at the gendered impact of large-scale migration', *Journal of International Development*, 8 (5) 655–66.
Dutton, M. R. (1992) *Policing and Punishment in China* (Cambridge University Press).
Goldstein, S. and Goldstein, A. (1990) 'Migration in China: Data Policies and Patterns', in Nam, C. B. Serrow, W. J. and Sly, D. F. *International Handbook on Internal Migration* (Westport CT: Greenwood Press).
Goldstein, S. and Goldstein, A. (1991) *Permanent and Temporary Migration Differentials in China*, papers of the East–West Population Institute no. 117, (Honolulu: East–West Center).
Han Min and J. S. Eades (1995) 'Brides, Bachelors and Brokers: The Marriage Market in Rural Anhui in an Era of Economic Reform', *Modern Asian Studies*, 29 (4) 841–69.
Ji Ping, Zhang Kaidi and Liu Dawei (1985) 'An analysis of marital migration among residents of the Beijing suburbs' (Beijing jiaoqu nongcun renkou hunyin qiianyi qianxi), *Zhongguo shehui kexue*, 3, 201–13.

Kuchler, J. (1990) 'On the establishment of a poverty-orientated development policy in China', in Delman, J. *et al.* (eds), *Remaking Peasant China* (Aarhus University Press).

Lavely, W. (1991) 'Marriage and Mobility under Rural Collectivisation', in Rubie S., Watson, R. S. and Ebrey, P. (eds)) *Marriage and Inequality in Chinese Society* (Berkeley: University of California Press).

Leeming, F. (1993) *The Changing Geography of China* (Oxford: Blackwell).

Lewis, W. A. (1954) 'Economic Development with Unlimited Supply of Labour', *Manchester School,* 12 (2) 139–91.

Ma, Z., Liaw, K. L., Zeng, Y. (1997) 'Migration in the Urban/Rural Hierarchy of China: Insights from the Micro Data of the 1987 Migration Survey', *Environment and Planning,* 29 (4) 707.

1990 Census (1993) *Tabulation of the 1990 Population Census of the People's Republic of China (Zhongguo 1990 nian renkou pucha ziliao)* (Beijing: National Census Office, Tongji Chubanshe, vols I–IV.

Overseas Development Institute (ODI) (1993) 'China's Economic Reforms', Briefing Paper (London) February.

Potter, S. H., and Potter, J. M. (1990) *China's Peasants: the Anthropology of a Revolution* (Cambridge University Press).

Riskin, C. (1987) *China's Political Economy: The Quest for Development Since 1949* (Oxford University Press).

Rong Zhigang and Wang Shanmai (1991) 'The Quality and Quantity of the Population', in Wang and Hull.

Scharping, T. (1987) 'Urbanization in China Since 1949: A Comment', *China Quarterly* 109 (March).

Sit, V. F. S. 1985 *Chinese Cities: The Growth of the Metropolis Since 1949* (Oxford University Press).

State Statistical Bureau (SSB) (1991a) *10 Percent Sampling Tabulation of the 1990 Population Census of the People's Republic of China ('Zhongguo 1990 nian renkou pucha 10% chouyang ziliao')* (Beijing: Statistical Publishing House).

State Statistical Bureau (SSB) (1991b) 1991 *China: Statistical Yearbook* (Beijing: Statistical Publishing House.

Yan Hao (1991) 'Population Distribution and Internal Migration in China Since the Early 1950s', in Wang and Hull.

Wang Jiye and Hull, T. H. (eds.) (1991) *Population and Development Planning in China* (Sydney: Allen and Unwin).

Zhao Zhongwei (1992) 'Household and Kinship in Recent and Very Recent Chinese History: Theory and Practice of Co-Residence in Three Chinese Villages in Beijing Area', unpublished PhD thesis, Cambridge.

4

The Floating Population in China's Cities: A New Ethnic Underclass?

Christopher J. Smith

Introduction

Chinese society has undergone a major transformation during the last two decades, as the old ideas about creating a socialist utopia have been cast aside in favour of what some observers have described as rampant capitalism (Schell 1994; Theroux 1993). The economy has been heated up to boiling point by the introduction of market-oriented reforms. Part of this process, as described in Chapter 3, has been the relaxation of the more draconian elements of migration control (see also Selden 1988; Cheng 1991), leading to an unprecedented increase in population mobility. The most dramatically visible component has been the movement of millions of peasants away from their homes in the countryside (Pannell 1995).

Many of the migrants headed for the biggest cities, in a process that has been referred to as a 'peasant flood' (Wan 1995). It is very rare for them to be granted permanent residence, so most have been fixed as temporary migrants. The marginalisation of this group, particularly in the housing and labour markets, has created what amounts to a new urban underclass, a situation comparable in some ways to the experiences of ethnic minorities and immigrants in the cities of the West. The major difference is that their status is not based on racial, religious or national terms: they are as Chinese as the permanent city residents they have joined. But their status as 'ethnic' minorities is ascribed to them largely because they are poor and from the countryside – in other words, because they are peasants.

This chapter begins with a discussion of the geographic patterns of the new mobility, and a brief account of the underlying forces (see also Chapters 3 and 5 in this volume). The major objective is to investigate the discourse that has been generated by the new patterns of mobility, which has been keenly debated by academics, policy-makers and city planners. The majority view is that migrants are acting as a force of change that will have a negative impact on the cities. It is possible, however, to put forward an alternative interpretation of the migrants having a more positive role in the urban transformation.

The geography of China's new population mobility

The census of 1990 attempted to provide an official count of the new mobility. Two types of movement were counted: permanent (*de jure*) and temporary *(de facto)* migrations. A permanent migrant is defined as someone whose move is officially sanctioned, in both the origin and the destination, by the granting of a household registration (*hukou*) in the new place of residence. The census data shows that this category remained stable throughout the 1980s, at less than 2 per cent of the population. Most of the new mobility has involved temporary migrants: individuals who lived in a place where they were not registered for more than a year, or who had been away from home, living in different places, for more than a year (Siu and Li 1993). The census figures are discussed in Chapter 3, and indicate that the total number of *de facto* migrants who in 1990 had permission to live somewhere different from their 1985 registration was in the order of 34 million (Table 3.1). But as is well known, this excludes many temporary and uncounted moves, including those who came and went during that interval of five years. The actual figure is often estimated at 70 million and sometimes much higher.[1]

The rate of temporary migration varies greatly across the country. The regions with the highest rate of in-migration in 1990 included Guangdong province and the major cities along the east coast, as well as the provinces and autonomous regions in border areas, where the government has been officially encouraging economic development and in-migration (including Heilongjiang, Xinjiang and Qinghai). The most attractive places for migrants have been the nation's largest cities and the most rapidly growing regions (Fan 1995). Close to half the total number of officially counted migrants (16 million) were moving from rural areas to urban areas (see Table 4.1), and Guangdong province was the nation's leading destination in 1990, with more than 3.3 million in-migrants, which represented 5.2 per cent of its total population. (The next highest rates were in the nation's biggest cities: Beijing, 4.8 per cent and Shanghai, 4.1 per cent; see Guangdong Population Census

Table 4.1 Migrants by origin and destination, 1985–90

	Number	% of total
Interprovincial migration		
Urban to urban	3 752 030	34.6
Urban to rural	492 930	4.6
Rural to rural	1 760 280	16.2
Rural to urban	4 831 020	44.6
	10 836 260	100.0
Intraprovincial migration		
Urban to urban	7 504 080	32.6
Urban to rural	910 400	3.9
Rural to rural	2 997 610	13.0
Rural to urban	11 592 260	50.4
	23 004 350	100.0
All migration		
Urban to urban	11 256 110	33.3
Urban to rural	1 403 330	4.2
Rural to rural	4 757 890	14.1
Rural to urban	16 423 280	48.5
	33 840 610	100.0

Source: Adapted from: State Statistical Bureau (Ten Percent Sampling Tabulation on the 1990 Population Census of the PRC).

Office 1990.) A marked 'distance decay' effect was evident in the pattern of migration, with the majority moving within the same province, and the numbers going further proportionately smaller. Of the 33.8 million total migrants who moved between 1985 and 1990, for example, more than 23 million (68 per cent) came from the same province, and the majority of the migrants from elsewhere came from adjacent provinces.[2] This was the case in all of the provinces that experienced significant amounts of net in-migration.

Migration throughout the late 1980s contributed significantly to urbanisation. In Guangdong province, for example, the percentage of the population officially designated as urban almost doubled, from 18.6 per cent in 1982 to 36.8 per cent in 1990 (Li 1993). However there are severe data problems, as the definition of what is 'urban' is frequently changed (Ma and Lin 1993; Chan 1994).[3] One researcher has estimated that as many as 45 per cent of the additional 2.6 million urban dwellers in Guangdong between 1985 and 1990 resulted from new definitions (Li 1993). With 14 per cent of the growth coming from natural increase of the population, this still leaves about 41 per cent of the new urbanisation in Guangdong province accounted for by migration, most of which came from the rural areas.

The factor most often identified as the cause of the new mobility is the rising surplus labour force in the countryside, which was generated by the new levels of economic efficiency associated with the economic reforms. An examination of agricultural statistics shows marked reductions in the average number of person-hours devoted to the cultivation of various crops (Chan 1994; White 1994; Taylor and Banister 1991). In fact, the surplus labour in the countryside was not created by the reforms *per se*, but was a legacy of the rural commune system. The 'iron rice bowl' security provided for the people during the collective era effectively guaranteed that everyone would have a job and food to eat, but at the same time it created a massive amount of hidden under-employment in the countryside. With the reforms, peasants were stimulated by the profit motive and higher procurement prices for agricultural products, and they had much easier access to 'free trade' markets to sell their wares. The lure of material gain gave the peasants the incentive to work more efficiently on the land, and within a relatively short period of time higher output levels were being achieved by far fewer agricultural workers than was ever the case in the collective era. The net effect was that millions of peasants were effectively redundant in the fields.

In addition to the efficiency argument a number of environmental, technological and demographic forces have contributed to the growing surplus of labour in the countryside. The amount of rural land available for farming declined steadily throughout the 1980s, partly as a result of overcropping and soil exhaustion, and partly as a result of urban and industrial encroachments (Smil 1993; Edmonds 1994). Combined with the introduction of machinery and other technological innovations in agriculture, this resulted in a significant reduction in the amount of labour used to produce most crops. It was reported, for example, that rice production required 22 per cent less labour between the years 1978 and 1985, and for wheat the figure was 53 per cent (Taylor and Banister 1991). A large cohort of peasants, born in the high-fertility period of the 1960s, reached working age in the late 1970s just as all of these other changes were starting to have an influence. The effect was that a significant proportion of the rural work force (15 to 40 per cent, depending on how the calculations are made) became surplus to requirements during the 1980s. This represents anywhere from 60 million to as many as 156 million people who would become potential migrants. The more lenient policies of the mid-1980s (see Chapter 3) effectively allowed the peasants to 'leave both the land and the countryside', on the understanding that they would be able to arrange for their own food supplies and support themselves (Zhou 1993, p. 208).

The immediate effect of the relaxation in the migration policies was a rapid population increase in many small towns, especially in the coastal provinces. The towns became increasingly industrialised as they attracted large numbers of redundant peasants. During this period the pattern of rural-to-urban migration adhered fairly closely to the government's preferred policy, which was to control the growth of the larger cities and allow a rapid expansion of smaller cities and towns. As Ma and Lin (1993) have observed, these towns became important centres for rural migrants and nodes of self-sustained industrial and commercial development. In spite of this, by the late 1980s large population increases were apparent in the largest cities, where the lure of better-paying jobs and the attraction of superior amenities and a higher quality of life provided a strong pull (Chan 1984).

The public discourse about migrants

Systematic attempts to assess the human consequences of the temporary migrant phenomenon are becoming more common, and Chinese scholars have produced a considerable literature on the topic.[4] In addition to academic works a wealth of information and opinion exists in newspaper articles published in all the larger cities that are experiencing an influx of rural migrants (Dai 1996a; China News Digest 1994a, 1994b, 1994c, Mallee 1988). These give the impression that the migrants, in such large numbers and within such a brief span of time, are being interpreted as a significant problem. Much of the public debate centres on the belief that migration to the cities at the present rates will seriously strain the capacity of the existing urban service infrastructure, with disadvantages and additional costs to all residents. It is thought that the excess numbers created by both migration and natural population increases will result in greater competition for scarce urban resources, with an overall reduction in the quality of city life. The impacts, it is feared, will be felt most critically in a continued shortage of adequate housing; a strain on transport and utilities such as water and electricity (Solinger 1996); and declining access to social services such as education and health care (White 1994; Bian 1994).[5]

There is also a feeling that the situation will get worse before it gets better. Demographers predict that the surplus rural population will reach 200 million before 2010 (Quan 1991; Taylor and Banister 1991). With such numbers it is likely that the itinerant population will continue to grow. During the boom era, jobs in all sectors of the urban economy have been plentiful, and the surplus labour has been easily absorbed. There is a lingering concern, however, that sooner or later economic growth will slow down. When jobs in the cities become hard to find, and effective demand is lowered by declining wages, it feared that competition between the newcomers and the long-term residents will accelerate.

These concerns have produced a discourse in which migrants are interpreted as a public problem. Three interrelated issues are involved in this discourse. The first is the idea that the new mobility is producing strife-torn cities, with the transients cast in the divisive role of a highly marginalised 'other' group. For a number of reasons the migrants are either being blamed for what is going wrong in the cities, or are pitied as the victims of uncontrollable structural forces. In an analogy with Western (particularly United States) cities, they are taking on the role of a new urban underclass (Massey 1990; Wilson 1987). A second theme involves the idea that Chinese cities are spinning out of control, with civic and social problems parallel with those of rapidly growing cities in other parts of the developing world (Devas and Rakodi 1993; Gilbert and Gugler 1992; Gugler 1986). In this sense, the recent transfer of population from the countryside to the cities is considered to have upset the delicate balance between city and countryside that had been maintained by deliberate urban planning policies in the pre-reform era (Pannell 1995). In less than one decade, mass migration out of the countryside has been accompanied by rapid urban growth that had been avoided in the two preceding decades (Kirkby 1985; Chan 1994). The horrors associated with rapid urbanisation in cities of the developing world – poverty, squalor, homelessness and public disorder – were largely absent until Mao's death, but in recent years they have started to appear (or reappear).

The first two strands of the discourse see cities becoming more like those in other parts of the world, but the third involves them shedding their unique characteristics as socialist cities. As some observers have argued, the very existence of huge new transient populations living and working outside the public domain signifies that the socialist state is no longer able to control the growth of its cities. In this sense, events in the cities can be seen as a reflection of what is occurring in Chinese society at large in the transition out of socialism. The state, according to this view, is no longer able either to direct the course of events, or to deal with the consequences.

A new urban underclass

The increasingly visible urban underclass stands in sharp contrast to the glitter of the new skyscrapers and the hum of capitalism (or 'market socialism') in the factories and on the streets. An investigation of the public discourse that has arisen around the new mobility reveals highly negative images of the migrants, both collectively and as individuals. Some of the migrants are easily identifiable in the cities: hanging around outside rail and bus stations; working on construction sites; and operating stalls or providing services on the streets. Perceptions of them by the permanent residents are a combination of preconceived notions of the peasantry, and observations of their working and living habits in the cities. As peasants the migrants are viewed as bumpkins or 'country cousins'. They look, speak, and behave differently; they are unsophisticated; and most importantly they are poor and to be avoided wherever possible (Honig 1992). To some extent these perceptions are nourished by the lifestyles of the transients. Those who work are forced to accept jobs that are too undesirable and low-paying for regular city residents, and as a result they often live in areas that are only marginally habitable. Others in search of work are forced to wander the streets and gather in public places, creating images of vagrancy and homelessness that are unsettling to the city's permanent residents.

Such images of the migrants are compounded by the reality of their transitoriness. To the permanent residents, migrants appear to be unable (or, some would argue, unwilling) to settle down to a life of stability. In this sense migrant lives are depicted at the polar opposite from those of the permanent residents, who consider themselves to be settled and urbane. The theme of mobility plays an important part in this characterisation. Migrants appear to be in constant motion, in search of work and places to live. Some are returning to their homes, either voluntarily or under pressure from the police; but they are constantly being replaced by newcomers eager to try their luck in the city. Onlookers have responded to the sudden appearance of peasants in the cities with a mixture of shock and sympathy. Solinger, for example, observed that

> China's transient population is ... unlinked from its legal domicile and set out on the loose. Pouring in waves and swelling in surges or

spewed out as flotsam [it] ... conjures up variegated images of anomic, atomized particles drifting and wandering without direction, also of aggregations billowing in huge masses and pounding at city walls (Solinger 1994, p. 128)

As a group, the migrants are referred to in the media and in local parlance as *liudong renkou* – that portion of the urban population that is 'temporary' or 'mobile'. This label has a two-part meaning. On the one hand it involves a largely neutral, geographical adjective describing their temporary status and mobility, but in public discourse the migrants are most often referred to as members of the 'floating population'. The use of the term 'floating' in English has been influenced by another frequently used label for this group, *mangliu*, which translates roughly as the 'blindly floating' population. In comparison to the relatively neutral terms 'temporary' or 'mobile', describing migrants as 'blindly floating' is considerably more pejorative, implying some degree of randomness of movement and even vagrancy. Labelling them in this way implies that they have left the countryside with little if any idea of where to settle or how to make a living.

Although this is no doubt the case for some of the migrants, many of them arrive with a clear purpose in mind, and some even have existing employment contracts. It is also important to point out that the degree of instability and transitoriness witnessed among the migrants is by no means a matter of choice. When they arrive, the majority of them are not granted registration permits (*hukou*) to legitimise their residence in the cities. In official terms, therefore, they are considered to be temporary migrants, although many of them have been *de facto* urban residents for years and have no plans to return to their homes in the countryside. They are assigned to a temporary living status that is both official and permanent, so the image of transitoriness is not one they can easily shake off.

Another dimension of the image of the 'floating populations' involves public health issues. There is a concern about the health of the migrants themselves, but more importantly there is a fear about the impact they have on health care services in the cities, and whether they will transmit diseases to an otherwise healthy urban population. The public health issue provides an image that is easy to comprehend, based on casual views of the way the migrants live and work. Many live in places that are dark, cramped, and dirty – adding to the existing public health hazards of life in cities that are already crowded, polluted and insanitary. In the largest cities such as Shanghai, Beijing and

Guangzhou, the rubbish, food waste and excrement added to the urban landscape by a million or more extra residents is difficult to ignore. It has been suggested that the presence of migrants has added to local air and water pollution problems, and has increased the potential for airborne disease transmission, especially during the hot and humid summer months. Among an already poor and ill-housed population, there are fears that new diseases will be introduced, and that 'old' diseases such as TB will reappear (Smith and Dai 1995). There have been reports that local food supplies have not been able to keep pace with growing demands, and in some cities shortages of water, gas, and electricity have been compounded by the pressure caused by so many new consumers (Solinger 1996). Although these images are certainly reasonable, very little hard data exists to support the assumptions on which they are based. As with many of the images of the new transients and their impact, concerns about public health are based almost entirely on individual journalistic accounts (Smith and Dai 1995).

Another acute source of potential conflict between the 'floaters' and the permanent city residents is the issue of birth control (Zhao and Zhang 1993). It is assumed that among the 'floating' population households birth rates will be significantly higher than for permanent city residents (see Chapter 5). Migrant women are mostly from the countryside, where birth control policies in general, and the one-child policy in particular, are not enforced to the same extent as in the cities. In addition, many of the migrant women working in the cities have no connection to established work units, so they have limited access to birth control devices. Without the formal control structures provided by workplace or neighbourhood organisations, there is a fear that nobody is available to counsel or harangue migrant women about unplanned and additional pregnancies (Whyte and Parish 1984). There are fears of rising birth rates in the cities, caused by transient women who are living 'outside the [one-child-per-family] plan' and having babies. On the basis of journalistic reports the image of huge numbers of 'black' babies (those born illegally in the cities) has become firmly lodged in public opinion. There is also a concern that few opportunities exist for health care, for mothers and their children, both before and after the births. In fact there is very little firm evidence to support any of the fears about rising birth rates, and according to Hoy (Chapter 5, this volume) fertility seems to decline among migrant women after they arrive in the cities. The extra demand placed on urban health care services by a rapid increase in the birth rate would indeed be a serious problem, but in fact few of the transients are eligible to use the subsidised facilities, on account of their rural *hukou* status. Those who can afford it have the choice of paying cash for such services; others, presumably, must do without or return to their homes in times of medical emergency.

Major conflicts also revolve around the living spaces of the new 'floating' populations. One of the most acute problems facing the transients is the shortage of housing. In spite of the market-inspired reforms during the last decade, the majority of decent housing is still state- or enterprise-owned, and access to it is controlled by the possession of a much-prized urban *hukou*. Only a small proportion of the transients are able to gain access to decent housing, either by buying (or otherwise attaining) an urban *hukou* or else by amassing sufficient resources to buy into the private housing market. The result is that many migrants have to share living quarters with relatives or other transients, in cheap and usually very dilapidated sections of the city. The lucky ones may be able to find accommodation in collective-unit shelters such as factory dormitories, especially if they have been recruited by specific enterprises on short-term work contracts. Others gravitate to more marginal spaces such as temporary workers' shacks and 'tent cities', which are usually visible on the edge of construction sites. Some flock to the cheap hotels and hostels of the city, but when their money runs out they may have to resort to a variety of nonresidential spaces such as squatter settlements, train station concourses, alcoves under bridges and even rubbish dumps. Many of the new transients are destined to live as and where they can, which reinforces the images of squalor and overcrowding, and increases the perceived and actual social distance between them and the permanent residents of the city.

The new urban disorder

The processes associated with the economic reforms since the early 1980s have resulted in a new level of cross-fertilisation between the rural and urban spheres. This first occurred with the spread of industrialisation in rural areas, then continued with the urbanisation of the countryside, as peasants began to spill off the land into rapidly growing small towns. The process has been completed by what has been described as the 'invasion' of the biggest cities by massive numbers of peasants, bringing about a comprehensive process of 'rustication'. In the case of Guangzhou, for example, it was estimated that by 1990 more than a million peasants had moved into the city, and there were probably many more living outside the law and out of sight of the census-takers (GPCO 1990; Vogel 1989).

To many observers, the rapid urban growth that has accompanied the economic reforms over the past two decades, and the emergence of the huge new migrant populations, are associated with a new level of public disorder that is reminiscent of the pre-communist era. The new urban trends, according to this argument, have rapidly undermined the efforts of the socialist urban planning of the late 1950s to the end of the 1970s. In the early 1990s, the cities have instead grown very rapidly through the migration of peasants from the countryside. This critique has two major components: first, the mass transfer of population from the countryside to the cities is considered to be largely responsible for upsetting the urban–rural separation that had been so carefully maintained during the Maoist era; and second, the new transients are being blamed for a resurgence of the urban social problems that had not been witnessed since the pre-revolutionary era.

It is reasonable to expect that such thorough changes have been accompanied by increased prevalence of urban social problems, particularly crime. A sharp rise in urban crime has been reported, and much of it has been attributed to migrants (Zhao and Zhang 1993). It has been suggested that the new migrants 'lack the identity and responsibility of city residents', and as a result 'they are prone to feel that they are treated unequally and are relatively deprived, and they resent this' (Tan and Li 1993, p. 355). These feelings of resentment, it is argued, result in a high rate of crime among the migrants. It is clear that without significant data such an assertion is questionable at best, and absurd at worst, yet such statements are widely accepted by the urban public. Perhaps city dwellers need to have someone to blame for their rising fear of public disorder, and their sense of imminent danger. In this sense, a constructed myth can easily become the basis for a widespread moral panic. The same group of researchers have stated, again without any corroborating evidence, that 'In the busiest districts of Beijing, 80 per cent of criminal offenses were committed by [the floating populations] ... in other big and medium sized cities and in the open coastal zones, the migrant population committed 40–60 per cent of all criminal offenses' (ibid.). Such connections are easily made in public debates and by newspaper editors, and the fact that they are so quickly accepted reflects the traditional fear among city dwellers all over the world toward newcomers and migrants (Skeldon 1990; Portes and Rumbaut 1990). In China special venom appears to be reserved for peasants, who are often characterised as crude, unsophisticated and untrustworthy. To many they are in fact the embodiment of the great rural wasteland that is detested and feared by city dwellers (Kirkby 1985). These public perceptions are fuelled by intermittent media stories sensationalising specific incidents involving members of the 'floating populations' (including rapes, murders and robberies), as well as newspaper reports about the rapidly eroding quality of urban life that is attributed to them (see Davin 1996).

If there is a kernel of truth in the connection between the transients and a new sense of public disorder, the association is reinforced especially by some of the less desirable public appearances of the floating populations, for example, the crowds gathering outside the railway stations. It would appear, however, that the pejorative nature of the labels 'floating' and 'blindly floating' is based on the characteristics of some but by no means all of the new migrants. The vast majority of migrants are hard-working, law-abiding people who have left their families behind in an attempt to better themselves. There are certainly far more 'floaters' earning their keep in factories, on construction sites and working as domestic helpers than there are disturbing the peace (Dai 1996b). This suggests that the images of squalor and disorder have a more powerful influence over public opinions than the image of people going about the everyday business of making a living.[6]

The demise of the state?

Some outsiders have suggested that the very success of the economic reforms now threatens to overwhelm and exhaust the cities and render them unworkable, signifying the inability of the state to maintain control and keep order. A visit to almost any rapidly growing city in China demonstrates that an ever-increasing proportion of urban dwellers are now openly living and surviving 'outside the plan' dictated by the state. They search for jobs, find places to live, do their shopping, and take care of their everyday needs on their own, with no help from the state. Their lives are effectively beyond the reach and purview of the state and the Communist Party – a situation that has not been the case since 1949. In the largest cities entire squatter settlements are emerging, as migrants slip in unnoticed from the countryside (Xiang 1996). Some reports suggest that in the face of such rapid growth of the transient populations, city bureaucrats and planners appear to be losing their grip, and have all but given up trying to control and extract taxes from many of the new residents.

The *hukou* system excludes the 'floating populations' from many of the publicly provided and subsidised services, but the presence of so many transients creates a massive 'free rider' problem. In reality it is impossible to exclude migrants from access to many city services such as water, gas, electricity, transport, sewers, garbage collection and parks. The expanded level of service provision to meet the extra demands can occur only at a significant cost to the cities in question, and to bear such costs it has been necessary for them to raise prices for all consumers. Fiscal crisis in some cities has also resulted in attempts by the state to withdraw from service provision, especially in such areas as health care, housing and transport (Smith 1996a; Hillier and Xiang 1994; Kirkby, 1994). It has also been necessary to maintain costly income subsidies to permanent city residents (both workers and students), to compensate for the rising cost of urban services. As a short-term palliative, cash subsidies have been a popular option, but in many cities the subsidies are now being eliminated as costs continue to rise (Kristoff and WuDunn 1994).

The blame for many if not all of these trends is being heaped on the transients. It is argued that their continued presence and growth seriously threaten the ability of the state both to control and to serve its workers in the provision of cheap and effective urban services. The state, it is feared, is no longer able to keep a lid on its urban problems.

In addition to the rising costs incurred by the migrants' presence, there is growing evidence that much of the modernisation process in the cities is occurring outside the domain of the state. Many factories now actually prefer to hire migrants as workers on construction teams and in factories, not only because they will work for less than the permanent city residents, but because they are usually docile and undemanding (Standing 1996). They neither expect nor demand the services and benefits typically provided to state workers. In this sense, therefore, the presence of the transients is contributing to a 'withering away' of the socialist socio-economic order in the cities, similar to what has already occurred in the countryside.

This interpretation represents perhaps the worst-case scenario of current events. But there is another way to interpret the huge rural-to-urban migration, from a perspective in which the mass exodus from the countryside serves rather than challenges the state, and helps it to survive rather than brings about its demise (Solinger 1994). The agricultural reforms contributed to the generation of a huge surplus labour force in the countryside, which is now being absorbed by the migration of peasants to the cities. In this sense the new mobility helps the state to ward off the potential for mass disgruntlement and instability in the countryside. The jobs in which many migrants are employed are essential to export-oriented industrialisation, which has played a key role in China's entry into the global economy. In addition, the jobs taken by the transients include the dirtiest, most dangerous, and least prestigious jobs in the city, jobs that might not otherwise be filled. In other words, migration fulfills many of the conditions for the modernisation process: it provides a safety valve for surplus labour; it ensures that even the worst jobs are filled; it generates income for consumption and savings; it allows money to be channelled into rural areas in the form of remittances; and it enables some migrants to receive education and training in the cities that will ultimately prove to be useful when and if they return to the countryside (Hugo 1996; Smith 1996a).

The transient populations provide an almost unlimited supply of workers who are able and willing to feed and house themselves, and take care of their own services. In the new China the market rewards those who are self-supporting, while those who fail must return to the countryside at their own expense. Migrants put far fewer demands on the state than would an equal number of permanent city residents, and with so many easily available there is less need for the state to institute costly programs of education, training or labour reform. On balance, as Solinger (1994) has suggested, the 'floaters' contribute at least as much to the state as they take from it, while at the same time they allow the state to remain as inefficient as ever.

There is still another function of the new transient populations that assists rather than challenges the authority of the state. As we have seen, members of the 'floating populations' are generally considered to be responsible for the increase in urban crime. In ordinary times the public security (police) forces are an extremely unpopular arm of the state's social control system, but in the face of the obvious need for heightened security and police surveillance that is generated by the transients, the social control function of the state is legitimised. The problem is huge, so even if the police operate twenty-four hours a day watching over and expelling migrants, their job will never be completed. They will, however, be given credit for attempting to control a problem they did not cause, and that is clearly in danger of getting out of control. In China, as anywhere else in the world, the public yearns for social order, and this translates into a demand for clean and safe streets. The public security arm of the state can help to provide this by inflicting its traditionally heavy-handed methods of social control on the citizens, whether they are migrants or not. Periodic efforts to round up transients and send them back home may appear to be ludicrous attempts to turn back the clock of progress, but visible efforts to deal with the problems are supported by the public.

Discussion and conclusion

Much of the public debate about the new mobility in China casts the 'floating populations' in a highly negative role, attributing to them much of the blame for the urban problems occurring during the explosive transition out of socialism. A critical analysis of this debate allows an alternative interpretation, one that looks more favourably upon the role of the new transients. From this perspective the migrants can be construed not as the cause of the failures in urban China but as the architects (or, more likely, the construction and production workers) of the successes. It is also important to put the events occurring in contemporary urban China into the larger context of migration on a global scale. Although the new population movements and the problems associated with them are exceptional in terms of the numbers involved and the speed of the changes, the fundamental patterns and processes of the recent migrations in China have been occurring in different parts of the world for centuries (Hugo 1996; Skeldon 1990).

The first part of this argument suggests that migrants from the countryside have contributed mightily to what one observer has called 'the rise of China' and the extraordinary economic growth that has taken the world by surprise in the 1990s (Overholt 1993; Lardy 1994). In its most extreme form this argument implies that the new wealth and the new urban landscapes of consumption have been built upon the frail and often unrewarded shoulders of the peasants. The 'floaters', in other words, have played a vital role in China's modernisation – in fact have made the whole thing possible. They respond quickly and efficiently to market signals; they work long and hard for extremely low wages; they are willing to put up with conditions most permanent city dwellers will not consider; and their enterprise has made possible a vast expansion of service and consumption-related activity. All of this contributes to effective demand and increases the circulation of capital; but in addition, migrant labour has allowed the urban middle classes some new freedoms. With a massive influx of young women from the countryside, for example, there is now a vast supply of maids to do housework and nannies to look after children. This is allowing parents to make choices about how to budget their time between work and leisure pursuits (Dai 1996a).

Most of the migration has occurred as a result of market forces, and the vast majority of the migrants remain in the cities on a temporary basis. This means that the state has not had to bear the extra costs associated with providing such services as education, housing and health care for the new residents. The emergence of the 'floating populations' has also presented the government with a way out of the dilemma it has created with its reform policies, by providing cheap labour without any official intervention to protect workers' rights or to finance and service the new labour market. As a result, the process of development has been relatively cheap and painless, and this has given China a crucial edge in the global marketplace. China has become one of the most attractive places in the world for investment, particularly from the so-called 'overseas Chinese', who are among the most capital-rich producers in the world. They already know the culture and the language, so the advantage of cheap and flexible labour, combined with the concessions offered in the special economic zones and open cities, has been a winning combination. Patrick Tyler, the China correspondent for the *New York Times,* interviewed an investor who observed that 'For all practical purposes the cost of labour in China is nothing' (quoted in Schell 1994, p. 399).

Exceptional though the current situation may appear, in many ways it is not dissimilar to what has occurred as a result of mass migrations in many parts of the world. It is clear that some of the newcomers are being exploited and marginalised, and that they represent a growing urban underclass. It is also possible, however, to interpret the current situation as simply part of the normal 'growing pains' associated with modernisation. What we see is part of a process that is occurring in all parts of the developing world, and that has been going on for centuries, as migrants have attempted to incorporate themselves into the modern urban world. The experiences of the 'floaters' in contemporary China are similar in many ways to those reported by other populations who have become minorities as a result of immigration. History demonstrates that in these situations it is quite usual for the newcomers to be defined as undesirable 'others', especially if one or more of the dominant groups fear their positions in the urban hierarchy are being challenged (Solinger 1993).

The members of migrant groups are attempting to make viable lives for themselves in the face of massive constraints and discrimination. In this sense what is happening to the 'floating populations' in China is similar to what is happening to their counterparts in the 'ethnic enclaves' of cities around the world. Studies of these enclaves, and of the way ethnic and racial minority groups are treated by the majority, have become popular research themes for urban studies researchers in a variety of academic disciplines (Portes and Rumbaut 1990; Gardner 1995). Such studies have recently started to catch on in China, as researchers have begun to explore the experiences of ethnic minority groups in China's cities (Harrell 1995; Gladney 1991, 1993; Jankowiak 1993; Guldin and Southall 1993). Unlike many other parts of the world, however, most of China's new migrants are not clearly defined as ethnic minority people, according to the traditional markers such as nationality, language, religion or race. But as Skinner (1977) observed, it is possible that even 'slight accents and ... minor mannerisms may serve as ethnic markers if either side finds it advantageous to maintain or erect ethnic boundaries' (p. 544). In other words, there is a precedent for categorising China's new transients as ethnic minorities, even though they belong to the Han majority.[7] For migrants in many different places around the world, such considerations have been crucial in their designation as 'others'. Placed in this context, the way the new transients have been received in China's cities, and their continued marginalisation, should come as no surprise. It is important to recall that many of the situations migrants find themselves in are not of their own making, and that the negative perceptions are often based on scant and incorrect information.

One last important concern is the transitory nature of China's newest migrants. Many of them return to their homes on a regular basis, sometimes several times each year; while others may return permanently after several years away. A number of experts have recently been persuaded that return migration is common (Hugo 1996; Fawcett 1989). Because of the marginal lives encountered by many migrants, as well as their lack of sophistication and skills, many of them have little choice but to return home.[8]

Return migration is often crucial to the 'sending' community, as migrants bring back resources in the form of cash remittances and skills, and provide useful information for potential new migrants (Massey *et al.*, 1987). Migration is also an important source of status and power for those who have been away to higher-status locations (in contemporary China this means the cities). Local empowerment often comes to individuals and households who have had access to places outside, so that migration helps to shape local culture and power relationships, and has become a measure of local inequality. As Gardner (1995) has observed, migration results in the emergence of a 'new axis of differentiation, based around people's access to places'. In China, it is reasonable to suggest that a similar transformation of local (home) culture is being renogotiated: having been to the city sets one apart from the rest. Hannerz comments that 'to have wealth and power is to have easy access to the metropolis ... and it is through one's relationship to the metropolis that one ... gains wealth and power in the periphery' (Hannerz 1992, p. 242). For Chinese peasants, going 'out' to work in one of the bustling new cities may represent the route to power after they return home. Even if they 'fail' to incorporate themselves into city life, they may in the long run turn out to be the new sophisticates at home, bringing money and ideas back with them, and eventually transforming and modernising the countryside.

Notes

1. The 70 million figure is reached by adding an estimate of people who were not counted by the census because they were away from home for less than a year. There is considerable disagreement and much confusion about the definitions involved and the methods of counting China's temporary migrant populations. The figure quoted here does not correspond to many of the other estimates being made of the so-called 'floating population' in China. The Ministry of Public Security, for example, includes all migrants, whereas the census counts only those who cross city or county lines. The larger estimates also include individuals who are away from home but are not seeking work and accommodation in the new locality, including those visiting relatives, seeking hospital treatment and attending meetings, in addition to tourists and students. All of these people are required to get a temporary residential registration card from the public security bureau if they are away from home for more than three days, but in fact many do not. There is also another category, known as 'vagrants', who are people wandering around with no fixed abode, and who generally do not register with the local public security office, even temporarily (see *China News Analysis* 1991, pp. 1–2).

   Another way to calculate temporary migrants is to aggregate from the number estimated to be living in the 11 largest cities in 1990, which was more than 8 million (see Li and Hu 1991). This also produces an overall estimate of about 70 million. Other estimates are lower; for example, the Foreign Broadcasting Information Service (FBIS) in 1990 estimated 50 million. Most scholars agree that it is almost impossible to count the 'temporary' migrant population accurately, because of the vast numbers involved; the rate at which new migrants enter cities, and others leave; and their tendency to hide away from the authorities. For a discussion of some of the difficulties involved in making an accurate count, see Wong (1994).

2. In the 1990s public concern about the rate of in-migration from the countryside produced a number of attempts to exclude people from other provinces, which means that in the future an increasing share of the 'temporary' migrants will be coming from the same province. For example, Wong (1994)

discusses the attempts to make employees in the Pearl River Delta cities hire workers from within Guangdong province.

3. It is important to note the definitional changes that have contributed to the apparent rapid increase in the rate of urbanisation during the last decade. In a number of provinces, prefectural centres and county seats have been redefined as cities (*shi*). This gives them jurisdiction over a number of surrounding counties, many of which are largely rural in character but whose people are then counted as urban. Many villages and market towns have been upgraded to towns (see Kirkby 1994); and in some cases township boundaries have been expanded beyond the built-up area, to provide leadership for the small towns within the jurisdiction (Tan 1993). The goal of these strategies was to bring about greater geographical integration in terms of economic and demographic interaction between the urban and rural areas (Prime 1991).

   To some extent these were artefactual changes, and they tended to produce unrealistically large jumps in the rate of urbanisation and suggest that China was urbanising faster than anywhere else in the world. It is also evident, however, that many of the towns selected for upgrades had experienced significant population growth, often fuelled by migration from the surrounding countryside, which reflects a bona fide increase in the rate of 'natural' urbanisation (Chan 1994).

4. Much of it is reviewed in Dai (1996a). See as examples Huang 1992; Gui and Liu 1992; Chan 1988; Chan and Xu 1985; Wu 1993; Wu and Xu 1990. One of the best sources of information about recent studies conducted on the topic of the 'floating populations' was a workshop in Oxford (July 1996), proceedings of which are published in Pieke and Mallee (1998) – see especially the papers by Scharping and by Jinhong Ding and Norman Stockman.

5. Solinger (1994, 1996) has concluded that these concerns are considerably exaggerated, perhaps because of the need to find someone to blame for all of the problems associated with the transition from 'plan' to 'market'. For an opposing viewpoint see Zhao and Zhang's (1993) study conducted in Shenzhen.

6. A partial explanantion for the connection between migrants and crime is the dominant image of the new migrants as young men with low education levels. It is generally assumed that such men are willing and able to work at almost any job, no matter how dirty or dangerous, and the image of a male-dominated group of rough and ready transients is inherently threatening to most people's sense of public order. The image of male dominance in the recent migration streams appears to have been influenced by a partial observation of the workers on construction sites, where the vast majority of workers are young men from the countryside. The ubiquity of construction sites acts as a symbol of prosperity and a metaphor for modernisation – the higher the rate of new construction, the faster is the (assumed) growth rate (Schell 1994). The construction sites, however, are only one source of employment for migrants. The majority of the new jobs being taken up by transients are in the consumption and service sectors of the urban economy, as well as many of the new factory jobs (many of which are held by women). Guangdong Province, which is the number one destination for migrants, receives more than the national average proportion of women as temporary migrants, many of whom are attracted (or recruited) into jobs in the heavily

'feminised' manufacturing sector, especially in factories making textiles, clothing, and electronic products (see Smith and Dai 1995; Gao 1994; Croll 1994). The gender ratio among temporary migrants in the province varies significantly from place to place, according to the structure of local industry. The city of Guangzhou's temporary migrant population is male-dominated (the gender ratio is 128.5 men per 100 women), but in the special economic zone (SEZ) cities of Shenzhen and Zhuhai, as well as in other rapidly growing cities such as Foshan and Donguan, women make up the majority of the migrants (GPCO 1990).

7. In her Shanghai study, Honig (1992) observed that migrants from the north of Jiangsu province were labelled as a single entity – 'Subei' people – even though they came from many different parts of the province. The label was used by Shanghai's elite, particularly those from the southern parts of Jiangsu, to denote a distinctly lower class and undesirable group of poor migrants from the north – which was seen and spoken about as a place of difference and 'otherness', and which was considered to be decidely inferior from their own place of origin.

8. It is important to point out that returning should not necessarily denote 'failure' among migrants – in fact it can often be seen as a measure of success, in the sense that returners may be able to take advantage of their experiences. This is suggested by Hamilton (1978, 1985) in the case of migrants from south China throughout the latter part of the nineteenth century, a group he refers to as 'adventurers'. Hamilton observed that the home places of the 'adventurers' were not random, in fact some societies or regions were much more likely than others to send out large numbers of them. From this, he was able to generalise some of the features of localities that make them structurally more conducive than others to send out large numbers of 'adventurers'. Such places are generally ones where coming back rich and successful is seen as both possible and desirable, and this is characteristic of many parts of the Chinese countryside. In other words, it is acceptable to leave and easy to get back, but to improve one's social standing in the home area it is important to have made some noticeable gains, typically measured in monetary terms. In contemporary times some parts of China (at the local and provincial level) appear to send a higher proportion of rural migrants to the cities – and in addition to absolute poverty and lack of local opportunities, it is possible that certain areas, in Hamilton's terms, are more likely than others to send out what he refers to as 'adventurers'.

References

Bian, Y. J. (1994) *Work and Inequality in Urban China* (Albany, NY: State University of New York Press).

Chan, K. W. (1994) *Cities with Invisible Walls: Reinterpreting Urbanisation in Post-1949 China* (Hong Kong: Oxford University Press).

Chan, K. W. (1988), 'Rural–Urban Migration in China, 1952 –1982: Estimates and Analysis' *Urban Geography*, 9, (1) 53–84.

Chan, K. W. and Xu, X. Q. (1985). 'Urban Population Growth and Urbanisation in China Since 1949: Reconstructing a Baseline', *China Quarterly*, 104, 583–613.

Cheng, T. J. (1991), 'Dialectics of Control: The Household Registration (Hukou) System in Contemporary China'. Unpublished PhD Dissertation, State University of New York at Binghampton, Department of Sociology.

China News Analysis (1991) 'From and in the Villages: New Migrants and Old Clans', 1462, January 1.

China News Digest (1994a) 'With Millions of Underclass Migrants, Will China's System Collapse?', from *Washington Post*, 9 October, by Lena H. Sun.

China News Digest (1994b) 'Government Begins Counting 'Floating Population' from the *Los Angeles Times*, 19 November, by Rone Tempest.

China News Digest (1994c) 'Corrupt Officials, Foreign Businesses Spell Doom for Workers: Profit – First Mentality Overlooks Safety Needs', from *Chicago Tribune*, 5 October, by Uli Schmetzer.

Croll, E. (1994) *From Heaven to Earth: Images and Experience of Development in China* (London: Routledge).

Dai, F. (1996a) 'Internal Migration in the Reform Era in China: With Case Studies in Guangdong Province', MA thesis, Department of Geography and Planning, University at Albany, State University of New York, Albany.

Dai, F. (1996b) 'The Feminization of Migration in the Pearl River Delta', paper presented at the Annual Meetings of the Association of American Geographers, Charlotte, North Carolina

Davin, D. (1996) 'Affreux, sales et mechants: les migrants dans les medias chinois', *Perspectives Chinois*, 38, pp. 6–12.

Devas, N. and Rakodi, C. (1993) *Managing Fast Growing Cities: New Approaches to Urban Planning and Management in the Developing World* (New York: Longman).

Edmonds, R. L. (1994) *Patterns China's Lost Harmony: A Survey of the Country's Environmental Degradation and Protection* (London: Routledge).

Fawcett, J. T. (1989) 'Networks, Linkages, and Migration Systems', *International Migration Review*, 23 (3) 671–80.

Foreign Broadcast Information Service (FBIS) (1990) 'Floating Population Exceeds 50 Million', 19 January (Washington, DC).

Gao, X. X. (1994) 'China's Modernisation and Changes in the Social Status of Rural Women', pp. 80–97 in C. K. Gilmartin, G. Hershatter, L. Rofel and T. White (eds) *Engendering China: Women, Culture, and the State* (Cambridge, MA: Harvard University Press).

Gardner, K. (1995) *Global Migrants, Local Lives: Travel and Transformation in Rural Bangladesh* (Oxford: Clarendon Press).

Gilbert, A. and Gugler, J. (1992) *Cities, Poverty and Development: Urbanisation in the Third World*, 2nd edn (New York: Oxford University Press).

Gladney, D. C. (1991) *Muslim Chinese: Ethnic Nationalism in the People's Republic* (Cambridge, MA: Council on East Asian Studies, Harvard University Press).

Gladney, D. (1993) 'Hui Urban Entrepreneurialism in Beijing: State Policy, Ethno-religious Identity and the Chinese City', pp. 278-307 in G. Guldin and A. Southall (eds) *Urban Anthropology in China* (New York: E. J. Brill Publishing Co.)

Goldstein, A., Goldstein, S., and Guo, S. Z. (1991) 'Rural Industrialisation and Migration in the People's Republic of China', *Social Science History*, 15, (3) (Fall), 289–314.

Goldstein, S. (1990) 'Urbanisation in China, 1982–1987: Effects of Migration and Reclassification', *Population and Development Review*, 16 (4) (Dec), pp. 673–701.

Guangdong Population Census Office (GPCO) (1990) *The Floating Population Census in Guangdong Province, 1990* (Guangzhou, Guangdong Province).

G. Guldin and A. Southall (eds) (1993) *Urban Anthropology in China* (Leiden: E. J. Brill).

Gugler, J. (1986) 'Internal Migration in the Third World', pp. 194-223 in M. Pacione (ed.) *Population Geography: Progress and Prospect* (London: Croom Helm).

Gui, S. X., and Liu, X. (1992) 'Urban Migration in Shanghai, 1950–1988: Trends and Characteristics', *Population and Development Review*. 18 (Spring), pp. 533–48.

Hamilton, G. G. (1985) 'Temporary Migration and the Institutionalization of Strategy', *International Journal of Intercultural Relations*, 9, 405–25.

Hamilton, G. G. (1978) 'The Structural Sources of Adventurism: The Case of the California Gold Rush', *American Journal of Sociology*, 83, (6) 1466–490.

Hannerz, U. (1992) *Cultural Complexity: Studies in the Social Organization of Meaning* (New York: Columbia University Press).

Harrell, S. (ed.) (1995) *Cultural Encounters on China's Ethnic Frontiers* (Seattle, WA: University of Washington Press).

Hillier, S. and Xiang, Z. (1994) 'Rural Health Care in China: Past, Present and Future', pp. 95–115 in D. Dwyer (ed.) *China: The Next Decades* (Harlow: Longman).

Honig, E. (1992) *Creating Chinese Ethnicity: Subei People in Shanghai, 1850–1980* (New Haven: Yale University Press).

Huang, W. T. (1992) *China's Hidden Economy* (Beijing: Zhongguo Shangye Chubanshe).

Hugo, G. (1996) 'Asia on the Move: Research Challenges for Population Geography', *International Journal of Population Geography*, 2, 95–118.

International Journal of Urban and Regional Research, 14, (1), pp. 49–69.

Jankowiak, W. (1993) 'Urban Mongols: The Search for Dignity and Gain', pp. 316–38 in G. Guldin and A. Southall (eds) *Urban Anthropology in China* (New York: E. J. Brill Publishing Co.).

Kelliher, D. (1992) *Peasant Power in China: The Era of Rural Reform, 1979–1989* (New Haven, CT: Yale University Press).

Kirkby, R. J. R. (1985) *Urbanisation in China: Town and Country in a Developing Economy 1949–2000 AD* (London: Croom Helm, and New York: Columbia University Press).

Kirkby, R. J. R. (1994) 'Dilemmas of Urbanisation: Review and Prospects', pp. 128–55 in D. Dwyer (ed.) *China: The Next Decades* (Harlow: Longman).

Kristoff, N. D. and WuDunn S. (1994) *China Wakes: The Struggle for the Soul of a Rising Power* (New York: Times Books (Random House)).

Lardy, N. R. (1994) *China in the World Economy* (Washington DC: Institute for International Economics).

Li, L. (1993) 'An Analysis of the Floating Population in Guangdong Province', *Economic Geography*, 1, 31–4.

Li, M. B. and Hu, Y. (1991) *Impact of Floating Population on the Development of Large Cities and Recommended Policy* (in Chinese) (Beijing: Jingi Ribao Chubanshe).

Ma, L. J. C. and Lin, C. S. (1993) 'Development of Towns in China: A Case Study of Guangdong Province', *Population and Development Review*, 19, (3) 583–606.

Mallee, H. (1988) 'Rural-Urban Migration Control in the People's Republic of China: Effects of the Recent Reform' *China Information*. Vol. 11, No. 4, pp. 12–22.

Massey, D. S. (1990) 'American Apartheid: Segregation and the Making of the Underclass', *American Journal of Sociolog*, 9 (2) 329–57.

Massey, D. S., Alarcon, R., Durant, J. and Gonzalez, H. (1987) *Return to Aztlan: The Social Process of International Migration from West Mexico* (Berkley, CA: University of California Press).

Overholt, W. H. (1993) *The Rise of China: How Economic Reform is Creating a New Superpower* (New York: W. W. Norton).

Pannell, C. (1995) 'China's Urban Transition', *Journal of Geography*, 94 (3) 394–403.

Pieke, F. and H. Mallee (eds) (1998) *Internal and International Migration: Chinese Perspectives* (Richmond, Surrey: Curzon Press).

Portes, A. and R. G. Rumbaut (1990) *Immigrant America: A Portrait* (Berkeley, CA: University of California Press).

Prime, P. B. (1991) 'China's Economic Reforms in Regional Perspective', pp. 9–28 in Veeck (ed.) *The Uneven Landscape,* Baton Rouge, LA: Louisiana State University Press.

Quan, X. Q. (1991) 'Urbanisation in China', *Urban Studies*, 28, (1) (February) 41–51.

Schell, O. (1994) *Mandate of Heaven: A New Generation of Entrepreneurs, Dissidents, Bohemians, and Technocrats Lays Claim to China's Future* (New York: Simon & Schuster).

Selden, M. (1988) *The Political Economy of Chinese Socialism* (Armonk, NY: M. E. Sharpe).

Siu, Y. M. and Li, S. M. (1993) 'Population Mobility in the 1980s: China on the Road to an Open Society', ch. 19 in Cheng, J. Y. S. and Brosseau, M. (eds) *China Review 1993* (Hong Kong: Chinese University Press).

Skeldon, R. (1990) *Population Mobility in Developing Countries: A Reinterpretation* (London: Belhaven Press).

Skinner, G. W. (ed.) (1977) *The City in Late Imperial China* (Stanford University Press).

Smil, V. (1993) *China's Environmental Crisis: An Inquiry into the Limits of National Development* (Armonk, NY: M. E. Sharpe).

Smith, C. J. (1996a) 'Migration as an Agent of Change in Contemporary China', *Chinese Environment and Development*, 7 (1–2) 14–55.

Smith, C. (1996b) 'China's New Multiculturalism: The Flowering of Ethnicity in the Peoples' Republic', unpublished paper, Department of Geography, State University of New York.

Smith, C. J. (1996c) 'The Two Faces of Economic Reform in Contemporary China: Economic Growth Versus Human Development', unpublished paper, Department of Geography, State University of New York.

Smith, C. J. and Dai, F. (1995) 'Health, Wealth, and Inequality in the Chinese City', *Journal of Health and Place*, 1 (2) 167–77.

Solinger, D. (1985) 'Temporary Residence Certificate Regulations in Wuhan, May 1983', *China Quarterly*, 101 (March), 98–104.

Solinger, D. (1993) 'China's Transients and the State: A Form of Civil Society?', *Politics and Society*, 21 (1) 91–122.

Solinger, D. (1994) 'China's Urban Transients in the Transition from Socialism and the Collapse of the Communist Urban Public Goods Regime', *Comparative Politics*, 27 (2) 127–146.

Solinger, D. (1996) 'The Impact of Migrants on City Services', *Chinese Environment and Development*, 7, (1–2) 118–143.

Standing, G. (1996) 'Global Feminization Through Flexible Labour', pp. 405–30 in K. P. Jameson and C. K. Wilbur (eds) *The Political Economy of Development and Underdevelopment*, 6th edn (New York: McGraw-Hill).

Tan, K. C. (1993) 'Rural-Urban Segregation in China', *Geography Research Forum* 13, 71–83.

Tan, S. and Li, D. (1993) 'Urban Development and Crime in China', pp. 345–52 in Guldin, G. and Southall, A.(eds) *Urban Anthropology in China* (New York: E. J. Brill).

Taylor, J. R. and Banister, J. (1991) 'Surplus Rural Labour in the People's Republic of China', pp. 87–120 in Veeck, G. (ed.) *The Uneven Landscape: Geographic Studies in Post-Reform China* (Baton Rouge, LA: Louisiana State University, GeoScience Publications, vol. 30).

Theroux, P. (1993) 'Going to See the Dragon', *Harpers Magazine*, October, 33–56.

Vogel, E. (1989) *One Step Ahead in China: Guangdong Under Reform* (Cambridge, MA: Harvard University Press).

Wan, G. H. (1995) 'Peasant Flood in China: Internal Migration and its Policy Determinants', *Third World Quarterly*, 16, (2), 173–96.

Wong, L. (1994) 'China's Urban Migrants: The Public Policy Challenge', *Pacific Affairs*, 67 (3), 335-55.

White, L. T. III (1994) 'Migration and Politics on the Shanghai Delta', *Issues and Studies*, 39 (9) 63–94.

Whyte, M. K. and Parish, W. L. (1984) *Urban Life in Contemporary China* (University of Chicago Press).

Wilson, W. J. (1987) *The Truly Disadvantaged: The Inner City, the Underclass and Public Policy* (University of Chicago Press).

Wu, C. T. and Xu, X. Q. (1990) 'Economic Reforms and Rural to Urban Migration', pp. 129–143 in Linge, G. J. R. and Forbes, D. K. (eds) *China's Spatial Economy: Recent Developments and Reforms* (Hong Kong: Oxford University Press).

Wu, H. X. Y. (1993) 'Policy Effects on Labour Force Rural-to-Urban Migration and Sectoral Transformation in the Economic Development of a Centrally-Planned Economy: the Case of China', PhD dissertation, University of Waikato, Hamilton, New Zealand.

Xiang, B. (1996) 'How to Create a Visible "Non-State Space" Through Migration and Marketized Traditional Networks: An Account of a Migrant Community in China', paper prepared for the Oxford Workshop on Migration, St Antony's College, 3–5 June, 1996.

Zhao, S. and Zhang, M. (1993) 'Population Migration and Flow in Shenzhen', pp. 131–140 in Ma, X. and Wang, W. Z. (eds) *Migration and Urbanisation in China* (Beijing: New World Press).

Zhou, D. M. (1993) 'An Approach to the Problem of Population Movement and Cultural Adaptation in the Urbanizing Pearl River Delta', pp. 205–15 in Guldin, G. and Southall, A. (eds) *Urban Anthropology in China* (Leiden: E. J. Brill).

5

Family Planning and Fertility Among Temporary Migrants

Caroline Hoy

Introduction

This chapter describes the development of marriage and family planning legislation in response to the great increase in population mobility. I show that descriptions of migrants' supposed 'deviant' behaviour in relation to marriage or births (such as marriage below the legal ages, or births out of plan) tend to be exaggerated and are in fact characteristic of the wider population. I explore the impact of fertility on migration and specifically the number of children migrants may be expected to have, according to the results of a small survey of temporary registered migrants I conducted in Beijing in June 1994 (referred to as the 1994 Beijing migrant survey). The chapter begins with a description of the survey population and the role of micro-demographic techniques. A history of the household registration system that controls mobility is outlined before the in-depth discussion of marriage and fertility.

During summer 1994, 403 migrants holding Beijing temporary residence permits were surveyed in two areas of Beijing: Haidian (an inner suburb) and Mentougou (an outer suburb). The target population were women who had been married at some point in their lives and whose proper household registration was outside the Beijing metropolitan area. (During the analysis it was found that the survey population included women who were cohabiting in *de facto* marriages.) No woman originated from Beijing city itself or from any of the city's suburbs or counties. The aim of the survey was to collect detailed migration histories both pre- and post-migration to Beijing. (A migration event was defined as a movement from one residence to another even within an administrative unit, for example, between villages within the same township or streets within urban areas.)

Microdemographic approaches

Microscale investigations are particularly suitable for examination of the experiences of subpopulations within a larger demographic phenomenon such as migration (Fulton and Randall 1988). Demographic analysis of migration will only ever capture a selection of population movement. A smaller-scale approach allows for greater flexibility in identifying the distance and duration thresholds that define migration, and allows investigation to be made in context (Hugo 1988).

There is a need to be aware of the pitfalls inherent in any scaling-up of results or expectation of macrobehavioural patterns based on findings from micro data (Caldwell and Hill 1988). Microdemographic work will, by its nature, always address inadequately the other sections of the population. However, if it is to provide an adequate picture of a society, especially one so opaque as that of China, each study must be seen as a stage in a detailed, complex and careful analysis. Thus microdemography is a step in the explanation of wider demographic processes (Caldwell *et al.* 1988; Hugo 1988). It is invaluable in establishing individual motives and reasoning within the larger-scale processes. 'If we are going to understand population process in China, we are going to have to study the process at the individual and family level' (Harrell 1995, p. 2). In addition, microdemography can identify differences in what has been called 'cultural geography' of China (Lavely *et al.* 1990, p. 819), which can pinpoint variations in society. Micro-demographic analysis has been particularly significant in analysing and reinterpreting the family forms found in China. Where society is in a state of flux and relationships are being negotiated, as between the urban and rural in China, macro work can easily miss small undercurrents that may become more significant in the future.

History of the household registration system

Systems for the enumeration and administration of the population, based on the household, can be traced back to pre-unification China (Dutton 1993). In contemporary China a system of household registration called the *hukou* has provided the structure for the administration of the population and the medium through which mobility is regulated. Household registration was introduced as a unified system for rural and urban areas in 1958, overtly for the 'preservation of social order'. The household registration system was designed to reduce urban population in a situation in which the state took on full responsibility of provision of basic foodstuffs, housing and facilities for its urban population (Dutton 1993; Cheng and Selden 1994).

Under the household registration system every household is defined as urban or rural, and, in addition, either agricultural and responsible for provision of its own basic foodstuffs, or non-agricultural and subsidised by the state. Household registers require the following pieces of information on individuals and the demographics of their household:

- whether an individual is the head of the household;
- if not, their relationship with the household head (e.g. wife, son);
- sex, name, birth place and date, and marital status.

When she marries, a woman's details are deleted from the records of her natal household and re-entered into the register of her marital household. Mobility, for any member of the population, is commensurate with movement from one household to another. The household registration system aimed to control migration in four ways:

1. Rural-to-urban migration was prohibited.
2. Mobility up the urban hierarchy was severely restricted.
3. Sideways movement from town to town, city to city was permitted, but in practice could be difficult unless it involved rural-to-rural migration.
4. Movement down the hierarchy, for example and especially, from cities to rural areas, was positively encouraged.

Marriage does not give a man or a woman with a rural registration the right to live with a partner with an urban registration in an urban area. Both, however, can live in a rural area.

The function of the registration system shifted over time. From being a tool of social control it became a taxonomy of social strata. Rather than reflecting economic activity and opportunities, the *hukou* dictated it (Gong 1989; Christiansen 1990). Each stratum was determined by household location and the benefits and disadvantages associated with that location within the urban hierarchy (Gong 1989), the apex of which was the province-level municipalities (Beijing, Shanghai and Tianjin). The prohibitions on personal mobility (and thereby social mobility) ensured that there was very little communication and exchanges of population and information between each level. By the late 1970s, restrictions on migration to urban locations had reduced the number of people who held rural registration, but who lived for any periods of time in urban areas, to a small minority (Wu 1994).

The household registration system and migration in the reform period

Guiding policy behind rural and urban reforms was introduced at the Third Plenum of the Eleventh National Party Congress in 1978. These reforms, spoken of as if revolutionary in character (SWB 1993; Qingnian Bao 1994), are the accepted catalyst for migration (Goldstein *et al.* 1991; Mallee 1995). Rural areas are the predominant source of the migrant population (Huang 1989; Chen 1991; CNA 1991; Ma and Lin 1993; Guang 1995). The transformation of agriculture into a productive and wealth-producing activity involved a rapid increase in labour productivity and the need to shed labour surpluses. Pressure built up in rural areas for migration to alternative economic opportunities (Shen 1994). This surplus population was partially absorbed by the development of non-agricultural activities, the town and village enterprises (TVEs). By the end of 1985, 10 per cent of rural labour was employed by such businesses (Goldstein 1990). But TVEs were unable to give guarantees of employment (Bowles and Dong 1994), and the numbers seeking work proved too large.

People turned toward urban centres in search of jobs, some of these created by official endorsement of private enterprise in 1983 (Solinger 1993). The increasing transportation and communication network also promoted population circulation. Out-migration from provinces such as Sichuan, Anhui and Guangxi was encouraged by mismanagement of agricultural land. Ma and Lin (1993) suggest that, overall, the reforms contributed to a significant spatial redistribution of rural labour.

This large-scale movement began to put pressure on household registration and resource allocation systems. One of the first official indications of this pressure occurred in 1981: a State Council order calling for strict control over rural-to-urban migration (Solinger 1985). But a period of flexibility in the way in which the household registration system controlled mobility had begun, which Ma (1993, p. 3) calls the period of 'half open migration' (from 1984 to the present). Its inception was marked by a 1984 State Council circular that was significant for several reasons, but especially as it allowed peasants to move into smaller cities and towns. Peasant families who requested transfers to work in towns below the level of the county town (*zhen*) would be granted them if they could demonstrate that they had a settled residence and were self-supporting. They would then be granted a certificate of self-sufficiency in grain (*zili kouliang hukou bu*), counted as members of the non-agricultural population at destination and have equal access with residents to urban facilities (Solinger 1991).

Significantly, this new policy granted permission for dependants to migrate with the worker. The circular stated that 'Public Security departments should grant permanent resident status to all peasants and their dependents who apply for engagement ... in towns' (FBIS 1984, p. K19). This was in direct opposition to the regulations laid down for the rest of the population, which did not normally allow family members to migrate as a unit, even if, for example, one was allocated to a job in a different area. The joint migration of partners was not challenged in later legislation such as the national regulations on temporary residence laid down in 1985 by the Ministry of Public Security.

By the end of 1988, it was reported that 5 million people had migrated under this scheme. However, the importance of this regulation should not be overestimated, as the certificate of self-sufficiency did not appear to be particularly popular with peasants (Mallee 1995) and was applicable only to towns below the county level. Neither did it make a great difference to patterns or levels of rural to urban migration. It had, however, created a precedent for the migration of couples, and this did not allay fears of high fertility rates in this population.

The new regulations granted a degree of legitimisation for migrants. Under the terms of this legislation, a migrant is required to register their presence if they are resident for between 3 and 30 days and to arrange for a temporary residence card (*zanzhuzheng*) if remaining for longer than 30 days. Registration for a temporary residence permit can be undertaken by anyone over the age of sixteen and must take place in person. Proof of identity is required along with a family planning card for a married woman of childbearing age, and recent photographs of the applicant. A permit is a legal document that allows the holder to stay in the location the permit is issued for a period of up to six months or a year, and can be renewed. Registration details are held in the police station of the area in which the migrant is resident, and the card is valid only for that area. A fee is required when the card is issued, and there are reports of migrants having to pay additional monthly 'protection' fees. Many migrants have found the registration card irrelevant or impractical. In 1995 it was estimated that 45 per cent of the 80 million migrants had not registered (*Renmin Ribao [People's Daily]* 1995). Since migrants are required to self-report, registration procedures are problematic. There are no regulatory mechanisms to identify mobility events independently of these procedures. In addition, personnel and budgets were insufficient in the struggle for up-to-date information on migrants.

A migrant (*qianyi renkou*) is in official terms anyone who has approval for movement that crosses an administrative boundary, such as a county border, and their household registration moves with them (Goldstein *et al.* 1991). Approval must be granted by work units and public security bureaux in both source and destination. Applications for migration must be submitted at origin prior to migration. The floating population (*liudong renkou*) have no permission to move. A member of the floating population is defined as someone absent from their place of registration or usual place of residence for one night, if they have not moved, or do not intend to apply to move, their household registration (Gui 1992; Tang 1993). Their registration remains at origin and they are classed as a resident of that origin, irrespective of the duration of their absence (Goldstein *et al.* 1991). Lacking legal residence status at destination, they are not eligible for benefits. Terms such as 'temporary' or 'transient' are semantically and politically expedient, calming the fears of urban residents and avoiding planning requirements that would be an acknowledgement of the need to accommodate this population permanently. In this chapter the floating, transient or temporary registered population (*liudong renkou*) are referred to as migrants, while those who have formally applied to move their household registration (*qianyi renkou*) are referred to as formal migrants.

Other terms for the migrant population are common. For example, migrants who stay for less than three days in an urban areas are called *guowang renkou*, or 'comers and goers'. Those seeking jobs are known as *dagong zi* (if male) and *dagong mei* (female). There are many more, pejorative, terms. Boundaries between these distinctions are fluid. A family visitor may slip easily into the permanent migrant category. Classifications such as these are in essence another form of control, but have not really become established as a tool in migration administrative policy, partly through their diversity and partly as their utility has not been proven.

After 1985 a process of smaller adjustments to the household registration policy at all levels occurred. Further, but limited, experimentation with the registration system took place such as the introduction of red-seal and blue-seal cards in Shanghai and counties of Beijing during the early 1990s (*China Daily*, 1994a; Laodong Bao 1994). These were a form or temporary residence permit, granting the holder access to benefits as if they were urban residents but without giving the right to permanent residence. They received some harsh criticisms: 'In the face of the surging waves of the floating population, the limited Blue Seal residence cards are like a cup of water unable to put out a load of burning wood' (FBIS 1994a, p. 11). Such comments were part of a larger public debate on the abolition of the *hukou* system, which would give those migrating security of residence in urban areas and produce a reformation of the land allocation system whereby those accepting urban residence would be required to yield their land to the market (*China Daily* 1994b, 1994c).

The impression of such measures is of legislation and regulation that is reactive rather than proactive, lacking integration with overall development strategy (Zweig *et al.*, 1987). The 1985 temporary registration system proved inflexible, and was ignored by many migrants. Many were staying well beyond the expected year residence (Goldstein 1992; Kuhn and Kaye 1994; Guang 1995). In response, a system of reliance on marriage, non-marriage and family planning certificates developed as a means of population control. This is discussed in the following two sections.

Marriage

Concerns about the timing of marriage, and the importance of marriage rather than cohabitation in the creation of unions, are connected to the function of marriage as a legitimisation of childbearing. The family planning system relies on a stable marriage pattern, and cannot accommodate relationships that would enable the couple to evade the extended process of accounting for, planning for, and disseminating information about, fertility.

It is frequently suggested that the migrant population is engaged in forms of 'illegal' marriage above the average rate. They are supposed to be more of them in 'early' marriage (below the legal age of 20 for women and 22 for men) and marriages which have not been formally registered (cohabitation). For example, in Xiaoshan city in Zhejiang in 1988–9, 24 per cent of in-migrants were reportedly cohabiting (Liu 1990). In Panshi county in Jilin in 1990, 77 per cent of married women of childbearing age among in-migrants did not have marriage certificates, and their attitude towards marriage was described as 'relatively backward'. Only 8 per cent of women in the 1994 Beijing migrant survey had not signed a marriage certificate; 14 per cent had married 'early'.

In response to these concerns and as part of a wider movement towards the regulation of migrant fertility, 'Measures for the Management of Family Planning of the Floating Population' were promulgated in late 1991. These required potential migrants to carry family planning cards that supplied proof of marital status (*China Population Today* 1992). Couples who arrived without such proof could be sent back to their place of origin. Provincial regulations supported these measures. For example, chapter 3, article 19, of regulations on the Jiangsu migrant population, published in 1994 stated that 'home owners are strictly forbidden to permit the co-habitation of a man and a women without marriage' (FBIS 1994b). Since 1990 Guangdong has required unmarried people to show proof of their bachelor- or spinsterhood.

The marital relationship also controlled other aspects of life. Migrant married women who did not register at an appointed hospital to receive family planning measures would, in certain areas, not be permitted to remain or work. In such way marriage was used to control the mobile population and in particular women, on whom the burden of proof seems to fall.

Closer examination of data shows such illegal marriages are present in wider society, that cohabitation and early marriage are in fact common among the resident population and are not a characteristic of migrants. Early marriage in the general population has been described as a matter of extreme urgency (Li and Zhang 1994). The classifications of marital status outlined by the State Family Planning Association in 1990 showed a pragmatic definition of marital status: unmarried (*weihun*), married (*you pei'ou*), widowed (*sang'ou*) and divorced (*lihun*). To these were added *de facto* marriages (*shishi hunyin*) that had not been registered but which were to be counted as marriages for administration purposes (Gui 1992, p. 211).

Li (1993) suggests that up to 25 per cent of all marriages between 1982 and 1990 were illegal. Some 5 per cent of the population aged 15 to 19 years at the time of the 1990 census were married (Liu 1992). The proportions marrying early have fluctuated. In 1980, 16 per cent of marriages took place before the legal age for one or both the marriage partners. At their peak, two years later, 28 per cent of marriages were described as 'early'. The problem is exacerbated by the practice of falsely elevating the age of one or both partners (Banister 1987). As for cohabitation, one report put the proportion of *de facto* unions at the end of the 1980s at a third of all new marriages (ICM 1990).

In response, the government and the Family Planning Commission established programmes which drew a closer association between pre-marital training, education and marriage registration (Li and Zhang 1994). Finally, in 1994, new marriage registration procedures were announced, replacing those of 1986. These measures reinforced the aims of the 1980 marriage law in ensuring freedom in marriage. It also outlined the role of registration offices and registration procedures. On the problem of illegal marriages, article 24 stated:

> Where Citizens who have not reached the legal marriage age but live together as husband and wife or parties who meet the require-ments for marriage and live as husband and wife but have not applied for marriage registration, their marriage relations are invalid and not protected by law. (FBIS 1994c, p. 40)

Promulgated on February 1, these regulations reportedly allowed for the separation of couples whose marriage was not conducted in accord-ance with the law. Their marriages would be considered valid if they subsequently registered (FBIS 1994d). The new regulations also targeted other forms of illegal marriages, including bigamous and arranged marriages.

In this context, the proportions of women in the migration popula-tion reported as engaged in some form of illegal marriage seem un-remarkable. For example in a survey of the migrant population in Xiaoshan in 1989, only 2 per cent of women married before the age of 20 (Liu 1990). Migrants are an easy population for the government to target and more likely to have their demographic patterns examined.

Family planning

Attempts to manage the fertility of the floating population varied considerably in space and time, often reflecting local conditions and experience. The earliest measures were introduced in 1985 in parts of Ningxia, Fujian and Guizhou, and by 1988 nearly forty provinces, counties and cities had devised measures for the control of the fertility of the migrant population between different areas (Gui 1992). Differences developed in the administration of family planning in the migrant population between areas. For example, definitions of migrants' origins and destinations varied, and so did the target popula-tion for family planning (whether the mobile population as a whole, or a highly selective group of married women of childbearing age). Measures by which work permits could be refused to migrants who were unable to produce family planning certificates were introduced in

Zhejiang, Beijing, Tianjin, Shanghai and Fujian in the second half of the 1980s (Hardee-Cleaveland and Banister 1988). Responsibility for migrants at destination varied between government departments, work units and neighbourhood offices (Gui 1992). At the end of 1987 a symposium was held in Guangzhou on establishing national regulations. Family planning was one issue on the agenda, particularly policy evasion and inadequacies in local implementation (Bao 1992). A commission was set up in 1987 to explore the issue of migrant fertility (Gui 1992).

Under the 1991 family planning regulations, administration of fertility behaviour became the joint responsibility of destination and permanent household registration areas. The target migrant population was defined broadly as those for whom 'the places of their permanent registration are not the places where their habitual residence is registered' (*China Population Today* 1992, p. 2), and, with no distinction by sex or marital status, simply 'who are fertile' (ibid.). Migrant family planning was governed according to the legislation implemented in the area of permanent registration. The family planning card, which provided proof of marriage, permitted the holder to have children at the place they moved to. Migrant source areas promoted contraception and issued family planning cards (FBIS 1990). Destination areas were responsible for propaganda organisation and collating information. They also had the important task of examining family planning cards prior to issuing residential and business licences (FBIS 1990), as well as upholding the marriage card in determining access to resources. If there were only low proportions of migrants using contraception, or high fertility levels, these were blamed on poor management in their areas origin.

The family planning card provided proof of identify in addition to marital status and its main role was in policing fertility. It defined access to opportunities: those who could not show one on demand would be refused accommodation or a work permit. The card's advantage lay in its transferability: the household register is not mobile, the identity card instituted in the mid-1980s has proved problematic and there are no birth certificates. But the family planning card requires a high degree of synchronisation between migration source and destination areas.

Figures 5.1 and 5.2 are examples of legislation and documentation associated with the management of marriage and contraception in the floating population. Figure 5.1 is the translation of a notice displayed in a county town in Hubei in 1994, and results from the responsibil-

Concerning the administration of family planning certificates among the floating population

Notice

In order to implement the 'Methods for the implementation of measures for the administration of the family planning of the floating population of Hubei province', and to improve the work of our county in family planning among the floating population, combining the present work of ordering and rectification of the administration of family planning of the floating population of our county, the following items relating to the arrangements for the handling of the floating population's planned fertility card, examination of cards, and exchanging cards are currently being carried out:

1. *On handling*: The floating population of this county, who by the time of out-migration have not arranged for a 'Hubei province floating population planned fertility card'must go the to the county office for administration of the floating population's planned fertility and arrange for a card. Members of the floating population who do not have a 'floating population planned fertility card', must return to their place of usual residence and, at the planned fertility administrative department of the county or above level, arrange for a certificate to be issued.

2. *Checking certificates*: Those members of the floating population who are here, have previously arranged a 'floating population planned fertility card' and have obtained employment should now go to the floating population planned fertility office to have their certificate checked.

3. *Certificate exchange*: The 'floating population planned fertility certificate'has a life of three years. Normally, those members of the floating population whose card is already three years old should return to their place of usual residence and at the planned fertility administrative department at county level or above or should arrange to exchange it for a new certificate.

4. The work of issuing and examination of certificates should be completed by 20 August; at this time, those who have not requested such work shall be subject to a fine, and must replace their card. Those who refuse will have their employment licence cancelled.

Floating population planned fertility
administration reorganisation committee
1 August 1994

Figure 5.1   Poster announcing changes to the administration of the planned fertility of the floating population of a county town in Hubei Province, 1994.

Source: 1994 fieldwork.

In-migrants Contraception Registration Card

No. 000000

Name   Identity Card number

Place of registration   Temporary Address

Current *danwei* and address

Husband's migration status

Husband's name and *danwei*

Current number of

    Sons   Date of birth of youngest child
                                        year/month

    Daughters

Current contraceptive status   Current pregnancy status

If pregnant out-of-plan at arrival, number of months pregnant

Pregnancy quota   Date of planned pregnancy

                                        Yeay   Month

Reason

Date of completion

19___ Year   Month_____   Day_____

Figure 5.2   Contraceptive registration card for in-floaters

Source: Gui (1992, p. 103).

ities outlined in the 1991 regulations. Potential migrants must arrange for a card proving contraceptive practice prior to leaving. In-migrants without cards have to return to arrange for the card to be issued. Those who fail to undertake these regulations face having their work permits revoked. Figure 5.2 shows the text on reverse of a contraceptive registration card for female migrants at destination. It contains information about the migrant and her husband, and her fertility and contraception history. It also shows the number of children a migrant is entitled to. The front of the card contains details of the area in which the card was issued and the validity dates.

As for marriage, provincial regulations, such as the 1993 'Measures for the Administration of the Floating Population' in Guangdong (Miao and Zhang 1995) supported the 1991 family planning regulations. In addition, local areas started their own initiatives. Two counties in Fujian and Zhejiang sent medical and family planning personnel to Beijing to provide contraceptive services to migrants from their areas (*Keji Ribao* 1994; *Beijing Ribao* 1994). However, these are wealthy provinces and these measures may also underline their independence from central authority; they could not necessarily be repeated by poorer provinces.

Migrant women and fertility

Women in the migrant population are often called the 'excess birth guerrilla corps' (CNA 1991; *Keji Ribao* 1994), since mobility potentially allows for self-determination of fertility. The threat of pregnancy is underlined by the continuous identification of women of childbearing age as a distinct population group. For example, nearly 90 per cent of migrant women in Xiamen (Fujian Province) were 'women of child bearing age'. This relationship is not always quite so explicitly stated, commentators simply noting the latent potential for high fertility rates in the migrant population in situations where *hukou* and family planning systems were relaxed (Liaoning Daxue 1992).

As in marriage, the migrant population is portrayed as the most susceptible to deviant behaviour such as pre-marital births (Liu 1990). For example, one street, the smallest administrative unit in urban areas, in a Heilongjiang city was reported to have 276 transient households. Of these, over three-quarters had 'excess' births (JPRS 1991). Some 6 per cent of transients migrating to Panshi county (Jilin Province) were women with three or more children and 11 per cent of those pregnant at the time of the survey in 1992 were 'out-of-plan' pregnancies. In the year before the survey, 29 per cent of births had been 'out-of-plan' whether they were first, second or third parity births. An article quoted a 1987 survey of 2000 households in the migrant population in Shiyuan (Hubei Province), a fifth of which had two or more children (*China Daily* 1989). Prior to the establishment of a special family planning centre, an economic zone in Yiwu city (Zhejiang province), was described as an 'air raid shelter' *(fangkongdong)* or 'haven' *(bifenggang)* for those wishing to evade the family planning regulations (Wang 1992, p. 60) and methods by which migrants can evade the regulations, for example, by hiding in villages set up for the purpose, have been described.

Comparisons between the rates of excess births in migrant and resident population are common to discussions of migrant fertility. The percentage of births in the resident population is often set at less than 1 percent. Excess births reportedly accounted for 14 per cent of births to married women migrants in Shanghai in 1988 (JPRS 1991) and 14 per cent in Xian in 1990 (Gui 1992, p. 2). In 1991 half of the excess births in Guangdong were to migrants, who made up 8 per cent of the population (CNA 1991). In 1991 in China as a whole, 13 per cent of excess births were ascribed the migrants (CNA 1991).

Such comparisons between resident and migrant communities can be questioned from two perspectives. First, perceptions of high fertility in the migrant population reflect the unfamiliarity of urban family planning personnel with the realities of rural fertility behaviour. Substantial differences in policy can exist between origin and destination area, and personnel are expected to be familiar with the regulations of each area of origin of migrants under their jurisdiction. Migrants are reluctant to conform with both urban quotas and urban timetables. Their subsequent fertility, while acceptable at origin, may be described as excess in urban reports.

Second, underestimation of the proportions of births counted as 'excess' in the resident population is likely to be large. In a 1991 survey in Hubei province, 7 per cent of births to the resident population were 'out-of-plan' (Chen 1993); 13 per cent of births to women aged 20–24 years were 'out-of-plan'. In 1988–9, 40 per cent of resident women in a county in Anhui had three or more children compared with 28 per cent of women who had migrated out (Bao 1992), although this pattern may reflect the differing age structure of migrants and non-migrants.

In contrast, in 1994 fertility rates of migrant women were lower than women in the resident population in Guangdong, and their peak of childbearing was some two years older *(Yangcheng Wanbao,* 1994). That low fertility rates were compatible with migration was established as early as 1986 (Tian 1991). One population institute suggested that 'migration of the rural population to urban areas is beneficial in lowering fertility ... migration itself is not to be viewed as a new form of contraceptive' (SHKX 1988, p. 9).

The idea that migrant fertility may in fact be lower than previously expected or even lower than that of the resident population is emerging only slowly into public consciousness. One newspaper announced the discovery of low fertility rates in a migrant population with the words: 'Excess birth guerrilla corps? Not necessarily! Low fertility corps? Exactly!' (*Yangcheng Ribao*, 1994). But there are no indications that the government will relax its vigilance on birth issues in the migrant population. In the face of such contradictory evidence, the question is therefore: what is happening to the fertility of migrants? The opportunity to explore this topic further comes from information supplied from the 1994 Beijing migrant survey.

Fertility in the sample population

A total of 584 births (576 surviving) were reported among the women in the 1994 Beijing migrant survey. Some 13 per cent of women had no children at the time of the survey, many of them having been married only in the calendar year before the survey, and their lack of a child being probably attributable to time. Around 14 per cent of women had one child and a third had two children. The mean number of pregnancies for this population was 1.4. Of those with children, it was unusual to find a women who had not had her first child within two years of marriage. The average length of the first birth interval was just under 16 months.

First birth intervals have never been targeted by family planning programmes, which have instead concentrated on the timing of marriage and longer intervals between later births (Feeney and Wang 1993). There is a trend towards decreasing the length of the first birth interval (Coale *et al.* 1988; Feeney and Wang 1993). Tu (1993) suggests a median first birth interval of approximately 15 months. Increased coital frequency, and unwillingness to use the limited range of available contraceptives, such as the intra-uterine device (IUD), have been cited as causes for this reduction (Honig and Hershatter 1988; Cleland and Shen 1991; Coale *et al.*, 1988; Cai *et al.* 1993; Feeney and Wang 1993).

In order to try and assess the impact of migration on fertility, the mean number of children according to birth cohort in sample subpopulations were distinguished by the relative timing of marriage, migration and birth of the first child. Five subpopulations were created by this method, as shown in Table 5.1. Six five-year birth cohorts were also established. Each five-year cohort runs from June of one year to

Table 5.1 Mean number of children ever born, by migrant subpopulation

Birth cohort[a]	Migrant subpopulation					Cohort mean
	1 Migration occurred before marriage	2 Migration occurred after birth of first child	3 Migration occurred between marriage and birth of first child	4 Migration and marriage occurred at the same time	5 Other	
1945–50	—	2.9	3.0	2.0	2.4	2.6
1950–5	—	2.6	—	—	2.4	2.5
1955–60	1.4	1.9	1.3	—	1.7	1.8
1960–5	0.9	1.7	1.2	2.5	1.6	1.6
1965–70	0.5	1.4	0.7	1.3	1.2	1.1
1970–5		1.0	0.2	1.2	0.9	0.6
Mean	0.9	1.8	0.7	1.4	1.7	1.4
Total	47	210	72	21	53	403

[a] The five-year periods in which the women sampled were born. Each five-year cohort runs from June of one year to May of the fifth year.
Source: 1994 Beijing migrant survey.

Explanation of categories:
1. The first sub-population consisted of women whose first migration occurred before their marriage, irrespective of later births. Thus, women in this group may not have any children or may have been near completion of their family.
2. Women who migrated at some point after the birth of their first child. Migration could have taken place immediately after the birth of this child or after the birth of subsequent children. The key event was the onset of childbearing.
3. This group consisted of women who migrated after marriage but before the birth of their first child, that is, in the first birth interval, irrespective of the total number of births. It also included women who had no children.
4. Women who had at least one child and whose migration took place at the same time as their marriage.
5. The final subpopulation consisted of those women whose life histories fell outside the preceding patterns of behaviour, such as women with 'early births'.

May of the fifth year, the reference point provided by the date of the survey. Women in the younger cohorts are more likely to have migrated before marriage and those in the older cohorts after the birth of their first child. The mean number of children for each subpopulation within each cohort was established. Means are shown in Table 5.1. Means were compared using one-way analysis of variance (ANOVA) and differences were tested for significance using a Bonferroni test (see the appendix to this chapter for procedures).

The smallest mean number of children born to any cohort occurred to women born in 1970–5 and who migrated between marriage and the birth of their first child (0.2 children). The largest mean (3.0 children) occurred in the same subpopulation, but for those born a quarter of a century earlier in 1945–50. Clearly, this is not a population characterised by high fertility.

There are no significant differences between the mean number of children ever born for any woman born before 1960. No significant differences existed between subpopulations in the cohort born 1960–5, but there are apparent visual differences between the mean number of children ever born to women who migrated in the interval between marriage and the birth of their first child, which is lower than in other populations. Significant differences occurred between means of children in the cohorts of women born in 1965–70 and 1970–75. Women in the 1965–70 birth cohort who migrated during the marriage-to-birth interval had a significantly lower mean number of children than those whose migration took place at some point after the birth of their first child. They also had a significantly lower mean number of children than women who married concurrently with migration. Women in the 1970–5 birth cohort who migrated between marriage and the birth of their first child had a significantly lower mean number of children than those in all other categories.

The most common area of differentiation lay between women who migrated after marriage but before their first child was born, and the other subpopulations. These women had lower mean numbers of children than the other subpopulations. It appears that migration is acting to reduce fertility. Whether this is a result of delaying first births and extending subsequent birth intervals, or of changes in fertility objectives, is discussed later in this chapter.

Differences are more apparent in younger cohorts. Migration opportunities have expanded in recent years. Social acceptance of different behaviour has increased, and a wider range of experiences has been created by younger women. Political suppression of migration means that older women are more likely to have had similar (restricted) mobility opportunities. An initial conclusion would suggest that where migration takes place in a less structured environment it is likely to reduce mean numbers of children ever born, lowering mean numbers of children most effectively where migration takes place before marriage and between marriage and first birth.

The experiences of the two youngest cohorts, born in 1965–70 and 1970–75, have been truncated by the demands of the survey, which only includes members of these cohorts who have married and migrated relatively early and rapidly. Thus the survey does not, and cannot, show the complete picture for women in these cohorts. The results are a 'snapshot' reflection of the subpopulations at the date of the survey. However, the fact that significant differences are apparent for these youngest of cohorts is further evidence of the impact on fertility of migration and changing opportunities in migration. The pattern is strong enough to survive the effects imposed by data collection. While mean numbers of children are expected to rise for women in the younger cohorts, at this stage it is reasonable to suggest that the patterns of migration and fertility will hold.

Comparisons between the mean number of children between the 1994 Beijing migrant survey and other survey subpopulations can be problematic, because of different sampling procedures and identified migrant subpopulations, but are still instructive. There are two sample subpopulations available for comparison procedures. In both cases there are insufficient data to undertake detailed analysis of age-specific fertility rates, and we have to rely on estimates of mean number of births by cohort. The data sets are married women in the Chinese Academy of Social Sciences 1986 survey of 74 cities and towns (CASS 1988), the 1993 Horizon survey of migrants in Beijing (Horizon 1993) and the 1994 Beijing migrant survey. Statistics from these data sets are displayed in Table 5.2.

Figures in Table 5.2 are not directly comparable, as the 1993 Horizon survey does not use standard five-year age groupings. Age groups for the 1994 Beijing migrant survey are also shifted six months from the usual year-end division. The low mean number of children born in all of these surveys is perhaps the most striking aspect, with consistency of results despite the time differential, and the differences between the surveys. The 1986 survey is more likely to have included a higher proportion of formal migrants, the 1993 survey a high proportion of non-registered migrants, and the 1994 more temporary registered migrants. In all populations, women below the age of 40 years have less than two

Table 5.2   Mean number of children reported in three migrant surveys

Age group	Sample survey		Age group	
	1994 Beijing[a]	1986 Cities and towns[b]	Age group	1993 Horizon[c]
20–24	0.6	0.6	19 to 25	0.7
25–29	1.1	0.9		
30–34	1.6	1.2	26 to 35	1.4
35–39	1.8	1.7		
40–44	2.5	2.4	36 to 45	2.1
45–49	2.6	3.0	> 46	3.3
Mean	1.4	1.6		1.5

Sources:
[a] 1994 Beijing migrant survey, N = 403
[b] Column 2 calculated from: CASS (1988), 1986 China migration of 74 Cities and Towns sampling survey data (1986) (Computer tabulation): pp. 37, 42. Migrants to metropolises, N = 3474
[c] Calculated from: Horizon (1993), Computer data set: m9305a, N = 229.

children. These results are all supporting information for the hypotheses that migration depresses fertility levels, and is not a mask for high-fertility behaviour.

Conclusion

I have suggested and shown how migrant control is being established through the use of mobile documentation such as the family planning certificate. Publicity ensures that the issue of high fertility rates in the migrant population is kept to the forefront of public awareness, despite evidence that fertility rates are low. Many migrants choose to ignore the requirements of registration and marriage, and time their own births, but they are perhaps not unusual compared with the population as a whole.

Even from the evidence provided by such a specialised survey population, it seems that despite the best intentions of the family planning offices it is the migrants who control their fertility, and any successes in family planning are due to changing expectations of the women and not the work of the family planning office. The impacts of the family planning office would be greatest in stable populations of migrant women who can be closely monitored – for example the wives of miners in the Mentougou district of Beijing, who will be resident for several years as their husbands work under contract to the mining companies.

In a society such as China, where fertility is prominent on both political and personal agendas, those with similar views or desires relating to fertility may congregate, for example, in areas where control is more lax or sympathetic towards their situation Those for whom fertility is not as vital a concern may be content to reside in areas that place a higher priority on conformity with policy. The 1994 Beijing migrant survey involved migrants who generally act in accordance with regulations. They will therefore not necessarily be representative of the more unregulated migrants. Regulated migrants, however, make up a substantial part of the population.

Urban areas with mainly registered migrants may differ from others because the groups are self-selecting of their habitation. Different groups are willing to accept varying degrees of authoritarian control over (the inhibition of) their movement (actual and social), and the degree to which they are willing to accept 'interference' in their fertility behaviour. Migrants who are unwilling to accept such interference will not be captured by this survey. We may suggest that migrants who remain in these areas belong to one or more types. First are those willing to be controlled by the government of the area, once the area has accepted their status as in-migrants. Second are those who are unwilling to accept control as a long-term component of their lives, but are able to accept it temporarily and who will leave once the degree of control has gone beyond a perceived threshold or time limit. This threshold of tolerance is likely to change as circumstances and experiences of urban life change. Third are those for whom the state control over fertility coincides with their own wishes and for whom the policy has no personal significance. This will include those who have completed their child bearing to their own satisfaction. Before arriving in the area they may have exceeded birth policy guidelines, but there is little the local government can do about it except restrict access to housing or schooling.

Women among the migrants, whether they have completed their childbearing or not, will be influenced by urban fertility policy. Its effects, combined with the experience of migration, may be transmitted to their children or to those with whom they come into contact. The overall impact may therefore be to lower fertility in China as a whole, if not in urban areas. Thus migration may be one of strongest forces in the demographic history, replacing family planning policies as the medium of change.

Appendix

ANOVA (analysis of variation) allows sample subpopulations represented by their means to be compared using the null hypothesis. The null hypothesis states that all subpopulation means are equal and the procedure tests this assumption. Differences between means may be observed, but it is important to be able to say whether these differences are valid or have occurred by chance (Norusis 1983). ANOVA allows for this multiple comparison procedure.

ANOVA assumes samples are random and independent, approximately normally distributed and that variances of subpopulations are equal. While the population of migrants fulfils the normal distribution requirement, the selection of the sample population was such that the random requirement has not been completely fulfilled. Sites were 'not randomly chosen but ... the opportunity was usually seized when some favourable circumstances made it possible to work in a particular area' (Caldwell 1988 p. 459). Sites tended to be determined by the negotiation process between the researcher, the government agency and the local government of the area in which the survey was held. These results should be regarded as indicative of the types of processes that may be found in a migrant population.

A fixed effect model was used in the testing procedures. This means that each of the migrant subpopulations was not considered to be a sample subpopulation from all possible types of migrant subpopulations (Norusis 1983).

Analysis of variance divides observed variability into variability about means within groups, and variability between group means (Norusis 1983). Thus, the mean number of children may not vary for individuals within the same subpopulation, but the means of each subpopulations may vary. If so, it is likely that the subpopulations are not equal in the defined characteristic. ANOVA produces an F-ratio which allows us to determine whether variance is real. This is the ratio of mean squares and is greater than 1.0 if there are real differences between subpopulations, and 1.0 or less if subpopulations are similar (Kirkwood 1988). A probability that the F-ratio is valid is also produced. Significance levels were set at 95 per cent (0.05) for all comparison procedures throughout this chapter. The F-ratio does not provide an indication of where differences occur.

Not all means are necessarily unequal. For example, only one pair of means may be significantly different. To identify where the differences lay a Bonferroni test was employed. This compares the variability of the group means and produces a matrix indicating the pairs of populations which are significantly different from each other at the 0.05 level (Norusis 1983). Tests were carried out for subpopulation within cohorts and not between cohorts.

References

Banister, J. (1987) *China's Changing Population* (Stanford University Press).

Bao, S. X. (1992) 'Introduction', in S. X. Bao (ed.), *Da Chengshi Liudong Renkou Yanjiu* (*Research on the Floating Population in Large Cities*) (Beijing: Zhongguo Shehui Chubanshe).

Beijing Ribao (1994) 'Ganjiakou yu Wenling Xian Chengli Jisheng Lianhehui' ('Ganjiankou and Wenling County Form a Planned Fertility Association'), 15 July, p. 6.

Bowles, P. and Dong, X-Y. (1994) 'Current Successes and Future Challenges in China's Economic Reforms', *New Left Review,* 208, pp. 49–76.

Chinese Academy of Social Sciences (CASS) (1988) '1986 China Migration of 74 Cities and Towns Sampling Survey Data (Computer Tabulation)', *Population Science of China,* Special Issue (Beijing: Population Research Institute).

Cai, W. M., Yu, S. Z., Sheng, Y. Z., Gao, N. S., Wang, Z. D. and Wang, M. N. (1993) 'Da Chengshi Zhouwei Nongcun Chuji Weisheng Baojian Gongzuo Mianlin de Xin Tiaozhan' ('Work of Preserving Basic Hygiene Faces up to a New Challenge in Rural Areas Around Large Cities') (Shanghai: Centre for the Preservation of Basic Hygiene).

Caldwell, J. C. (1988) 'Micro-Approaches: Similarities and Differences, Strengths and Weaknesses', in Caldwell, J. C., Hill, A. G. and Hull, V. J. (eds), *Micro-Approaches to Demographic Research* (London: Kegan Paul International) 458–70.

Caldwell, J. C. and Hill, A. G. (1988) 'Introduction to Recent Developments Using Micro-Approaches to Demographic Research', in Caldwell, J. C., Hill, A. G. and Hull, V. J. (eds) *Micro-Approaches to Demographic Research* (London: Kegan Paul International) 1–9.

Caldwell, J. C., Reddy, P. H. and Caldwell, P. (1988) 'Investigating the Nature of Population Change in South India: Experimenting with a Micro Approach', in Caldwell, C., Hill, A. G. and Hull, V. J. (eds), *Micro-Approaches to Demographic Research* (London: Kegan Paul International) 37.

Chen, Q. L. (1991) 'Guanyu Bada Chengshi Liudong Renkou Wenti de Zonghe Baogao' (Summary Report on the Problems of the Floating Population in Eight Large Cities) *Shehuixue Yanjiu* (*Sociological Research*), 3, 20–4.

Chen, H. D. (1993) 'Nongcun Yihun Funnu Jihua Wai Shou Yun de Dechan ji Jie Yun Cuoshi de Yingxiang Fenxi' (Characteristics of Without Plan Pregnancies and Impacts of Contraceptive Measures in Rural Areas), *Renkou Yanjiu,* 2, 62–4.

Cheng, T. J. and Selden, M. (1994) 'The Origins and Social Consequences of China's Hukou System', *China Quarterly,* 139, 644–68.

China Daily (1989) 'Transients Dodge Family Policy', 4 August, p. 3.

China Daily (1994a) 'Cities Set Looser Rules on Residency', March 3, p. 3.

China Daily (1994b) 'Household Registration System Faces Overhaul', February 1, p. 1.

China Daily (1994c) 'Ending Residence Registration', 17 May, 4.

China Population Today (1992) 'Measures for the Management of Family Planning of the Floating Population', 9, (1) 2–5.

Christiansen, F. (1990) 'Social Division and Peasant Mobility in Mainland China: The Implications of the Hu-k'ou System', *Issues and Studies,* 26 (4) 23–42.

Cleland, J. G. and Shen, Y. M. (1991) 'Later and fewer but no Longer: Fertility Change in Hebei, Shaanxi and Shanghai 1965–1985, in *Proceedings of the International Seminar on China's In-depth Fertility Survey, Beijing, February 13–17* (Voorburg: International Statistics Institute) 273–91.

CNA (1991) 'From and In the Villages: New Migrants and Old Clans', *China News Analysis,* 1426, 1 January.

Coale, A. J., Li, S. M. and Han, J. Q. (1988) 'The Distribution of Inter-Birth Intervals in Rural China, 1940s–1970s', Papers of the East-West Institute, 190 (Honolulu: East West Institute).

Dutton, M. R. (1993) *Policing and Punishment in China: From Patriarchy to 'the People'* (Cambridge University Press).

Foreign Broadcasting Information Service (FBIS) (1984) 'State Council on Peasants Settling in Towns', FBIS–CHI–84–206, 1,206 23 October, p. K18–20.

Foreign Broadcasting Information Service (FBIS) (1990) 'Transient Population Family Planning Stressed', FBIS–CHI–90–237, 10 December, pp. 29–30.

Foreign Broadcasting Information Service (FBIS) (1994a) 'Article Urges Household Registration Reform, FBIS–CHI–94–151, 5 August, pp.10–12.

Foreign Broadcasting Information Service (FBIS) (1994b) 'Regulations on Jiangsu Transient Population', FBIS–CHI–90–069, 11 April, pp.60–2.

Foreign Broadcasting Information Service (FBIS) (1994c) 'Xinhua Publishes Marriage Registration Regulations', FBIS–CHI–94–046, 9 March, pp. 38–41.

Foreign Broadcasting Information Service (FBIS) (1994) 'Government to Curb Illegal Marriages', FBIS–CHI–94–040, 1 March, p. 23.

Feeney, G. and Wang, F. (1993) 'Parity Progression and Birth Intervals in China: The Influence of Policy in Hastening Fertility Decline', *Population and Development Review*, 19, 161–201.

Fulton, D. and Randall, S. (1988) 'Households, Women's Roles and Prestige as Factors Determining Nuptiality and Fertility Differentials in Mali', in Caldwell, J. C., Hill, A. G. and Hull, V. J. (eds) *Micro-Approaches to Demographic Research* (London: Kegan Paul International).

Goldstein, S. (1990) 'Urbanisation in China, 1982–87: Effects of Migration and Reclassification', *Population and Development Review*, 16 (4) 673–701.

Goldstein, S., Goldstein, A. and Guo, S. (1991) 'Temporary Migrants in Shanghai Households, 1984', *Demography*, 28 (2) 275–91.

Gong, X. K. (1989) 'Zhongguo Xianxing Huji Zhidu Touxian' (One Perspective on the Current Household Registration System in China), *Shehui Kexue* (*Social Science*), 102, 32–6.

Guang, H. W. (1995) 'Peasant Flood in China: Internal Migration and its Policy Determinants', *Third World Quarterly*, 16 (2) 173–96.

Gui Shixun (1992) *Zhongguo Liudong Renkou Jihua Shengyu Guanli Yanjiu* (*Administration of Family Planning in the Floating Population of China*) (Shanghai: Huadong Shifan Daxue) 1–2, 62–75, 103, 211.

Hardee-Cleaveland, K. and Banister, J. (1988) 'Fertility Policy and Implementation in China, 1986–1988', *Population and Development Review*, 14 (2) 245–86.

Harrell, S. (1995) 'Introduction: Microdemography and the Modelling of Population Process in Late Imperial China', in Harrell, S. (ed.) *Chinese Historical Micro-Demography* (Berkeley and London: University of California Press).

Honig, E. and Hershatter, G. (1988) *Personal Voices: Chinese Women in the 1980s* (Stanford University Press).

Horizon (1993) *Horizon Survey of Migrant Life in Beijing and Shanghai 1993*, (Beijing: Horizon Market Research Company, 5th Floor Service Centre, CIEC, 6 Bei San Huan Dong Road, Beijing, 100028).

Huang, J. L. (1989) 'Ziliu Wenti Qiansi' (An Examination of the Problems of Transience), *Guangdong Shehui Kexue* (*Guangdong Social Science*),3, 138–41.

Hugo, G. (1988) 'Micro-Approaches to the Study of Population Movement: An Indonesian Case Study', in Caldwell, J. C., Hill, A. G. and Hull, V. J. (eds) *Micro-Approaches to Demographic Research* (London: Kegan Paul International, 1988) pp. 376–8.

ICM (1990) 'A 'Merry-Go-Round' the Law', *Inside China Mainland,* July, 27–8.

JPRS (1991) 'Floating Population Causes Social Problems', JPRS-CAR–91–060 (30 October) 55–56.

Keji Ribao (1994) 'Putian Xian Guanhao Waichu Renkou Jisheng Gongzuo' (Putian County Attends to Family Planning Work of its Out-Migrants), 9 June, p. 4.

Kirkwood, B. R. (1988) *Essentials of Medical Statistics* (Oxford: Blackwell).

Kuhn, A. and Kaye, L. (1994) 'Bursting at the Seams', *Far Eastern Economic Review,* 10 March, 27–8.

Laodong Bao (1994) 'Yiqian Babai Ren Shenqing Shanghai Ji' (One Thousand Eight Hundred People Request Shanghai Residence), 15 May, p. 1.

Lavely, W., Lee, J. and Wang, F. (1990) 'Chinese Demography: The State of the Field', *Journal of Asian Studies,* 4, 807–34.

Li, R. (1993) 'A Study of Early Marriage in China', *China Population Today,* February, 4–9.

Li, Y. and Zhang, H. (1994) 'Nongcun Zaohun Zaoyu Wenti Jidai Jiejue' (The Problem of Early Marriage and Early Births in Rural Areas Urgently Waits a Solution), *Renkou Yanjiu (Population Research),* 14 (4) 60–1.

Liaoning Daxue (1992) 'Shenyangshi Zanzhu Renkou Zhuangkuang Fenxi' (An Analysis of the Temporary Resident Population in Shenyang City), *Renkou Yanjiu (Population Research),* 6 (78) 24–8.

Liu Guanyu, X. (1990) 'Xiaoshan Shi "Wailai nu" Zhuangkuang Jiqi Guanli Wenti' (Situation of 'Women from Outside' in Xiaoshan City and Administration Problems), *Renkou Yanjiu (Population Research),* 6 (November) 31–6.

Liu, Q. (1992) 'Characteristics of China's Early Married Population'

Ma, L. J. C. and Lin, C. (1993) 'Development of Towns in China: A Case Study of Guangdong province', *Population and Development Review,* 19 (3) 583–606.

Ma, X. (1993) 'Migration Pattern and its Change in Urban China', in Ma, X. (ed.) *Migration and Urbanisation in China* (Beijing: New World Press).

Mallee, H. (1995) 'China's Household Registration System under Reform', *Development and Change,* 26, 1–29.

Miao, J. and Zhang, X. (1995) 'Guangdong Liudong Renkou Jihua Shengyu Gongzuo Tanlun' (Discussion on the Planned Fertility and Work of the Floating Population in Guangdong Province), *Renkou Yanjiu,* 19 (3) 18–19.

Norusis, M. J. (1983) *SPSSX: Introductory Statistics Guide* (Chicago: SPSS).

Qingnian Bao (1994) 'Di Sanci Jiefang' (The Third Revolution), *Zhongguo Qingnian Bao,* 18 March, p. 4.

Renmin Ribao (1995) 'Tongyi Renshi Qizhua Gongguan Youxu Liudong' (Unify Understanding and the Joint Administration and Order of Floaters), *Renmin Ribao,* 9 July. Re-published in *Renkou Xue Yu Jihua Shengyu (Population and Planned Fertility),* 5 (4) 4–7.

Shen, Jianfa (1994) 'Analysis and Projection of Multi-Regional Population Dynamics in China: 1950-2087', PhD thesis, Department of Geography, London School of Economics and Political Science.

SHKX (Zhongguo Shehui Kexueyuan Renkou Yanjiusuo) (1988) Zhongguo Qianyi Yu Chengshi Hua Yanjiu (Research on Migration and Urbanisation in China) (Beijing: Beijing Jingji Xueyuan Chubanshe) 9.

Solinger, D. J. (1985) "Temporary Residence Certificate' Regulations in Wuhan, May 1983', Research Note, *China Quarterly,* 101, 98–104.

Solinger, D. J. (1991) 'China's Transients and the State: a Form of Civil Society?', Hong Kong Institute of Asia-Pacific Studies, Seminar Series, 1.

Solinger, D. J. (1993) *China's Transformation from Socialism* (Armonk, NY: M. E. Sharpe).

SWB (1993) Internal Affairs (7), CCP Third Plenary Session, Third Plenary Session Seen as China's 'Second Revolution', *Summary of World Broadcasts, Third Series, FE/1844,* 12 November, pp. 4–5.

Tang Xuemei, X. (1993) 'The Flow and Movement of Population in Beijing', *Renkou Yanjiu,* 4, 52–5.

Tian, X. (1991) 'Population Movement, Marriage and Fertility Change', *Chinese Journal of Population Science,* 30 (1) 27–44.

Tu, P. (1993) 'Contraceptive Use Patterns Amongst Young Rural Women in Four Counties of China', Working Paper, Institute of Population Research, Beijing.

Wang, D. (1992) 'Shilun Chengxiang Jingji Maoyi Qu De Liudong Renkou Tezheng He Jihua Shengyu Guanli Duice' (Characteristics of the Floating Population in Urban Rural Economic Trade Zones and Countermeasures in Birth Control), *Renkou Yanjiu,* 5 (77) 60–2.

White, L. T. III (1994) 'Migration and Politics on the Shanghai Delta', *Issues and Studies,* 30 (98) 63–94.

Zweig, D., Hartford, K., Feinerman, J. and Deng Jianxu (1987) 'Law, Contracts and Economic Modernization: Lessons from Recent Chinese Rural reforms' *Stanford Journal of International Law,* 23 (2), 319–64.

Part II

Economic Growth and Environmental Problems

6
Wuhan: Policies for the Management and Improvement of a Polluted City

John G. Taylor and Xie Qingshu

Although China has a long record of dealing with ecological problems, it is currently facing forms of environmental degradation for which it is neither fully equipped nor prepared, thrust upon it by the rapidity of its industrial growth. The air in most cities is polluted by particulates and sulphur dioxide; waste water from industries and cities is dumped untreated into rivers and lakes; solid waste is piled on city boundaries; drinking water is polluted, with shortages exacerbated by industrial overuse of ground water.

In recent years, commentators have tended to focus on analysing the extent and impact of these areas of environmental pollution, rather than examining policies aimed at improving them. China has an array of environmental laws covering in detail most areas of pollution, together with an established institutional framework through which these laws and regulations can be implemented. The key problem, however, is that these laws do not seem to be being implemented adequately.

A project undertaken recently enabled us to address this problem of inadequate implementation by examining the environmental situation in Wuhan, a major industrial city.[1] We investigated the main forms of pollution, combining this with an examination of the regulatory framework governing its control. We then constructed a sample of city enterprises, subjecting them to analysis on the basis of our environmental findings. In addition to our having contacts with university environmental researchers, Wuhan was selected because (at both national and municipal level) it is seen as having a reasonably rigorous environmental legal framework, and a fairly comprehensive monitoring system. Indeed, in areas such as air quality, its municipal policies are presented as a model for Chinese cities. Additionally, Wuhan is beginning to receive international attention, with increases in foreign investment and loans from multilateral agencies such as the Asian Development Bank and the World Bank. Given its rapid industrial growth and pivotal role in the development of China's central provinces, its importance will increase, as will the need to deal with the environmental problems accompanying its industrial development.

Objectives

Our initial hypothesis was that, despite detailed regulations and an environmental monitoring system, the institutional framework for implementation remains inadequate for dealing with the main environmental problems faced by the city of Wuhan. On the basis of this hypothesis, our initial aims were the following:

1. Assess the current state of environmental pollution and the impact of policies to deal with this.
2. Calculate the environmental impact of changes occurring in the city's industrial and commercial structures as a result of its planned expansion in the coming decade.
3. Investigate why policies drawn up by the municipality have not been taken up extensively by the enterprises for which they were designed.
4. Make recommendations as to how both the existing regulatory framework and its implementation can be improved.

Initially we encountered considerable difficulties in obtaining relevant environmental data. Much of what was available from the city's bureaux was too general, and related only to a limited number of years; additionally, there were crucial gaps in the data. As a result, we had to spend much more time than had been envisaged collecting data from a variety of sources, before proceeding to the investigation of our enterprise sample. Additionally, the regulatory framework proved more complex than we had conceived, combining elements from provincial and municipal sources in different ways in the main areas of environmental control. Our aim of calculating the future impact of environmental changes became somewhat secondary, as our main task became that of assessing the extent of pollution and the efficacy of the regulatory framework.

Methods

During the project's first year, data were collected from a variety of primary sources, including official municipal publications, environmental bulletins, local newspapers and journals, and data provided on selected topics from the city's environmental protection bureau. We also accompanied officials on their visits to inspect enterprise monitoring equipment. We then tabulated data for selected years, giving us a reasonably detailed picture of the city's environmental state. Information on the regulatory framework was provided from publications by Hubei Province Environmental Protection Committee and Bureau, and by bureaux in Wuhan city and its districts.

Our representative sample of twenty enterprises was taken from the 64 most seriously polluting state-owned enterprises (SOEs) in the city. These were monitored by the Wuhan Environmental Protection Bureau in 1993. Variables were selected on the basis of enterprise district and scale, and the sample contained 15 industrial types (paper-making, metallurgical, leather, pharmaceuticals, dyestuffs, dyeing, textiles, textile printing, enamelling, engineering, cement, coal-fired electricity, glass, building materials, foodstuffs). Comparisons were also made between these sampled enterprises and 4 non-state rural enterprises on the periphery of the city. Additionally, the sampled enterprises were compared with a foreign enterprise, established in the city in 1986. Our questionnaire was followed up by interviews at each of the enterprises, to explore further the answers given.

Wuhan in context

At the beginning of our research, we collected general economic data on Wuhan, and on its role within Hubei province. Initially, we had hypothesised that implementation of the regulatory framework might be affected by inadequate funding, or (more generally) an unwillingness by enterprise managers to innovate. Our early findings suggested that both these issues were more complex than we had originally conceived.

Throughout the 1980s, the city appears to have suffered economically as a result of its relations with both provincial and national governments.[2] For example, in a typical year (1985) the city's total income was 1.44 billion yuan, from which 1.22 billion was taken by the provincial and national governments. The retention rates (revenue that lower government levels keep and are not passed up to higher levels) for most other large cities were much higher (24 per cent for Shanghai, for example). This alerted us to an important point: until recently Wuhan seems to have suffered economically as a result of its relations with central and especially provincial government. In most economic

Table 6.1   Central extraction as a percentage of local revenue. Wuhan 1984, 1990, 1991 and 1992 (billion yuan)

Year	Total revenue	Local revenue	Local expenditure	Central (and provincial) extraction	as % of total revenue	as % of local revenue
1984	1456	n.a.	n.a.	1220	84	n.a.
1990	3668	2947	1542	1979	54	67.15
1991	4417	3219	1594	2190	49.6	68.03
1992	4454	3402	1806	2468	55.4	72.54

Sources: D. J. Solinger, *China Quarterly*, 145, 25; also *Wuhan Yearbook* (1985, p. 167; 1991, pp. 2335–6; 1992, p. 255; 1993, p. 346).

areas, Hubei province seemed to have benefited from Wuhan's wealth, but to have provided little in return (Table 6.1).

It also appeared that in areas such as export promotion, the setting up of technology and development zones, and inward investment, Wuhan was disadvantaged by its relations with Hubei, and by preferential treatment given to other cities by the central government. This only began to change in 1992, with the start of the Yangtze Development Plan, for which the central government gave Wuhan a pivotal role.

In addition to limiting its ability to retain wealth, Wuhan's relations with province and centre also seem to have restricted its ability to innovate. In the 1980s, for example, Wuhan was one of the first cities to introduce stock-sharing, leasing and bidding; in 1988, it organised a pioneering system of enterprise mergers, following this in 1992 with a unique scheme by which foreign investors could purchase enterprises at reduced rates in return for introducing modern management systems. Consequently, the picture (of a technologically outmoded, economically conservative and bureaucratically minded city, unwilling to innovate) suggested in much of the literature seemed to need considerable modification. Rather, we found a city whose ability to generate wealth to realise its innovative ability was continually restricted. This had serious environmental implications: funds that could have been used for environmental investment were unavailable, and environmental innovations were either discouraged or had only limited application.

This aspect of Wuhan's recent history explained much of the hesitancy and reluctance of environmental managers to innovate, which we repeatedly came across in our interviews; it also explained their somewhat cynical and dismissive attitudes to the collection and use of pollution levies and funds in the city.

The regulatory system

Our investigation of the environmental regulations and standards in the city revealed a complex and fairly detailed system. China has environmental laws covering most areas, from atmospheric, water, and coastal pollution to work noise. These laws are accompanied by detailed sets of regulations for each of these areas, with national, provincial and city requirements. To deal with atmospheric pollution, for example, urban areas are divided into zones, each of which must meet specific standards in relation to levels of total suspended particulate (TSP), dust, sulphur dioxide (SO_2), oxides of nitrogen (NO_x) and carbon monoxide (CO). Standards are set for daily, monthly, and average emissions. Accompanying these laws is a comprehensive institutional framework for their implementation, overseen by the National Environmental Protection Agency. In addition to these regulations, Wuhan has at its disposal an array of provincial and city-level laws and ordinances, implemented by institutions with seemingly wide powers to monitor and sanction. For example, at the provincial level, there are detailed laws on environmental management, together with specific regulations on urban noise control, emission levels, environmental impact assessment, pollution levies, fines, waste disposal and the management of town and village enterprises.

At the municipal level, there are additional regulations dealing with details of environmental impact assessment in city areas, water management of river zones, smoke-dust control, industrial relocation, transport of solid waste, the issuing of pollution permits, the raising of levies and fines, and (as one would expect, given the city's heavy industrial base) detailed provisions on the operation of industrial boilers. These ordinances and regulations are directed by a Municipal Environmental Commission and overseen by an Environmental Protection Bureau (EPB), which has bureaux in each of the city's districts. These bureaux formulate local environmental standards and organise environmental monitoring; the city's EPB is responsible for the collection of data and the compilation of an annual environmental report. Additionally, many industrial enterprises have set up their own environmental protection departments, and government units operate environmental responsibility systems, with targets to be met in particular environmental areas.

Control over enterprises operates largely through a system of fines on units whose emissions of particular pollutants exceed the standards for the zones in which they are located. The fines are paid into a fund which, in addition to subsidising the costs of monitoring, provides low-interest loans to enterprises for improving existing equipment or purchasing cleaner technology. Since 1993, the city has begun to issue pollution permits to selected enterprises, mostly located in tourist zones, and related to the provision of drinking water. To examine the adequacy of this system for the city's environmental needs, we collected data for a number of environmental factors for 1993, and then compared both pollution levels and their treatment with the years 1988 and 1984. In some cases, we had access to monitoring results for 1994, and where possible these are included. In what follows, we outline the main trends.

Atmospheric pollution

Data on zonal air quality and the monitoring of air pollutants indicate that (despite improvements in purification rates achieved for waste gas and particulate removal in the 1980s) severe problems remained in the early 1990s. Based on Chinese air quality standards (which are themselves lower than World Health Organisation (WHO) standards) we have the following illustrations for Wuhan's commercial zone in 1993:

Annual daily average
TSP: 383 micrograms /m^3, Chinese Standard 300, WHO 90.
SO_2: 117 micrograms/m^3, Chinese standard 60, WHO 60.
NO_x:147 micrograms/m^3, Chinese standard 100.

From such data, and from those covering the years 1984, 1988 and 1993, it is clear that high concentrations of sulphur dioxide and oxides of nitrogen exist in Wuhan's commercial zone, together with high levels of NO_x in areas of denser traffic. High levels of TSP exist in all the main city zones, but are exceptionally high in the industrial zone. In autumn and winter, almost all districts have unacceptably high levels of TSP, SO_2 and NO_x; indeed, it could be concluded that, in reality, emissions of SO_2 and NO_x remain uncontrolled.

Water pollution

Data on water pollution control during the last decade suggest that Wuhan has made some progress in its treatment of industrial wastewater. However, about a third remains untreated, and 26 per cent of the treated water did not meet relevant national standards in 1993. Furthermore, an investigation of wastewater treatment at 22 state enterprises undertaken by a group of EPB officials during 1994, found that only 55 per cent were operating normally, with the remainder temporarily inoperative due to lack of parts, funding, or violation of local regulations. The main pollutants discharged from these industries were mercury, chromium, cadmium, lead, arsenic, cyanide, phenol, sulphide, suspended oil, and oil substances.

During the 1980s, severely polluting industries such as electroplating, printing and dyeing, and casting, were relocated away from the populated areas of the city, to development zones or peripheral areas. By this stage, however, the damage to much of Wuhan's surface water had been considerable (Map 6.1). East Lake, the largest lake in Wuhan, has experienced heavy eutrophication, and is now graded class IV.[3] Other large lakes, such as Moshui and Nantaizi, with class V, are waste sinks, and Nanhu lake has BOD5[4] and cyanide levels over class V standards. As one would expect, given the size and rate of flow of the Yangtze River, it has been much less affected. However, monitoring of the water quality of the Yangtze river by the Wuhan EPB from 1986 to 1992 found that dissolved oxygen (DO) and ammonia nitrogen (NH_3–N) levels exceeded national class ii standards for 1986–8, and that chemical oxygen demand (COD) remained high. The data on water pollution control also shows an increase in domestic wastewater, from 32.6 per cent of the total wastewater in 1984 to 39.7 per cent in 1993. Only 0.82 per cent of this was treated in 1994. A wastewater treatment plant with 50,000 cubic metres daily capacity was built recently in Wuchang district, but it only seems to operate sporadically, owing (officially) to lack of funds. Given the restrictions placed by national government on the discharge of domestic wastewater into the Yangtze river, there is an urgent need to expand the sewerage system, and set up new wastewater treatment plants.

Waste disposal

Data on the disposal and use of solid wastes indicate that much of the waste has been 'comprehensively used', with strategies for recycling, composting, incineration and landfilling enabling an increase in comprehensive use from 67.4 per cent in 1984 to 90.7 per cent in 1993. A major problem for composting and incineration, however, is that over half the waste stream is inorganic, with coal ash as the

150

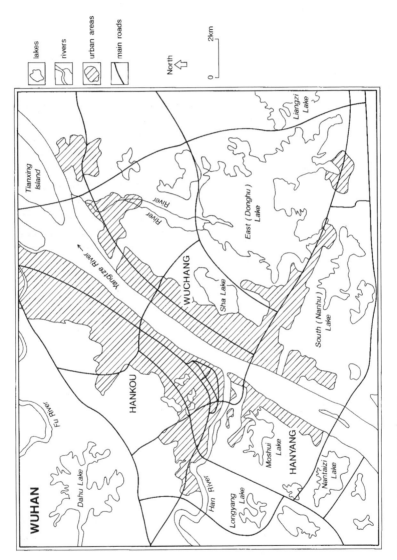

Map 6.1   Wuhan conurbation

dominant component. Used in areas such as brick-making, road-fill and fertiliser production, the ash then contributes to the already high dustfall levels. Additionally, only a very small number of the city's landfills appear to meet either national or international standards. Most dumps inspected in our research had no means of protection from leachate contamination of surface water or aquifers, and much of the burning seemed uncontrolled. The city appears to be running short of landfill sites, particularly when faced with an increase in the area occupied by industrial solid waste from 1.39 million square metres in 1992 to 3.49 million square metres in 1993. In 1993, domestic garbage totalled 1.55 million tons, with treatment levels being about a quarter of the total.

Environmental assessment

From a general assessment of comprehensive urban environmental control in Wuhan for 1989 to 1993 we drew a number of conclusions from our survey of the city's environmental state. These guided us in the design and delivery of our questionnaire:

1. TSP, SO_2 and NO_x levels exceed national quality standards in individual urban districts, and in autumn and winter in almost all districts. Additionally, SO_2 and NO_x emissions are virtually uncontrolled. Dustfall levels are high, and vehicle emissions are increasing rapidly.
2. Treatment levels of industrial wastewater are less satisfactory than claimed by the municipality, and domestic wastewater is largely untreated. Much of the surface water is severely polluted.
3. Solid waste disposal does not meet national standards, and landfills are reaching capacity. Domestic garbage is not adequately treated.
4. While there have been improvements in some areas (notably controls over air pollution) the environmental position remains critical.
5. Although our research centred on the urban districts of the city, we also visited a number of sites of rural industrial pollution in peripheral areas, from which we were able to draw a number of tentative conclusions: an investigating collective rural enterprises in the sectors of brickmaking, smelting, casting, electroplating and ceramics, we found that of those examined only 28.2 per cent treated industrial wastewater, of which only 19 per cent met municipal standards. Similarly the purification rate of industrial waste gas averaged 6.83 per cent. There was little evidence of any monitoring or

environmental management of these enterprises. Although town and village enterprises do not appear to have developed in Wuhan as rapidly as in other areas adjacent to major cities, their output is likely to increase considerably during the coming years, and their lack of pollution control systems will become a major problem.[5]

Wuhan's enterprise: an environmental summary

The picture portrayed by Wuhan's official environmental publications is one of state enterprises with active environmental departments, promoting environmental education for employees; most are said to operate environmental responsibility systems,[6] give priority to the environmental impact of their activities, participate in the pollution levy or (more recently) permit system, and cooperate environmentally with neighbouring enterprises; they use environmental facilities to the full, and have been particularly successful in controlling air and water pollution. These environmental achievements of state enterprises are contrasted with the failures of rural enterprises to control pollution. Our findings presented a rather different picture.

Environmental information

Although 23 of the 25 sampled enterprises claimed to be involved in disseminating environmental information on a regular basis, further discussions revealed that this was concerned largely with organising meetings at irregular intervals[7] and with distributing general information provided by the EPB. With the exception of the foreign enterprise (Anheuser Busch International Brewery) no environmental handbook or set of specific guidelines as produced for workers (and even for this brewery it was rather basic). Eleven enterprises had internal environmental protection departments, with the remainder giving environmental policy to non-environmental departments. 84 per cent of the enterprises had drawn up environmental plans in the period since 1990, but only 66.7 per cent of these had been implemented, owing (it was stated) to lack of funds. Seven of the enterprises claimed that they simply did not have sufficient funds to engage in environmental protection. A lack of funds was also given as a major reason by the 52 per cent who had not managed to set up environmental protection responsibility systems; they also claimed that there was no clear requirement from above to set up such systems. Whilst 44 per cent of managers stated that they gave 'top priority' to the environmental impact of new industrial equipment, 40 per cent agreed that they gave it only 'general consideration'. As opposed to the case with enterprise managers, a substantial proportion of the managers of internal environmental departments stated in further discussions that their advice on the environmental impact of new equipment was generally ignored, and that they were usually overruled by their enterprises' technical departments. From the responses to our questions on general environmental organisation, it seems to be the case that environmental considerations are not accorded the priorities claimed.

Environmental impact assessment

Turning to policy implementation, we find a similar picture: 84 per cent of the enterprises had environmental impact assessments (EIAs) on all projects undertaken, and 85 per cent of managers claim that they have details of these EIAs. Similarly, 76 per cent of the enterprises have implemented the *santongshi*, or 'three simultaneous' points policy.[8] However, further enquiries indicated that the quality of the assessments was poor (as can be seen from an example translated and summarised in Figure 6.1), and that some assessments were begun only after construction had started. There was also a tendency to have EIAs undertaken by external experts, with very limited involvement by some enterprises in the actual assessment process. For the rural industries in the sample, no EIAs had been undertaken for any projects. Perhaps we can conclude that, whilst compliance rates seem high, there remain questions both about the quality of the assessments and about enterprise managers' knowledge of them.

Control and disposal

Responding to questions on air and water pollution and solid waste disposal, our findings on low rates of sulphur removal were borne out by the fact that only 15.8 per cent of enterprises had desulphurisation facilities. Additionally, industrial briquettes were not used by any enterprise. Whilst a variety of methods of smoke dust removal were in operation (water membranes, electronic precipitators, bag filters, and cyclonic dust separators), underlining the city's progress in this area during the last decade, 25 per cent of the sample had seriously deficient boilers and kilns.

Responses to questions on waste water control revealed that for most enterprises the level of fines is much lower than the cost of wastewater treatment; hence there seemed to be little incentive to control effluent emissions. Indeed almost 50 per cent of the sampled managers

---

Summary of an environmental impact assessment proposal for a sulphuric acid project proposed by the managers and work force of a phosphate fertiliser factory in a suburban county.

The proposal was undertaken in 1988. It is divided into seven sections: introduction; engineering analysis; the project's environment; atmospheric projections; environmental impact of main pollutants; measures for environmental protection; conclusions.

The introduction outlines the basis for the EIA proposal, principles and methods. It stresses the importance of the EJA, the standards used, and targets to be achieved.

The engineering analysis deals mainly with the introduction of the proposed new technology, and examines the impact of the consumption of new raw materials, fuel, water, and electricity. It predicts future pollutant emissions, with particular reference to increased water emissions resulting from the extension of the enterprise.

The section dealing with the impact of the extension on the immediate environment deals only in the most general way with the effect of water emissions on the natural environment. It outlines the main sources of atmospheric pollution, and develops a model for prediction. levels of air pollution.

The analysis of the environmental impact of the main pollutants focuses on wastewater, noise, and solid waste disposal, but does so in a very general way.

The section outlining measures for environmental protection devotes most of its analysis to the impact of fines and the effects of tree planting.

Figure 6.1   Summary of an environmental impact

---

stated that the current wastewater effluent fee was too low. Only four enterprises produced hazardous toxic waste, and this seemed to be stored satisfactorily. Some solid waste was sold to other factories as raw material (slag and coal ash is used to make cement, coal ash to manufacture bricks; sodium carbonate is recycled in paper-making, phenol and sulphuric acid in manufacturing dyes), but there was little further evidence of the multiple use of waste. Despite this, all enterprises benefited from tax reductions resulting from the adoption of multiple-use strategies.

50 per cent of the sampled enterprises had unused environmental equipment, and a high proportion had experienced breakdowns in recent months. The most-cited reasons were high operational costs and a lack of technical knowledge. Our investigation of this low use rate in more depth, and random inspections of wastewater treatment facilities of 44 enterprises during the course of 1994 revealed that only 30 per cent were operating adequately. Several managers concluded that landfill sites were inadequate, and that most were reaching capacity. On the basis of our findings, we concluded that the operational use of environmental equipment in the city's enterprises is probably at quite a low level.

Pollution land permits

Respondents' answers to questions on the operation of the pollution levy and permit system highlighted several key problems. Whilst 84 per cent of the sample had registered as polluting enterprises, the remainder cited a lack of monitoring equipment as the main reason for non-registration. Managers of rural enterprises all argued that they did not pollute, and thus saw no need to register. Only 12 enterprises had obtained pollution permits, and most of these were temporary, for a two-year period. Whilst 92 per cent of the sampled enterprises had obtained subsidies from the environmental protection fund, there was evidence from some enterprises that funds had been used for non-environmental investment and projects. According to many managers, environmental cooperation with neighbouring enterprises in meeting pollution emission standards was restricted by the ability of these enterprises to contribute financially to the purchase of less-polluting technology. Only two enterprises had been given a clean bill of health through being awarded the title of 'Clean and Hazardousless Factory' by the municipal government. Seven had been fined during the last two years, and eleven had been required to control severe pollution. Further local investigation in the neighbourhoods of sampled enterprises revealed that these cases were very severe, and included extensive leakages of ammonia due to cracked pipes, heavy losses of nitric acid during transportation, bromine loss as a result of a cracked tank, severe air pollution as a result of prolonged 'black carbon' emissions, and waste water regularly discharged into fish ponds.

Environmental priorities

Investigating the extent to which managers prioritise environmental issues revealed a consensus both for this and for the lack of finances to achieve it. When presented with descriptions of cases of varying degrees of pollution, however, managers disagreed markedly on their severity. For example, for many respondents descriptions of reasonably serious ground water pollution were not recognised as such.

Whilst most knew the main environmental laws, they had little understanding of their particular contents except in relation to issues of safety, labour protection, and the collection and re-use of solid waste. Similarly, they seemed to have only a very limited understanding of the effects of air and water pollution. 84 per cent of the sample disagreed with the statement that 'responsibility for eliminating pollution should rest largely with the enterprise', seeing it as a task to be undertaken almost wholly by the EPB. Managers of the larger enterprises stated that they usually received sufficient funding to deal with the most important environmental problems, but managers of smaller units felt that, owing to a serious shortage of financial resources, they were pushed continually into a position of relegating environmental problems, faced with an urgent need to upgrade and modernise their plant. A small number of managers (17 per cent) agreed that old, polluting technology could be sold to rural enterprises.

Of the rural enterprises sampled, only one had begun to implement a degree of environmental protection. It had introduced a basic environmental responsibility system, established a simple wastewater treatment station, and constructed an NO_x and SO_2 absorption tower. Apart from this case, managers of rural enterprises had little environmental understanding, and little knowledge of environmental management issues. Environmental officials from the counties in which the enterprises were located admitted that their staffing levels were woefully inadequate for dealing with the environmental problems produced by numerous and widespread small-scale enterprises.

Environmental complaints

In looking briefly at public awareness of environmental issues, we examined the complaints made to Wuhan's constituent environmental bureaux during 1994. In total, they received 650 complaints, and followed these up with 658 visits. This seems a relatively small number for a city of 6.92 million. Most complaints dealt with noise levels (42.4 per cent) and air pollution (21.7 per cent). Only 3.6 per cent of complaints dealt with wastewater pollution. Monitoring one newspaper, the *Chanjiang Daily*, revealed an average of two environmental articles each week. Apart from the well-known case of the UN 'Global 500' award being made to four pupils at the city's Daxinglu Primary School in early 1995, there seemed to be little evidence of systematic environmental education in schools.

Conclusions

On the basis of these findings, we reached a number of general conclusions concerning environmental policy and its implementation in the city:

1. Wuhan's ability to deal with its environmental problems in the years since 1978 has been restricted by its economic and political relations with both the Hubei provincial and national governments. This has changed since 1992, and resultant improvements in retention rates and inward investment are enhancing the possibilities for the city to improve its pollution levels. This tendency will increase in the coming years.
2. The city's environment is seriously degraded, with an urgent need to treat high concentrations of sulphur dioxide, nitrogen oxides and dustfall levels. Much of its surface waters are highly polluted, resulting largely from poor treatment of wastewater. In all areas there is an urgent need for improvement. Although pollution from rural industries will increase in coming years, the main polluters remain the city's state-owned enterprises.
3. Wuhan has a detailed and complex system of laws and regulations covering most areas, combined with a framework for environmental monitoring and a system of rewards, sanctions and environmental funding.
4. This system is inadequate for meeting the city's current environmental needs, for the following reasons:
    (i) Despite initial appearances, dissemination of environmental information is poor, and both enterprise managers and heads of environmental departments have only a limited general knowledge of environmental issues.
    (ii) Many enterprises do not prioritise environmental objectives, and advice given by environmental departments to both enterprise managers and technical departments is often ignored.
    (iii) Consequently, many enterprises have neither environmental plans nor environmental responsibility systems, and the impact of environmental planning is limited by its being implemented at too general a level.

(iv) In a crucial area of implementation, environmental impact assessments seem to be of poor quality, and have only limited enterprise involvement.

(v) Whilst planning and implementation are limited by a lack of funds, they are also affected by a lack of clarity in requirements from both the municipal government and its EPB.

(vi) Pollution fines are set too low for their objectives to be met in any meaningful way.

(vii) As a result, limited funds are available for pollution control and abatement, and some of these funds appear to be being used for non-environmental purposes.

5. Environmental monitoring of rural enterprises is woefully inadequate.

Policy recommendations

On the basis of our analysis of the present state of environmental pollution, and our conclusions on environmental planning and implementation, a number of issues can be raised concerning the future development of environmental policies in the city:

1. The pollution levy system in Wuhan is not meeting its objectives, and there is considerable scope for improvement. Pollution fees could be increased gradually until they reached the marginal cost of control for each pollutant, thereby encouraging improvements in maintenance and operation. Fines could also be paid from profits rather than being passed on in price increases. To meet the costs of increased fees, enterprises could be allowed to retain a greater proportion of their profits than is presently the case. Increases in fees paid into the pollution levy could generate increased loans for longer-term solutions, since much of the funding is used currently for short-term technical solutions.

2. Implementing such policies in Wuhan, however, is easier said than done. From our research it is clear that, given greater autonomy, many of Wuhan's state enterprises would not survive the ensuing increase in competition (both with each other and with enterprises from other Chinese cities) for investment, markets and access to raw materials. The city would also have difficulties coping with the social impact of the accompanying increases in unemployment and the dismantling of the welfare services currently provided by state enterprises to their workforces. Consequently, what seems to be an obvious way of improving a crucial area of the environmental

control system would have a chance of success only if it was accompanied by a comprehensive plan for the generation of new, less-polluting industries, and for the development of a welfare system to replace current enterprise provision. Given the increases in inward investment in recent years, following the policy changes from 1992, and the more substantial increases likely in coming years, gradual implementation within a comprehensively planned and financed restructuring may be achieved in a way that has not been possible since the late 1970s.

3. In the longer term, the quality of Wuhan's air will be improved by the construction of the Sanxia (Three Gorges) Dam on the Yangtze River, but even then there will be a continuing reliance on coal. Clearly, energy use could be made more efficient through increases in the price of coal, attempting to get industries to use less, and of a higher quality. Stricter standards applied to the quality of coal, a rigorous monitoring of its washing, and a gradual introduction of a tax on the sulphur content of coal might be more relevant and less dramatic in their social and economic impact. Treating coal in this way would reduce emissions of fine and ultrafine particulate and smoke dust. Additionally, relatively cheap pre-combustion policies could focus more on systematic descaling of boilers and plants. This, together with more regular adjustments in temperatures, pressures, oxygen availability and mixing rates could also reduce emissions of sulphur dioxide and nitrogen oxides.

4. In addition to providing adequate funding, the environmental monitoring system could also be improved through the provision of serious incentives for undertaking environmental impact assessments. Since, at present, the only incentive is to pass through the assessment process, managers usually conclude that their energies are best put into negotiating with the municipal government to provide general guarantees, rather than undertaking detailed analyses.

5. The planning and inspection undertaken by the city's environmental protection bureaux could be improved at relatively little cost. Although they devise plans for improving air and water quality, they do not appear to analyse alternative strategies, nor do they seriously estimate the costs of investments needed, to ensure that the controls are affordable. Consequently, planning could be developed rather more comprehensively, with a greater emphasis on devising and assessing least-cost strategies. With regard to inspection, ways need to be found to monitor bureaux work more rigorously, ensuring that regulations are applied uniformly.

6. From our very limited survey of rural enterprises, suggestions for improvement could involve selecting sectors for priority treatment; these could comprise the most serious polluters (smelting, brick-making and electroplating). Emission levels and pollution levies could be enforced more rigorously if more of these industries could be located in zoned areas. Incentives to relocate could be provided by the construction of basic infrastructural facilities, providing access to water and collective waste disposal at subsidised rates.

Notes

1. Entitled 'Policies for the Management and Improvement of a Polluted Urban Environment: A Case-Study of the City of Wuhan', the project lasted for two years, and was funded by the Global Environmental Change Programme of the UK Economic and Social Research Council, whose support is gratefully acknowledged by the authors. We would also like to thank the officials of the Wuhan Environmental Protection Bureau who assisted us in the project, and the enterprise managers and heads of enterprise environmental departments who participated in our interviews and questionnaires. Full sources of data referred to in this chapter are available in the project report.
2. This point has also been made recently in an article by Dorothy Solinger ('Despite Decentralisation: Disadvantages, Dependence and Ongoing Central Power in the Inland – the Case of Wuhan', *China Quarterly*, 145, March 1996), pp. 1–34.
3. The water classification system operative in Wuhan, as in the rest of China, is as follows: classes i and ii: high quality, suitable as a source of drinking water; class III: usable for drinking water after treatment; class IV: boating, fishing, and industrial water supply; class V: irrigation and industrial cooling.
4. Biological oxygen demand, or BOD, is a general term that describes the overall demand on dissolved oxygen from oxygen-depleting processes such as re-aeration, bacterial decomposition of organic matter, or (in the case of Wuhan) inadequate sewerage treatment. A commonly used measure of BOD over time is called BOD5, where the '5' stands for 5 days. BOD5 is a standard waste limit, adopted internationally.
5. In 1993, Wuhan's industrial types were as follows: rural industries by village, 4329; rural co-operative enterprises, 1345; Rural Individual Enterprises, 21 990. This last figure is two-thirds of all industrial enterprises. State enterprises in Wuhan numbered 1108, with a further 2826 ollective enterprises.
6. In Wuhan, these systems give specific responsibilities to units within the production process. Each enterprise has an environmental protection committee and an internal environmental department, establishing and implementing internal environmental rules and inspection standards. Each section of the enterprise is set environmental targets, and is rewarded with certificates of attainment and money; failure to meet targets can result in fines.
7. Since 1990, enterprises had averaged four environmental meetings.
8. Under this policy, no project can be approved unless its design, construction, and operational investments satisfy environmental protection standards, and the required pollution control equipment is included.

7
Recent Developments and Prospects for the Sanxia (Three Gorges) Dam

Richard Louis Edmonds

Introduction

The wisdom of building large scale-dams as a solution to power generation and flood control problems is increasingly being questioned.[1] While the debates are highly polarised and many still see great benefits to be derived from large-scale dams, the drawbacks have become well known, so that projects are no longer automatically approved by governments and international funding agencies. However, the idea of building a dam in the Sanxia (Three Gorges) along the Chang (Yangtze) River in western Hubei province dates back to at least the 1920s and is deeply rooted in the psyche of those wishing to develop China rapidly (Map 7.1). Therefore, it should come as no surprise that the Chinese National People's Congress passed the Sanxia Key Water Control Project in April 1992. However, the fact that close to a third of the delegates to this rubber-stamp congress abstained or voted against this project represented considerable opposition to what was normally an automatic affair.[2] Moreover, since that date a considerable number of Chinese have written questioning the scientific and social value of this mega-project.

The history of the project has been discussed elsewhere (Edmonds 1992). Here I concentrate on recent developments in the project. I should point out, however, that through the years there have been opposition viewpoints by various agencies within the Chinese government towards the dam. The Chang River Valley Planning Office, the Ministry of Water Conservancy, the State Planning Commission and Hubei and Hunan provinces, together with other downstream provinces, generally supported the project, whereas the Ministry of Electric Power, the Ministry of Communications and Sichuan province

162

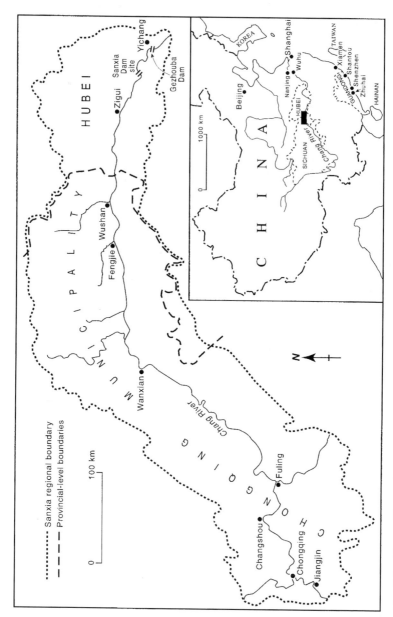

Map 7.1 Chang (Yangtze) River, Sanxia (Three Gorges) Dam site and region

generally opposed the project, while Chongqing and Shanghai muni-cipalities had mixed responses (Lieberthal and Oksenberg 1988, pp. 283–7). In general reporting on the dam has been more critical in the Sichuan/Chongqing press than in the Hubei, although criticism has been very limited since the blocking of the Chang River in November 1997 ('Major Problems in Three Gorges Dam Resettlement Program' 1998). Problems resolving these bureaucratic differences helped make it difficult for the central government to come down firmly in favour of the project for many years. However, the 1991 floods of the Chang and Huai rivers, caused in good part by govern-ment neglect of flood-control infrastructure, again brought the issue to the fore. The arrest of dissidents in the aftermath of the Tiananmen incident in the summer of 1989 helped to reduce opposition to the project.

After formal approval, the State Council formed the Sanxia Project Construction Committee as the project's decision-making body. Immediately afterwards, the Changjiang Three Gorges Project Development Corporation was established as the economic entity responsible for the project. Preparatory construction including the cof-ferdam project began in 1993 and formal official construction began in December 1994 with over 20,000 construction workers at work (6000 at the dam site), 20 million cubic metres of earth moved, and two temporary roads on both banks of the river built as of mid-1994 (Wu Naitao 1994, p. 15). In 1994 the State Council also approved the estab-lishment of a Sanxia 'Open Economic Zone' with all the policies and priorities given to special economic zones (Edmonds 1993). Yichang, Wan Xian and Fuling have been designated 'Open Cities'. The airport near the site was completed in October 1996 and all major transport links into the area are in place. In 1997 Chongqing city and a large area of its surroundings in east Sichuan were separated from the rest of the province and made a province-level municipality (equal to Beijing, Shanghai and Tianjin in the administrative hierarchy).

Contracts are being awarded on a bidding system and foreign com-panies have been invited to bid. The first contract went to the Bridge Bureau of the Ministry of Railways to build the Xiling Bridge, with another 22 approved by mid-1994. The most notable foreign-related contract was awarded for US$807 million, in August 1997, to a consor-tium of Chinese firms, Siemens of Germany and General Electric of Canada to provide generators and turbines for Phase Two.

The plans for development indicate that the Sanxia project will become the world's largest dam in terms of volume of concrete work

(185 metres high and 1983 metres wide), with a final reservoir surface area of 1060 square kilometres, a capacity of 39,300 million cubic metres, and a maximum flow rate of 100,000 cubic metres per second (cusecs). The 1996 floods in southern and eastern China affected the progress of the project, but not seriously. The 90-metre-high dam severed the Chang River in autumn 1997. It is hoped to begin filling the reservoir in 2002, to have the first generator in place in 2003, and for the dam to be completed in 2009 with reservoir water reaching its final level in 2010, eighteen years from the start of preparatory work, although the filling of the reservoir to its full height is likely to be delayed until 2019 because of 'resettlement problems'.

The four main reasons for construction

Public argument as to whether the dam should be constructed concentrated on several key technical questions: flood control, energy supply, navigation, and water supply. The dam is favoured by many senior officials and professionals in official capacities because it is supposed to improve navigation, to provide hydroelectric energy, and to help in flood control and in the transfer of Yangtze waters to water-deficient north China. In the post-Tiananmen political climate, experts and reporters inside China have been subtle in voicing dissent against the project. However, overseas Chinese intellectuals and foreign experts have advised the government not to proceed with the dam, and despite political pressure opposition statements from within China have appeared, one of the most impressive being an autumn 1996 appeal to Jiang Zemin and members of the standing committee of the Politbureau signed by 56 leading cultural figures, to intevene and ensure that cultural relics in the Sanxia area are preserved (Chen and Chen 1993; Tyler 1996b).[3]

Flood protection

In the run-up to approval of the project, flood protection seemed to be given top priority among the reasons for construction – presumably in part because of the serious flooding of 1991. Flood control is still listed as the first argument for constructing the dam in officially-published articles, and proponents insist that there is no substitute for a large reservoir dam at Sanxia. Today many stretches of the Yangtze River are only able to withstand floods occuring every ten to twenty years, and the repercussions of this low level of protection became apparent in the summers of 1991, 1995 and 1998. The Sanxia Reservoir is expected to have 22,150 million cubic metres floodwater storage capacity. The dam will control about half of the river valley's annual volume of flow, and it has been stated that it will be able to control all but the most serious of flood conditions in the Yangtze Valley. While such tremendous claims for flood protection have been made, it is considered reasonable that the 12 million people and 533,000 hectares of good fields in the Jianghan Plain just below the dam site will derive considerable flood protection. In addition, building a dam supposedly will help reduce flooding in the Dongting Lake Plain and save 970 million yuan in flood control expenses annually. The dam will reduce the silt in water flowing downstream, and reduce peak flows, giving some flood relief, although with so many tributaries entering the Yangtze River downstream it will not be able to control flooding to a significant degree. For example, the flood that occurred in the lower course in summer 1991 would have occurred even with the dam in place. The dam's likely impact on other flood-related aspects is also not clear, such as how much flooding upstream will be increased, how much clear water releases will lead to undercutting of downstream dikes, and to what degree flood prevention capabilities will be sacrificed to ensure hydro-generation and navigation capabilities. Flood retention requires empty capacity in the reservoir, while power generation is most efficient with water at the highest level.

Power generation

The hydroelectric potential of the dam is important because the country is short of electricity. It has become clear since formal approval that this is the government's key reason for constructing the dam. Sanxia is expected to have around 18,000 megawatts generating capacity, making it the world's largest hydroelectric generating plant with the 26 large turbines supplying an estimated one-eleventh of the 1994 total electricity supply (85,000 million kilowatt hours a year).[4] The electricity generation will equal fourteen 1200-megawatt thermal power plants, or 50 million tonnes coal equivalent. While China's coal reserves are significant, proponents have stressed that there is already a strain on the available coal supply. China will find it virtually impossible to meet its future planned energy needs simply by expanding coal production or nuclear power.

After approval of construction the energy role has become part of a general overall strategy perhaps best described by Yuan Guolin, who is vice-director of the China Changjiang Three Gorges Project Development Corporation as well as an employee of the Ministry of

Water Conservancy. Yuan restates the geographical view of China's development strategy in terms of a bow and arrow (Yuan Guolin 1995, p. 5). The bow is the east coast, with the string linking the northern and southern ends of the bow being the major north–south railways. The Yangtze River is the arrow. Although Yuan does not say it, using this imagery leaves the Sanxia Dam as the hand on the arrow. All indications are that most of the energy produced by the dam will be used up and down the river valley, with emphasis on down rather than up. In late 1995 the government gave the go-ahead for the project to construct a 9100-kilometre-long, 500 kilovolt transmission line and substation system to move the electricity eastward and westward towards Chongqing. In mid-1996, a state company to build the distribution network to nine provinces was established.

Opponents did express doubts about cost effectiveness of the dam in terms of electricity potential, since efficiency has been measured only in terms of cost per kilowatt hour of power versus excavation and concrete costs, without consideration of timing or political and environmental factors. Power will have to be transmitted over great distances to reach the energy-hungry east coast. The long lead time before generation starts means that the dam will not be able to solve immediate energy problems, and money could be better spent on smaller-scale hydropower generating dams on tributaries upstream. Official policy now promotes using funds raised by power generated from the dam to pay for construction costs of smaller upstream dams over the next 20 or 30 years.[5] One could speculate whether or not an offer of loans by the international community to build smaller upstream dams could have halted construction of Sanxia. My feeling is that Sanxia would still have gone ahead.

Navigation

Those who have suggested that the project will improve navigation have been on somewhat weak ground since even the Ministry of Communication was known not to strongly support the project before it was approved, claiming that construction will cause so much havoc with navigation in the short and medium terms that it will render any long-term benefits uneconomic. Many experts suggested that a series of small dams creating several reservoirs along tributaries would benefit navigation more than one big dam. The increases in silt load predicted by some suggest that a reservoir of the order of 175 metres deep will not keep bed load sediments low in the Chongqing area (at the head of the reservoir), even with the flushing techniques proposed, and that the reservoir would not have a long enough life to make construction worth while.[6] Although data varys slightly from source to source, between 1957 and 1986 the area in the river basin affected by soil erosion more than doubled (Chang 1990, p. 5; Chang 1993, p. 14). In addition, the project includes five sets of locks which began construction in April 1994 and are to raise ships to the reservoir level. These locks are scheduled to be completed in July 2003. There is no existing dam in the world with such a complex set of locks, and technical problems such as those related to cleaning out silt from the locks remain as yet unsolved.[7] In recent years, the much simpler Gezhouba dam locks downstream have been experiencing serious failures, which are due apparently to basic design faults and lack of maintenance. Just to take the Number 3 Gezhouba Lock as an example, a passenger vessel crashed into the lock gate in early August 1995. Fortunately, the vessel ran into a pedestrian bridge in the process, which reduced the damage to the gate to the degree that it did not burst. At the time there was a difference of 18 metres in the water level on each side of the lock. In the case of the future Sanxia Dam, with water depths of over 100 metres on either side of its locks, there could be a great disaster.

Supporters of the dam point out that the best that could be done to improve vessel navigation to Chongqing without the Sanxia Dam is to enable 2000 or 3000 dead-weight tonne (dwt) vessels to get there year round. Moreover, there would still be problems during the flood season. The dam and locks will allow 10,000 dwt vessels to travel to Chongqing for more than half the year, and 5000 dwt vessels to get there all year round (Wang Z. 1990, pp. 88–90). Other navigation works are to be undertaken on this stretch of the river in three stages, with final completion projected for 2030. The proponents feel that efforts now going on to afforest the upper valley will help reduce sedimentation upstream.[8]

The navigation factor has become more critical after the start of construction of the new major economic development zone in the Pudong district of Shanghai. Within days of the National Congress approval of the dam, the Zhongtongshe news agency announced plans for a Chang River economic community with regional nodes focusing on Shanghai, Nanjing, Wuhan and Chongqing.[9]

Water supplies

The ability of the Sanxia Dam to aid in water supply was raised as another major argument for construction rather later than flood control, energy generation, and navigation improvements, with its significance becoming more apparent since 1992, although most authors still cite only the other three factors as the main reasons for construction. The huge water storage capacity of the reservoir would facilitate plans for south–north water transfers from the Middle Yangtze Valley to the water-short North China Plain, as well as allow for irrigation of an additional 4 million hectares of farmland. Even though, as of early 1998, the government was again considering which of the three proposed south–north transfer routes would go ahead, the reservoir will benefit either of the two more likely routes. The central course of the south–north water transfer project was officially announced as 'going ahead' in January 1995 and has been called the 'new Grand Canal'. It will be the world's longest artificial waterway (1241 kilometres), and could be completed at the same time as the dam. It would make direct use of Sanxia Reservoir water after transferring it to the neighbouring Danjiangkou Dam. Even downstream pumping of water along the eastern route (which makes use of the old Grand Canal) would be steadier in the dry season, since the dam will release stored water in the dry season should that route be chosen. However, south–north water transfer plans are quite controversial, and may be cancelled or further altered.

Other points of contention surrounding the dam

Resettlement

Perhaps the most contentious point is what will happen to the people living in the area to be flooded by the long riverine reservoir. It is estimated that including the interim population growth at least 1.13 million people will have to be relocated when the water in the reservoir reaches the planned 175-metre level. Others give higher figures.[10] It is estimated that 40,000 million yuan (US$4800 million) is to be spent on resettlement. Some sources suggest this is as much as 40 per cent of the total budget for the project, and the figure is likely to climb to 80,000 million yuan by 2009. A total of nineteen county-level units, including 140 market towns, eleven county seats and the county-level municipalities of Wan Xian and Fuling, 326 villages, 657 factory and mining sites, 139 power stations and 956 km of roads will end up under water, and a total of 1600 enterprises and 600 schools will have to be moved.[11] Resettlement experiments began in 1985 prior to approval of the project. Between late 1992 and October 1994, 12,353 people were moved in a 15.28-square kilometre area of Yichang and Zigui Counties of Hubei.[12]

Since then the pace of resettlement has picked up, with 50,000 to 100,000 people resettled by March 1998 ('Major Problems in Three Gorges Dam' 1998). Another 67,000 were to be moved in the remainder of 1998 ('China Denies Dam Project Problem' 1998).[13] Fifty per cent of the resettlement is to be completed by 2003, and the remainder was to be finished by 2009, but it now looks as though that will be delayed ten years (Tyler 1996a).

Officials working on the dam point out that the area is the most ideal site along the course of the Yangtze. Since the reservoir will be in a deep gorge, it involves the least movement of people. Moreover, as many of the people are poor, the government would have to invest considerable amounts of money to improve their lives. As it is, several billion yuan out of the resettlement funds are to be devoted to development of secondary and tertiary industries.[14] By the end of 1995, twenty provinces and ten municipalities had 'donated' about 450 million yuan for resettlement projects in the reservoir area. Local governments are also providing training for officials of these relocation projects. It was announced that a life insurance company, with its headquarters in Beijing and branch offices in the reservoir area, will be set up to provide policies for the people who will be resettled. The government is so worried about the possible problems with resettlement that it granted Canada's Monenco Agra a US$34.5 million contract to provide a computer system for the resettlement planning during Premier Li Peng's October 1995 visit to Canada.[15] By late 1997 reports suggested that some people were complaining that the small resettlement payments were getting delayed in the pocket of local officials. There were reports that resettlement was not working smoothly due to lack of coordination of funds, job provision and decent housing, as well as corruption, misuse of funds, descrimination against rural residents in the allocation of resources, lack of local consultation, non-scaling of compensation to inflation, and ill-prepared undercover resettlement (Faison 1997; Tyler 1996a; 'Major Problems in Three Gorges Dam' 1998; 'Three Gorges Officials Reportedly Admit to Embezzlement' 1998).

Construction difficulties

Technological problems, the actual cost of the dam, and how to raise funds also remain contentious points. Opponents pointed out that results from the Gezhouba Dam, the Danjiangkou Dam and the Sanmenxia Dam on the Huang (Yellow) River, to say nothing of the numerous smaller dams that have collapsed, do not necessarily inspire confidence in the ability of the government to cost the Sanxia project

(Dai Qing *et al.* 1998, pp. 18–38). For example, instead of taking 5 years as planned, Gezhouba took 18 years to finish at a cost close to 4 times the original estimate. New technical problems such as the more sophisticated navigation locks than those at Gezhouba will make the Sanxia project far more difficult. Already 1200 workers toiled day and night for the first ten months of 1995 to prepare for the difficult cofferdam construction.

Funding and budget problems

It is thought that the dam may use up so much of the national budget that there will be little funding left to carry out any other basic water management projects. Discussion of the project stalled construction of smaller dams in the area, and it will never become clear what other projects might have been possible if construction of the dam had not begun. It appears that it has even slowed approval of the south–north water diversion project itself. In late 1995 China was saying it could only fund 60 to 70 per cent of the Sanxia project's total cost, with the remainder having to come from foreign sources. This represents a significant change from the idea that China could finance the project completely, as was being mooted in the early 1990s. In January 1997, six organisations underwrote a US\$330 million bond issue for the State Development Bank of Chuna (Becker 1997).[16]

Although 1997 price estimates for the project costs had risen to 210,000 million yuan (US\$25,000 million), opponents have suggested figures rising closer to 1,000,000 million yuan. It should be pointed out that the 1997 costing is far higher than previous costings; even in spring 1998 official budgetary estimates in Xinhua broadcasts were 50,000 million yuan (calculated at May 1993 prices) and the 1993 figure was up considerably on earlier estimates.[17] Although a Xinhua news agency release in April 1996 noted that the vice president of Changjiang Three Gorges Project Development Corporation said that Sanxia was the first case in China where the funding for a major capital project was ahead of cost, but he also said that more efforts must be made to raise money by issuing bonds, because the project is still expected to be short of 40,000 million yuan prior to 2007. The finance problem is made more serious by President Clinton's attempts to curb US financing of the project, and clear signs that Japan is avoiding investment. One source says that up to the beginning of February 1997 the project was consuming 10 million yuan of investment per day (Yun Shangfeng 1997, p. 8). Later in the year, Yuan Guolin stated that the dam will require 10,000 million yuan of investment annually to 2000, and between 15,000 and 20,000 million yuan after that (Wang Yiru 1997, p. 7).

Revenue for the dam is to be raised six ways: higher electricity consumption taxes, which are to be placed in the 'Sanxia Construction Fund' (*Sanxia jianshe jijin*), amounting to 45 per cent of the total;[18] first-phase power generation from the dam, a State Development Bank 'contribution', Gezhouba Dam power profits (5 per cent of the total), domestic and international loans, and offshore sales of convertible bonds. In July 1997, stocks were first sold on the Shanghai stock market and the Chinese began saying that there would be a need for fund-raising by issuing stock in Hong Kong prior to 2000, and perhaps on overseas markets. From these figures, and guesses that the cost of construction materials will rise more slowly than inflation, the government concludes there will be sufficient capital to repay loans with interest, and that profit will begin with project completion. However, some officials have suggested that the project could be breaking even by 2005, thanks to profits from power generation.

Environmental impacts

The government notes that environmental research on the project began in the 1950s, and resulted in an environmental impact assessment report supervised by the Environmental Protection Bureau during the 1980s. To cope with any possible environment problems, the National Environmental Protection Agency (NEPA) carried out investigations of major pollutant-discharging enterprises in the reservoir area in June 1994 and sent a national environmental law enforcement inspection group to look at the project area in October 1995. The government is also allocating 90 million yuan to establish an environmental monitoring network and has awarded the Chinese Academy of Sciences Institute of Remote Sensing (IRS) a 50,000 yuan grant to monitor vegetation change in the Sanxia area (NEPA 1995, p. 18). With this fund, the IRS has digitised nearly 60 maps into a digital terrain model for future satellite monitoring. Some contend that the dam will reduce ecological damage caused by flooding and downstream sedimentation. Moreover, the air and water pollution caused by the coal-fired power plants that would be necesssary otherwise will be avoided.[19] Although the government concedes that ecological damage will occur, they say that ecological benefits will outweigh that damage.

Independence and compliance

However, others voice the concern that assessment of environmental impacts were undertaken by organisations that will benefit from the dam's construction (Fearnside 1988, p. 627; International Water

Tribunal 1992, p. 3). Today it is the company in charge of the project (China Changjiang Three Gorges Project Development Corporation) that is responsible for environmental protection under its contract to construct the dam. While the government says environmental aspects will be monitored during construction, it remains worrying that no independent source is responsible for environmental aspects, and contract violations regarding environmental aspects of the project have already occurred. Moreover, there are known to be problems of coordination amongst local environmental protection departments in the monitoring of the area.

Already by May 1995 the Department of Environmental Appraisal of the Chinese Academy of Sciences had noted that new industries along the reservoir site were polluting the Sanxia area.[20] In October 1997, to dispel fears about reservoir pollution, the Xinhua news agency announced that China would spend US$481 million during the five-year period up to 2003 on sewage disposal projects to control Chongqing municipality waste water discharged into the Yangtze. All factories in Chongqing would be required to meet tougher environmental standards for sewage discharge by 2002. In addition to urban waste water, the potential for pollution from increased mining of potassium ore, limestone, and coal are also considerable as the surrounding area experiences economic growth. However, individual contracts such as that for the Xiling Bridge stipulate that all possible measures to control pollution should be undertaken. At least two on-site construction material processing plants have installed waste-water treatment facilities; and the development corporation claims that they are undertaking tree planting, installation of separate storm sewers and waste water discharge outlets, as well as sealed transportation of construction materials (Li Yuanbo 1995, p. 1). Others contend that environmental damage has already occured in the early stages of construction (Yun Shangfeng 1997, p. 8).

Agriculture and soil erosion

Issues concerning change to the agro-ecosystem continue to be debated, with most foreign specialists feeling that the project will have an overall negative effect on local agriculture, fishing and the general environment. For a start, it is estimated that 23,800 hectares of crop land and over 4900 hectares of orange groves will be under water. Losses from these rich alluvial fields cannot easily be compensated for by the new, less-fertile lands proposed for settlement.[21] Currently 18 per cent (202,300 hectares) of the cultivated land in the reservoir area is on slopes greater than 25 degrees and there is considerable potential for increase of soil erosion and mud flows from farming land with steeper slopes higher up the hillsides. Between 1988 and 1995, 18,800 square kilometres of erosion area were brought under comprehensive control in Sichuan province and Chongqing municipality and there are plans for another 17,500 square kilometres during the ninth five-year plan period. Yet the task is far from complete, as an estimated 40 per cent of the province suffers from soil erosion ('Sichuan' 1996, p. 4). The Chinese are now urging international financial agencies to invest in erosion control in the Upper Yangtze Valley but it appears that so far no agencies has lent funds. In addition, it has been pointed out that if the water level in the area is raised during the winter and spring, soils could become swamp-like and gleyed. This might lead to reduced agricultural production in waterlogged fields, and the irrigation with colder water from the reservoir could affect crop growth.

Fisheries

Much of the environment impact is unclear and negative aspects cannot be measured in economic terms. For example, fish breeding grounds would also change along the river, probably for the worse. And although fish ladders are to be built around the dam itself, it is thought that certain species of fish will not be able to use them.

Historic sites

As well as scenery, habitats of animals, some significant historic places will be destroyed, with at least ten famous sites out of an estimated 883 under water. All signs are that not enough funds are being devoted to preservation.[22] There are also worries about the effect of the dam on climate, the creation of disease-favourable habitats, and impacts on ecosystems downstream and in the neighbouring portions of the East China Sea.[23]

Species extinction

While it is generally agreed that the dam will not lead to the extinction of many species, there are worries about the future of some forms of wildlife. These include eighteen special types of upstream fish as well as the Yangtze (Chinese) sturgeon, the Yangtze (white) dolphin (*Lipotes vexillifer, baijitun*), the Chinese sucker (*Myxocyprinus asiaticus, yanzhiyu*), the grenadier or samli fish (*Macrura reevesii, shiyu*) and the Siberian crane (*Grus leucogeranus, baihe*).[24] There is even talk of rodents moving up into higher unsettled areas ahead of the reservoir waters and causing damage in the new settlement areas. As experiments cannot predict exactly what will happen, there is no way the proponents can assure the opposition that such negative ecological consequences will not occur. Many scholars feel that there is not yet conclusive research to either proceed with or halt the project, and that alternatives have been not been sufficiently researched.

Disaster inducement

Much debate has centred on the increased possibility of disasters after the building of the dam. Landslides or earthquakes induced by the large reservoir could threaten the dam directly or through wave surges, although some scientists have stated that even multiple landslides into the reservoir could not cause a serious enough wave surge to damage the dam. The geological structure of the region is not all that stable and landslides have been common. It has been postulated that a rise in the water table caused by the reservoir could trigger landslides. In August 1996, about sixty researchers and experts with the State Commission on Science and Technology drafted a report admitting that the dam might induce moderate earthquakes at the main construction site.

To a degree this report alleviated public concern that major earthquakes may be induced due to the reservoir's huge water storage capacity. However, earthquakes greater than 4.75 on the Richter scale have been recorded in the reservoir area 21 times, with the greatest reaching 6.5. Thus earthquakes exceeding the dam's supposed 5.5 safety level are possible. However, government experts point out that to their knowledge no dam has ever burst because of an earthquake induced by the weight of a reservoir, and only two such earthquakes have produced cracks near the tops of dams, which posed no major flood threats.[25]

Military threats

During the Sino-Soviet tensions of 1969–70, an article in a small-circulation magazine called *Qunyan* mentioned another possible disaster that could confront the dam: military attack. Although the Geneva Conventions prohibit destruction of dams, they still remain a common military target. Pessimists estimate that up to 38 per cent of China's infantry and 20 per cent of armoured units could be flooded were the dam to be destroyed. In fact, the Chinese have been conducting bomb tests on models for a long time, and have stated that the reinforced concrete used for the dam will have properties that help it to resist damage in an attack. It has been further stated that all that will be necessary is to lower the reservoir level to 145 metres (the flood control level) at times of military tension, and channel a certain amount of the waters into flood diversion paths. However, such a defence appears rather weak because it relies on considerable foresight.

The changing international stance

The Sanxia project has been widely condemned by environmental groups in the late 1980s and 1990s.[26] Major funding bodies steered clear of the project, but there has been a change of stance by the international community in recent years. During 1994 alone, over 500 group members from nineteen polities came to talk with officials of Changjiang Three Gorges Project Development Corporation about finance, management, and research. Moreover, corporation people visited seventeen foreign countries (Xu Keda 1995, p. 35). The Chinese have found foreigners to be interested in investing in construction equipment, components for the turbines and generators, transmission and transformer facilities, and consulting services. In November 1993, the USA sent a 250-member delegation (including environmental specialists and engineers) to look at the site and to discuss possible cooperation. Deals for equipment have already been signed totalling US$20 million with various foreign firms such as Caterpillar of the USA.

In 1995, the USA Export-Import Bank, in response to a request from American companies, asked the Canadian environmental group Probe International to prepare a document regarding financial, technical and environmental information to help it decide whether or not to subsidise exports related to the project by providing insurance and financial aid. This can be taken as an indication of the pressure on the US government to help and to allow US companies to fund the Sanxia project. But in May 1996, the US Export-Import Bank turned down the request from three American companies to provide financial backing because of ecological concerns.[27] Boris Yeltsin discussed possible Russian participation in the project during his Presidential visit to China in April 1996. The Chinese have said they were likely to spend close to US$800 million on foreign equipment in the near future. They now plan to use Hong Kong as the centre responsible for handling internal loans related to the project.

State of China's political geography and the dam

The political situation in the People's Republic of China remains such that domestic public opinion could not block a project if the leadership is in favour of it. As is often the case, political decisions rather than a careful look at the evidence have determined a project's future. With so many technical matters unclear and the difficulty of costing the project, the politicians are using the dam to fulfil the goals they deem most important. This dam will submerge land, change river hydrology, affect ecosystems, jeopardise cultural heritage, displace people in the valley and deprive them and many others of their subsistence livelihoods. However, others even outside the political elite have found construction to be to their immediate economic advantage, such as peasants who can rent rooms to construction workers. In 1995, it was reported that thieves have been taking advantage of construction work at the site to steal archaeological treasures to sell overseas.

Succesful construction can actually enhance the power of central authority at the expense of local autonomy. The creation of Chongqing municipality was one way the central government is able to divide and rule Sichuan as well as buy off concerns in the Chongqing area. The central government can use Sanxia to help keep wealthy coastal provinces, such as Guangdong and Shanghai, as well as wealthy companies in line, since these units are paying more than others for this project to develop central China. Guangdong provincial government, Guangzhou municipality, and the Shenzhen special administrative region have made 'contributions' to the project. A children's beverage company in Zhejiang gave millions of yuan in assistance (Dai Qing 1997, p. 76). In spite of these domestic contributions, lack of outside funding could cripple the project to such a degree that it might have to be scaled down, although the chances of its being cancelled is becoming less and less likely. Halting foreign funding has been the main strategy used by foreign opposition groups since construction began. But as time passes, memories of Tiananmen and of environmental concerns at the time of approval in 1992 have faded. The possibilities for obtaining foreign loans for the project have improved, with Canada, Germany, and Switzerland already supplying export guarantees for equipment, and some foreign banks also underwriting bond issues for the project.

In the final analysis the Sanxia dam, along with the south–north water transfer scheme to which it is now linked, seems to be part of another attempt to catch up rapidly with developed nations and solve problems with grand projects. The past construction of dams in China does not inspire confidence. The current leadership, however, sees more to be gained from appearing to do something spectacular about flooding and energy shortages, and in giving China something they feel will be a positive legacy, than from worrying about potential negative consequences. Yet it is traditional methods that will produce safer and more useful flood control and navigation improvement: soil conservation and afforestation, reservoir construction on tributaries, improvement of the central- and lower-course dikes, expansion of flood water retention districts, dredging of the river and adjoining lake beds, improving flood warning systems, and educating the local populace. Electricity generation could have come on line faster if smaller dams had been constructed on tributaries using the project funds. Water saving on the North China Plain and industrial relocation could also go some of the way to solving water shortages there.

Fortunately, the government is committed to undertaking most of these policies in conjunction with the dam construction and water diversion, provided there are funds. However, if faithfully carried out without construction of the dam, these efforts could go a long way towards improving flood control and rapidly generating hydroelectric power while facilitating navigation and supplying water without incurring the ecological, economic and social costs of the super dam.

Notes

1. An emotional wide ranging condemnation of large dams can be found in Goldsmith and Hildyard (1984). O'Riordan (1990 pp. 141–8) discusses the environmentalist bias against large projects.
2. Opposition came from many including: Qian Jiaju, a former communist official and prominent economist now resident in the USA; the reporter Dai Qing (imprisoned for writing against the project); Li Rui, the former vice-minister of electric power; Sun Yueqi (a senior hydrologist); physicist Zhou Peiyuan; Hou Xueyu (now deceased), the former head of the Institute of Botany (Chinese Academy of Sciences); and Wang Ganchang, atomic bomb specialist.
3. In May 1996 a preservation work draft asked the government for the equivalent of US$230 million up to 2006, yet funds were slow to appear.
4. Wu Naitao (1994 p. 18) gives a generation figure of 507,900 million kilowatt hours (kW h). The 85,000 million kWh per annum figure is from a 1996 Reuter news release.
5. Yuan Guolin (1995 p. 6) mentions some of the dams to be funded by Sanxia generation – Xiluodu, Xiangjiaba, Baihetan, and Hutiaoxia on the Jinsha River. These will have a total installed capacity above 40 million kW. (See Chapter 13 on the Hutiaoxia Gorge.)
6. Some proponents feel that siltation will not be a problem with the Sanxia Reservoir, because the water level can be altered to flush out much of the buildup of silt. The water level will be kept at 145 metres during the high-water and silt-depositing season (June to September); even at this height large tows will be able to make it to Chongqing. Once the high waters have

passed the reservoir can begin to be filled for the coming dry season. In the following April, towards the end of the dry season, the water level can attain at least 155 metres and then be dropped 10 metres in order to flush the relatively small amount of silt built up over the winter. It is thought that it will take 80 to 100 years for the reservoir to reach its dead storage volume. After that time, say proponents, incoming silt and outflowing silt will have achieved a balance and the depth of water at the tail end of the reservoir should still be three metres, which will allow shipping to continue to reach Chongqing.

7. A description of the 6442 metres of double-direction permanent shiplocks can be found in Pang Yongxiang (1995 pp. 8–9). It will take 12 minutes for a lock to lower its water level, or about one hour for a vessel to clear the locks and an estimated 2.35 hours to clear the lock system. The annual shipping capacity for the system will be 51.52 million tonnes.

8. Fearnside (1988 p. 622) points out the water pH at around 6.5 is in the range where fine silt particles are not likely to clump together and settle out. Yuan Guolin (1995 p. 6) states that calculations suggest that navigation costs in the upper valley will be reduced by 35 to 37 per cent by construction of the dam. According to a March 1998 report ('PRC to Develop Forest Belt in Three Gorges Reservoir Area', 1998) China will spend 6.6 billion yuan on the forest belt in the reservoir area. The completed forest belt is planned to be finished in 2010 and have an area exceeding 2 million hectares, increasing present coverage from 27 to 46 percent. However, Dai Qing (1997, pp. 77–8) mentions a report that suggests there will be heavy sedimentation in the Chongqing area after the first severe (one in a hundred years) flood.

9. One must remember that the idea of economic promotion has on occasion taken on a carnival atmosphere, and various economic schemes announced sometimes do not materialise. One example of local money-making schemes was the walk by Canada's self-proclaimed 'prince of the air', Jay Cochrane, on a tightrope suspended 1300 feet in the air above the gorges at Fengjie county in Sichuan province as a stunt on 29 October 1995. Hotels were packed, traffic rerouted, and schools suspended for this longest tightrope walk in history. An estimated US$1.02 million was spent on the event, with the government hoping tickets sold and TV rights would recover the costs. The All China Sports Federation had begun looking for somebody to undertake the walk in 1990.

10. For example Wang Ming (1992, p. 14) give figures as high as 1.4 to 1.6 million people, and Qi Ren (in Dai Qing *et al.* 1998, pp. 59–60) points out that the figure could go to 1.8 million. One can also find estimates of 1.9 million.

11. In total, about 200,000 students will have to be relocated. The State Education Commission is putting 240 million yuan into the school resettlement plan, with Wan Xian and Yichang the most affected areas. Yichang has already spent about 4 million yuan to move five schools since 1993.

12. Gao Jiaheng (1995, pp. 10–11) points to several lessons learned in this 1992–4 resettlement period: (1) government policy and corporate interests have taken a different view of the resettlement; (2) land management laws and budgetary regulations have been in contradiction; (3) several tens of fees have had to be paid in land acquisition and for resettlement which has

complicated procedures; and (4) relations of national government, enterprises, and individuals with local government have not always been what they should. In Dai Qing *et al.* (1998, p. 62) it is noted that as of February 1996 only 3000 million yuan had been spent on resettlement.

13. The first figure is only an estimate. According to Gan Yuping, a vice-mayor of Chongqing municipality, 80,000 people had been moved from the dam area by March 1998 ('China Denies Dam Project Problem' 1998). Writing by the pen-name of Wu Ming, a Chinese sociologist living abroad states that falsification of figures is common, with some local officials having stated that 200,000 had already been moved by January 1998. Wu Ming thinks that the actual figures are no more than half those given by the government, and more than likely about 50,000 – perhaps less if 'resettled' is to include properly housed, compensated and re-employed ('Major Problems in Three Gorges Dam Resettlement Program' 1998). According to a newspaper report in *Hubei Ribao* (28 February 1998), Hubei is to resettle 70,000 people – 42.68 per cent of the province's total resettlement number – between 1998 and 2003 (*Hubei Conference on Immigration for Three Gorges Project* 1998).

14. According the Yuan Guolin (1995, p. 6), industries to be developed number over 400, including: local speciality product processing, construction materials, silk and light industrial machinery. Massive rises in unemployemnt in the state sector during 1996 and 1997, with Sichuan and Chongqing one of the most seriously affected areas, suggest that job provision for the migrants will prove even more difficult than originally anticipated. Qi Ren (in Dai Qing *et al.* 1998, p. 62) estimates total cost for resettlement will be 170,000 million yuan, based on resettlement taking twenty years and inflation remaining at rates similar to those of the mid-1990s.

15. This contract appears to have broken the ice on Canadian funding restrictions, with a US$30 million soft loan likely to be made by the Canadian government to Monenco Agra in January 1996.

16. Opposition groups including a coalition of 45 international groups have tried to put pressure on American and Japanese financial institutions to refain from underwriting the Chinese bonds. Bonds directly for the Sanxia project are offered only in China, whereas foreign bonds are tied to multiple sources through the State Development Bank of China. In 1996 the first international State Development Bank of China bond was underwritten by Nomura Securities in Japan. Early in 1997 a second 30,000 million yen bond issue in Japan was cancelled, allegedly because it was thought the funding was for the Sanxia dam. This was the third time a bond issue had been cancelled due to a 'lack of investor interest'. On 12 November 1997 anti-dam campaign groups in the USA took out a full-page advertisement in *The New York Times* urging investors not to buy bonds for the Sanxia project. *The New York Times* ran an editorial on the same day criticising the dam. Further pressure was mounted in March 1998 by the International Rivers Network and Human Rights in China with their joint scathing report on resettlement and foreign funding ('Major Problems in the Three Gorges Dam' 1998). In contrast the World Bank (1994) has presented China's dam resettlement policies as a model. Currently European and Canadian export credit agencies have been supplying funds as well as Western investment firms who are channelling money to the State Development Bank of China.

17. Dai Qing (1997, p. 75) gives a series of official and estimated costs from 1983 to 1995. Between January 1993 and June 1995, a total of 9000 million yuan had been injected into Sanxia-related projects, and total investments in the project had reached 30,000 million yuan. 8000 million yuan of the related project investments were fixed asset investments of which 4100 million yuan were spent directly on the future dam, with other spending related to resettlement, design, research, management and bank interest payments.

18. A 2 per cent national electricity tax to pay for the dam has been imposed in over twenty provincial-level administrative units.

19. In contrast Wang Jiazhu (1992, p. 51) points out that pollution worries will be increased in the Chongqing area by the slowed flow of water.

20. Du Gang (1995, p. 6) notes that fifty different types of pollutants, including excessive amounts of phenol, potassium and cyanides, now enter the Yangtze in the reservoir area from industries that have virtually no water treatment facilities. The banks of the river and its tributaries have rubbish heaps and industrial sludge piled upon them. Scientists of the Chang River Resources Protection Institute have stated that unless something is done, the reservoir will be a pool of putrid water bringing serious problems for the local environment. A news release concerning construction of a new chemical plant in Sichuan that may provide jobs for displaced people from the reservoir area ('Jobs Slated for People Displaced by China Dam' 1996) suggests that sources of pollution are likely to increase through the resettlement programme. Open Chinese criticism of the lack of pollution concern from the city of Chongqing can be found in Tyler (1996a). Local engineers openly stated that the central government had glossed over the seriousness of Chongqing water pollution in their environmental impact statement given to the US embassy in Beijing.

21. According to Zheng (1992, p. 3), the Quaternary lands have a double cropping index of 250 or better and produce grain yields of 852 jin per mu per annum.

22. 'Qiangjiu Sanxia' (1996, p. 4) notes that attempts at historic preservation in the Sanxia area involves more workers than any other historical preservation project since 1949. On a visit to Taiwan, Mr Huang Kezhong, leader of the Sanxia Cultural Relic Preservation Planning Small Group (Sanxia Wenwu Baohuguihua Xiaozu), stated that only a small portion of what can be preserved will be saved but this will be well preserved. However, more than 60 prominent scholars still felt it necessary to sign a petition to Jiang Zemin in August 1996 asking him to support demands for increased aid to protect relics in the Sanxia area. In 1993 some scholars proposed turning one of the more famous sites, Baiheliang, into an underwater museum.

23. A slowed flow rate of the river might well lead to increased salinisation of water and land along the river banks at the mouth. Even proponents of the dam have admitted this possibility, but have argued that careful management of the water flow during the winter months would eliminate such a threat. A reduced flow rate should also reduce natural oxidation of the river water and the ability of the river to flush out pollutants.

24. In October 1996 the Research Institute for Artificial Breeding of the Chinese Sturgeon released 200,000 sturgeon fry at Yichang which should help main-

tain the stock for a while. As the Yangtze dolphin do not migrate upstream they are not directly harmed by changes brought about by the construction of Gezhouba or Sanxia. However, an increase in boats brought on by improved navigation, blockage of migration routes for fish upon which they feed, or changes in the river bed could further reduce their already small numbers. According to 'Protecting Plants' (1997, p. 27) the Sanxia region is a treasure trove of rare and precious plants, with 3964 different species, about one-seventh of China's total. The Chinese Academy of Sciences in cooperation with the Yichang government is building a botanical garden in the Yichang Jinyingang Experimental Forest Ground to help preserve species. Dai Qing (1998, p. 4) notes that there are less than a hundred white-fin dolphins in the world.

25. One crack occurred in India; the other was a 6.1 level earthquake at the Datou dam on the Xinfeng River in Guangdong province.
26. At a 1989 conference in San Francisco, the Sanxia Dam project was labelled the worst of the world's 20 most dangerous large dam projects. In February 1992 the independent jury of the Second International Water Tribunal in Amsterdam stated that the Sanxia project should be either greatly modified or stopped (International Water Tribunal, 1992). In 1992, the Canadian governments' decided to stop aid to the project.
27. See 'Mei jinchukou yinhang' (1996, p. 4). These included maintaining adequate reservoir water quality, protection of ecological resources, preserving endangered species, and population resettlement. The bank's decision does not limit US companies from privately participating in the project.

References

Becker, Jasper (1997) 'Shun Bonds Call Goes to Three Gorges Opponents', *South China Morning Post*, 14 November, 11.

Chang, William Y. B. (1990) 'Human Population, Modernization, and the Changing Face of China's Eastern Pacific Lowlands', *China Exchange News*, XVIII (4) 3–8.

Chang, William Y. B. (1993) 'Lake Management in China', *Asian Journal of Environmental Management*, I -(2) 11–21.

Chen Guojie and Chen Zhijian (1993) *Sanxia gongcheng dui shengtai yu huanjing yingxiang de zonghe pingjia yanjiu* (A Comprehensive Research Evaluation of the Ecological and Environmental Impact of the Sanxia Construction), 'China Denies Dam Project Problem', Associated Press (14 March) (Beijing: Kexue Chubanshe).

'China Denies Dam Project Problem', Associated Press (14 March).

Dai Qing *et al.* (1998) *The River Dragon Has Come! The Three Gorges Dam and the Fate of China's Yangtze River and Its People* (Armonk, NY, and London: M. E. Sharpe).

Dai Qing (1997) 'The Three Gorges Project and Sustainable Development in China', *Civil Engineering Practice*, Spring/Summer, 73–92.

Du Gang (1995) 'Water Polluted in Three Gorges', *China Environment News*, 15 May, p. 6.

Edmonds, Richard Louis (1993) 'China's Plans for a Special Economic Zone in the Sanxia Area', *Geography*, 78 (3) 309–11.

Edmonds, Richard Louis (1992) 'The Sanxia (Three Gorges) Project: the Environmental Argument Surrounding China's Super Dam', *Global Ecology and Biogeography Letters* IV (2) 105–25.

Faison, Seth (1997) 'Set to Build Dam, China Diverts Yangtze While Crowing About it', *New York Times*, 9 November, section 1.1.

Fearnside, Phillip (1988) 'China's Three Gorges Dam: "Fatal" Project or Step Toward Modernization?' *World Development*, 16 (5) 615–30.

Gao Jiaheng (1995) 'Sanxia gongcheng jianshe yongdi yu yimin anzhi' (Building Lot [sic.] and Emigrant [sic.] Employment for Three Gorges Project), *Zhongguo Sanxia jianshe*, V, 10–11.

Goldsmith, Edward and Hildyard, Nicholas (eds) (1984) *The Social and Environmental Effects of Large Dams, Vol. 1: Overview* (Camelford, UK: Wadebridge Ecological Centre).

Hubei Conference on Immigration for Three Gorges Project (1998) FBIS-CHI–98–071 (12 March).

International Water Tribunal (1992) 'Case Papers on the Three Gorges Dam Project, China and James Bay Hydroelectric Project, Quebec, Canada', in: *The Case Books*, 7 volumes, 2nd International Water Tribunal (Utrecht: International Books).

'Jobs Slated for People Displaced by China Dam' (1966) *Journal of Commerce* 1 February, section A p. 5.

Li Yuanbo (1995) 'Three Gorge Dam Project Considers its Impact', *China Environment News*, 15 November, p. 1.

Lieberthal, Kenneth and Oksenberg, Michael (1988) *Policy Making in China: Leaders, Structures, and Processes* (Princeton University Press).

'Major Problems in Three Gorges Dam Resettlement Program', Joint Report by International Rivers Network and Human Rights in China, 12 March.

'Mei jinchukou yinhang jueju daikuan gei Zhonggong' (1996) US Import Export Bank refuses to give a loan to the Chinese communists, *Zhongyang ribao* (International Edition), 24699 (2 June) 4.

NEPA (1995) *Report on the State of the Environment in China 1994* (Beijing: National Environmental Protection Agency).

O'Riordan, T. (1990) 'On the "greening" of Major Projects', *Geographical Journal*, CLVI, (2) 141–8.

Pang Yongxiang (1995) 'Xingjianzhong de Sanxia yongjiu chuanjia' (Permanent Shiplocks of the Three Gorges under Construction), *Zhongguo Sanxia jianshe*, V, 8–9.

'PRC to develop Forest Belt in Three Gorges Reservoir Area' (1998) FBIS-CHI98-071 (12 March 1998).

'Protecting plants' (1997) *Beijing Review*, 40, 41 (13–19 October) 27.

'Qiangjiu Sanxia wenwu qianjing kanyou' (1996) (Preliminary worries about saving Sanxia cultural relics), *Zhongyang ribao* (International edition), 24701 (4 June) 4.

'Sichuan shuitu liushi yanzhong weiji Sanxia gongcheng' (1996) (Sichuan's soil erosion is serious and threatens the Sanxia project), *Zhongyang ribao* (International edition), 24696 (30 May) 4.

'Three Gorges Officials Reportedly Admit to Embezzlement' (1988) FBIS-CHI-98-075 (16 March).

Tyler, P. E. (1996a) 'China Dam Project is Questioned', *Dallas Morning News* 21 January, 1A

Tyler, P. E. (1996b) 'Dam's Inexorable Future Spells Doom for Yangtze Valleys Rich Past', *New York Times*, 6 October, Section 1, 12.

Wang Jiazhu (1992) 'Sanxia jianku dui Chongqing Shi de yingxiang ji zhuyao duice' (Three Gorges Reservoirs [sic.]: Its Impact on Chongqing City and Relevant Measures), *Renmin Changjiang*, XXIII (December) 46–53.

Wang Ming (1992) 'Deng Xiaoping Zancheng jianba Sanxia shangma cheng dingju' (Deng Xiaoping Approves Dam Construction, the Commencement of Sanxia Becomes Fixed), *Guangjiaojing*, CXXXIV (March) 12–15.

Wang Yiru (1997) 'Sanxia gongcheng gupiao jiang zai haiwai shangshi' (Sanxia Project Stock Will Go into the Overseas Market), *Zhongyang Ribao* (international edition), 25191 (7 October) 7.

Wang Zuogao (1990) 'Navigation on Yangtze River and the Three Gorges Project', *Bulletin of the Permanent International Association of Navigation Congresses*/Bulletin de l'Association Internationale Permanente des Congres de Navigation, LXX, pp. 86–96 (in English with French résumé).

World Bank (1994) 'Resettlement and Development: The Bankwide Review of Projects Involving Involuntary Resettlement 1986–1993' (8 April).

Wu Naitao (1994) 'Three Gorges Project Proceeds Smoothly', *Beijing Review*, 37 (24) 14–20.

Xu Keda (1995) 'Qiaokai damen ying jiabin zhencheng hezuo jian weiye' (Open the Door and Let Guests Come and Participate in the Great Enterprise), *Zhongguo Sanxia jianshe*, V, 35–6.

Yuan Guolin (1995) 'Sanxia gongcheng de xingjian dui Changjiang liuyu jingji fazhan de ladong zuoyong' (A Pushing Effect of Three Gorges Project Construction on Regional Economic Development for [the] Yangtze Valley), *Zhongguo Sanxia jianshe*, V, 5–7.

Yun Shangfeng (1997) (J. C. Lewis, trans.) 'The Yangtze River is Congested', *China Focus* V (4) (April), 8.

Zheng Zhuyuan (1992) 'Yanmo fanduisheng keyi yao man'gan' (The voices opposed to flooding must make themselves heard), *Zhongyang ribao* (International edition), 23118 (28 January) 3.

8
World Bank Policies, Energy Conservation and Emissions Reduction

Lin Gan[1]

Introduction

In the early 1990s, international arrangements for the environment were broadened to include a new dimension: the protection of the global environment, in particular the reduction of greenhouse gas (GHG) emissions to the atmosphere due mostly to the burning of fossil fuels. Among many initiatives, improving energy efficiency was proposed as a cost-effective measure to eliminate global environmental risks, particularly with regard to the use of new technologies and processes in industry (Schipper and Meyers 1992, p. 73–118). After the 1992 United Nations Conference on Environment and Development (UNCED) in Rio, many initiatives were undertaken at the national and international levels to strengthen various mechanisms for action, including the Global Environment Facility (GEF), jointly managed by the World Bank, the UNDP and the United Nations Environment Programme (UNEP).[2]

As developing countries are increasingly being involved in various mechanisms to protect the global environment, many difficulties arise in project design and implementation, such as conflicts of interest, choice of priorities, emissions targets and barriers in human resources development, as well as institutional arrangement. It has been realised increasingly that effective financial transfer holds a key to addressing the energy and environmental dilemma in developing countries (Levine and Meyers 1992, p. 25). International aid agencies could play an important role to facilitate this development; this is especially relevant when issues contain a global dimension, and require collective actions across national boundaries.

Providing financial assistance to China for energy development was an important component of international development assistance in most of the 1980s, although it focused almost exclusively on building up physical energy supply capacities to meet energy demands. From the late 1980s, strengthening energy sector management received substantial attention in international development assistance. Energy conservation was stated as an important component at the time. However, there was a gap between the stated objectives and the commitment of projects, as many constraints arise from the conflict of interests between organisations and political preferences (Gan 1995).

Only in the last few years have international aid agencies developed their interests in supporting energy conservation and environmental protection in China. Degrees of interest and scales of involvement, however, vary considerably. The transition toward a market-oriented economy and associated structural reforms there have fostered important changes in aid policies and strategies. As a response, international aid agencies have shifted their interests from an overwhelming focus on hardware development, such as infrastructure buildup, to increased support for national capacity-building (e.g. human resource development) and technical assistance, although these initiatives still have a limited scope.

In this chapter I review the interactions between international aid agencies and the Chinese government in defining their policies to address energy and environmental problems. The process of project negotiation, contracting and implementation is discussed. The dynamics of policy change within international aid agencies, governmental institutions and industry are analysed accordingly. I examine the effects of operations supported by the World Bank and the UNDP, and how these two organisations affect the design and establishment of energy conservation and environmental projects. It addresses the contradictions and changing patterns of aid in relation to the role of governmental institutions and the energy industry, by comparing the strengths and weaknesses of institutional arrangements. For a better understanding of the domestic tensions, a brief review of the energy and environmental interaction is presented in the first section.

The following questions will be discussed:

1. Who are the main actors involved in project design and implementation, and what are their interests, capabilities and level of involvement?
2. What kind of bargaining process has occurred in developing financial transfer agreements? Has bargaining led to optimal or suboptimal outcomes, and why?

186 Energy Conservation and Emissions Reduction

3. How have transfer mechanisms changed over time? Has there been any convergence among institutions in the strategies and policies employed?
4. What changes in behaviour, attitude, and institutional forms can be linked to transfer mechanisms?
5. What kind of tensions exist between sectoral institutions, and why?

Energy conservation and environmental protection

In the past decade and a half, China has achieved the highest rates of economic growth in the world (10.2 per cent from 1980 to 1990, and 12.9 per cent in 1990–4). The industrial sector maintained an even higher rate of growth: 11.1 per cent in 1980–90 and 18.8 per cent in 1990–4 (World Bank 1996, p. 208). This development was sustained by the extensive use of coal as major energy source (about 76 per cent of the total energy supply). From 1980 to 1991, coal consumption increased from 434.9 to 789.8 million tons of coal equivalent (Mtce), a rise of 82 per cent (Yan 1994, p. 123). By the year 2015, it is projected to double to 1660 Mtce (Liu 1993, p. 47). With the increasing demands for energy supply and services, the energy shortage has become a big bottleneck in achieving economic development objectives (State Statistical Bureau 1994, p. 75). The problem was due mostly to the inefficient use of energy resources, especially during coal production and consumption processes. The average energy efficiency, including energy production, transportation, conversion and end use, is 30 to 33 per cent. This figure is much lower than those for Japan (57 per cent), USA (51 per cent) and Western Europe (42 per cent). In China, each unit of GDP output requires much more energy than in major industrial countries: 5 times that of France, 4.4 times that of Japan, 3 times that of the USA, and even 1.7 times that of India (Yan 1994, p. 240). At the same time, energy-related environmental problems, e.g. air and water pollution, led to serious side-effects in human health and billions of yuans' worth of economic damage (see this volume, Chapter 6).[3]

Since energy is the main determining factor in the pace of economic development, its development is considered as a strategic area for economic policy-making. Although the energy sector has experienced constant growth in the 1980s (with an average annual growth of 5.5 per cent), energy production has lagged far behind the needs for industrial development (World Bank 1992a). This serious energy shortage nationwide has limited the capacities of economic development (Gan 1990, p. 12).

The cost of economic development on the environment is high. According to statistics published in June 1992, the National Environmental Protection Agency (NEPA) warned that an increase of 4 to 9 per cent in air, water and solid waste pollution was observed in 1992. The report also said that pollution fouled more than 10 per cent of the arable farmland and was ruining 12 million tons of grain each year (*China News Digest*, 10 August 1993).

From 1980 to 1990, carbon dioxide (CO_2) emissions rose from 406 million tons to 660 million tons. China's global share of CO_2 emissions changed from 8 per cent in 1980 to 11 per cent in 1990 (Sinton 1996, pp. ix, 49–51). This share may increase up to 20 per cent by the middle of the twenty-first century, if the present trend of economic growth continues. Concerned about the potential impact of climate change on ecosystems, the Chinese government perceives its CO_2 emissions problem and associated climate-change risks to be a serious issue (Zhao *et al.* 1992). China is also concerned about its international image, and wants to be regarded as an environmentally friendly nation within the international community. All these factors have contributed to changes in governmental behaviour and attitude to redefine national security with respect to environmental risks. However, the government interest in energy conservation and environmental protection is motivated mostly by the deterioration of environmental quality caused by air and water pollution, and associated economic costs.

China has already developed an organisational base for energy and environmental management, linked by a sophisticated national network. There is also a technical and managemental capacity for project design and implementation that is rare among developing countries. The government has committed itself to solving energy and environmental problems, mostly through enforcement of management and regulatory measures. More recently, increasing the role of environmental technology has risen on the policy agenda, especially in relation to the development of clean technologies (CT) and products (SSTC and SPC 1994, p. 32).[4] (SSTC is the State Science and Technology Commission.) The government has also committed itself to increasing environmental expenditure in the next few years, and energy conservation has been regarded as an important priority by the government. In the 1980s, 27 billion yuan ($3.2 billion) was invested in energy conservation projects. Efforts were made to institutionalise energy conservation initiatives. As a result, more than 400 new technical innovation projects were developed and demonstrated nationwide. An energy-saving capacity of 56 Mtce was reached, and 370 Mtce was saved between 1980 and 1992 (SPC 1993b, pp. 71–2).

The State Planning Commission (SPC) estimates that the economic growth rate in China in the 1990s will remain around 8 to 9 per cent annually, and about 7 per cent in the years 2000–10. China needs to reach an energy-saving target of 500 Mtce in the 1990s, which means an average rate of energy-saving of 4.5 per cent, compared with 3.6 per cent in the 1980s. The measures proposed for meeting this goal are:

- energy price system reform;
- encouraging cost-effective adjustment in industrial structure;
- increasing the share of the service industry;
- increasing inputs for research, development and innovation of new technologies;
- adjusting energy conservation and cleaner coal technology measures;
- introducing energy conservation laws; and
- providing incentives to foreign aid for industrial investment (SSTC 1993, p. 102).

In the environmental sector, the impact of acid rain has become a critical issue recently, and has attracted the attention of the government. In 1993, SO_2 emissions from fossil fuel burning, mostly direct use of coal, reached a record high of 18 million tons (38 per cent higher than that in 1985) (Sinton 1996, pp. viii–11). The total area affected by acid rain has increased from 175 square kilometers in 1985 to 280 in 1993 (*People's Daily*, 10 January 1995). It has been estimated that annual SO_2 emissions may increase to more than 20 million tons by the year 2000, and 28 million tons by the year 2015. The associated environmental damage may cost as much as 1.6 billion yuan ($188 million) per year. To maintain SO_2 emissions at the 1990 level would require a total investment of 15 billion yuan ($1.8 billion).

It is important to take a close look at the sources of pollution and the main contributors. Two issues play an important role in energy conservation: the behaviour and attitude of industry and consumers; and the influence of governmental policy and institutions. Along with economic decentralisation, profitability and economic growth have been a dominant force, pushed by industrial enterprises and local governments. State-owned energy enterprises, such as coal mines and power plants, are pushed by the central government to reduce their deficit and increase productivity, although they are not energy-efficient and are big polluters (SPC *et al.* 1993a, p. 41).[5]

Meanwhile, energy consumers, including industrial enterprises and individual end users, are less interested in reducing their energy costs, mostly because of distorted low energy prices, which provide little economic incentive for energy conservation.[6] In addition, the fast growth of small-scale rural industries throughout the country has led to lower energy efficiency and slow response to technological innovation, because they tend to adopt outdated technologies, pushed by international investment by which some high-polluting industries are transferred from other countries. Internally, some high-pollution urban industries have shifted production to rural areas owing to stricter environmental controls in urban areas. Some rural industries have difficulty in investing in new and energy-efficient technology because of lack of funds.

Another tension exists within the Chinese government. It has chosen to speed up power supplies, particular in electricity generation, to meet growing energy demand. During 1991–5, heavy investment was targeted in areas such as coal-burning power plant, large hydro-electric power generation (e.g. the Three Gorges Dam project), and nuclear power generation.[7] By contrast, state investment in energy conservation has been declining. In recent years, investment in energy conservation (1.1 billion yuan per year) accounts for only 1 per cent of the total investment in infrastructure projects. In the early 1980s, investment on technology innovation for energy conservation was 640 million yuan per year. By 1989, it was reduced to 160 million yuan (Liu *et al.* 1993, p. 108). These problems reflect a strong tension among industrial leaders and state policymakers. Their overwhelming priority seems to be dominated by the desire to push growth and meet energy demand. This constraint will be likely to increase, because of the growing regionalism and liberalisation of the economy. In brief, the economic policies implemented have:

1. encouraged the increase of small-scale rural enterprises that are less energy-efficient and more polluting than large industries;
2. reduced the effectiveness of the central government in enforcing laws and putting effective control in place;
3. increased the incentives for enterprises to maximise value-added and to treat the environment as a low priority, or an externality;
4. increased the pressure for loss-making state-owned enterprises to reduce their subsidies, so reducing their interest in emission controls.

It is only in the last few years that the interrelationship of economy, energy and the environment has become increasingly recognised by the government. The concept of sustainable development is being translated into policy components and integrated into various sectoral policies. This is particularly seen in assessment, selection and transfer of energy technologies for environmentally sound development. Emphasis is given to increasing energy-efficiency in the use of coal. For that, choice of technology is the vital part of governmental policy-making (*People's Daily*, 23 August 1991, p. 3).

There has been progress in environmental protection (discussed in more detail in Chapter 6). For instance, from 1985 to 1990, a total of 47.7 billion yuan ($5.6 billion) was invested in environmental pollution control, which was equivalent to 0.7 per cent of the gross national product (GNP). Between 1991 and 1995, investments in pollution control increased to 87 billion yuan ($10.2 billion), or 0.85 per cent of GNP (Liu *et al.* 1993, p. 19). However, total investment needed for pollution control in old industries (those constructed before 1980) was estimated at some 200 billion yuan, or $23.5 billion (NEPA 1992, p. 116). It was estimated that in order to keep the environmental pollution under control by the year 2000, the total environmental investment needed will be 420 billion yuan, or 1.6 per cent of the GNP in the same year (SPC *et al.* 1993a, p. 43). Just a few years ago the government stated the difficulties in meeting the investment needs for the environment because of economic and political considerations (e.g. fear of reducing growth rates and massive layoffs of workers; (*China News Digest*, 13 October 1992).[8] To complement this, China also openly admitted its interest in receiving international development assistance for the environment and the improvement of energy efficiency.

Energy conservation and environmental protection can complement each other. In the early 1980s, measures for tackling energy and environmental problems were developed with short- and medium-term objectives, aimed primarily at solving energy shortage and pollution problems at the local and regional levels. In the 1990s, concern has refocused on the harmonisation of long-term development, or the so-called environmentally sustainable development. An international perspective, with a commitment to solving global environmental problems, has been incorporated into development objectives (SSTC 1994). In this context, proposals submitted to international agencies are increasing, with encouragement from governmental policy. International debates on the global environment further reinforced these concerns, particularly with the push provided by the UNCED meeting at Rio, and the resulting activities, such as the implementation of national Agenda 21 and associated priority projects.

In the early 1980s, the scientific community played a critical role in increasing governmental concerns for energy conservation and environmental protection. From the mid-1980s to the early 1990s, more than 600 regulations and standards for energy conservation in various sectors were introduced, and the Energy Conservation Law was promulgated in 1995 (*People's Daily*, 10 January 1995). In the environmental sector, 142 state environmental standards were set up by 1991. The Air Pollution Prevention Law and the Water Pollution Prevention Law were reviewed by the People's Congress in 1994 (*China Environmental Year Book* 1995, pp. 127–9). Since then the government has mobilised economic institutions such as banks to adopt stricter control of loans to prevent industrial pollution from spreading in rural areas (Greenwire, 24 January 1997).

So far, measures to tackle energy inefficiency have led to partial success. It is obvious that with limited public funds it will be very difficult to reach the government's energy conservation and environmental objectives. In addition, conflicting interests exist between high-level political commitments and the practical implementation of policies, particularly with polluting rural industries at the local level (*China Environmental News*, 18 October 1988, p. 1). In many respects, the central government has difficulty in controlling what is going on at the regional and local levels where priorities are usually given to projects that could produce maximum economic returns. The same tension also exists between local authorities and industrial enterprises.

Financial transfer mechanisms

In development assistance, the success of project implementation depends largely on national capacities for project management. China differs from many developing countries in its competence in project design and management. This can be credited to its well-established institutional networks for project management, its trained technicians and research and development (R&D) expertise. Between 1988 and 1991, the total number of science and technology (S&T) personnel in the public sector almost doubled from 9.7 million to 17 million. By 1992, more than 40.8 million scientists and engineers were involved in R&D activities, and China ranked fourth in international comparison, after the former USSR, the USA and Japan (SSTC 1993, pp. 28–36). China has also developed expertise in conducting project appraisal and evaluation, e.g., in Environmental Impact Assessment (EIA).

The growth of its economic power and its potential for R&D self-reliance, promoted by growing nationalism, made the Chinese government believe that development assistance should do no more than provide additional funds, relying mainly on its own resources to fulfill its development objectives.[9] This belief has an obvious impact on many officials and policymakers who are involved in aid negotiations and project management.

In the past, China managed to organise large-scale development projects by mobilising resources from the government budget. This situation is changing, owing to the growth of regional autonomy which has led to a reduction of the central authority (Jia and Lin 1994) and the decline of the financial capacity of the central government to invest in the public-goods sector (Wang and Hu 1993, pp. 38–54). This has led central government to be very interested in searching for external assistance from multilateral and bilateral aid agencies for support in the public-goods sector.

Having realised the potential role China could play in balancing the international equation on energy production, consumption and the environment, international aid agencies have made important adjustments in their policies and operations in the country. Both sides have realised the opportunities and constraints in energy sector management and environmental protection, and the associated costs of policy intervention, although each side perceives the need and scope for resource allocation differently, particularly with regard to different sectoral demands.

For international aid organisations, an international consensus has caused environmental protection to increase in status in recent years. This is exemplified by such initiatives as the adoption of environmental assessment procedures for project management at the World Bank, and in the joint operation of GEF projects. But it can be argued that energy conservation has been to some extent overlooked. Some experts have already warned that international responses to energy conservation have been slower than what was expected at Rio, particularly in multilateral aid agencies.[10]

It is clear that political commitments on global environmental protection, such as the UN Framework Convention on Climate Change, cannot guarantee allocation of financial resources, although these commitments provide an opportunity for energy conservation and environmental protection to be better integrated into aid policies and practices. An important issue is how to operate international aid effectively and in consistence with domestic concerns. Clearly, there are constraints in China at the institutional level, where concern is mainly to increase production, often at the cost of environmental quality and human health. This is especially so in urban areas, where energy production and consumption often undermine conservation and environmental objectives (Qu 1992, p. 132).

Under the established institutional framework for project negotiation and management, the World Bank and the UNDP have each developed a formal partnership relationship with their Chinese counterparts: the World Bank with the Ministry of Finance and the UNDP with the Ministry for Foreign Trade and Economic Cooperation. Financial resources are channelled through these arrangements, which often reinforces central government capacity, but has limited effects in strengthening regional capacities, local communities or non-governemntal organisations (NGOs).

Energy conservation and environmental protection have been vitalised in international organisations in recent years, although each organisation reacts differently in its agenda setting, priority selection, project appraisal procedures, and attached conditionalities. As China is in the middle of a massive economic and social transition, new areas for aid transfer have been identified, such as providing support for cleaner coal technologies, energy end-use efficiency management and[11] capacity-building for the environment, plus new and renewable energy technologies.[12]

The World Bank

China regained its membership of the World Bank in 1980, and began to receive loans in 1981. Between 1983 and 1994, the bank's lending to China grew more than 40 times, from $70 million to $3.1 billion (*China Foreign Economic Statistics: 1979–1991*, 1993, p. 343–4). China is by far the largest recipient of loans and credits, and accounted for 15 per cent of the total $20.8 billion approved by the bank in 1994 (*China News Digest*, 27 September, 1994).[13] The bank's lending priorities in China are based on the results of a number of large-scale studies conducted in the 1980s, which analysed the needs of various sectors. Table 8.1 indicates the share of the loans by sector between 1982 and 1992.

In the environment sector, total resource allocation between 1982 and 1993 was $735 million, which accounted for about 4.5 per cent of the total $16.3 billion in loans from the bank. Out of a total of 126 projects approved by the bank during this period, only six were classified as environmental projects (4.8 per cent). Two of them were

Table 8.1 World Bank loans to China by sector, 1982–92

Sector	Loans	
	($ bn)	%
Agriculture	3.3	23.8
Transportation	3.3	23.5
Energy	2.5	18.1
Social development[a]	2.2	15.8
Industry	2.1	15.2
Forestry	0.4	2.8
Technical assistance	0.1	0.7
Total	13.9	99.9

[a] Including education, healthcare, urban development, poverty reduction, and environmental protection.
Source: Luo and Ning (1993, pp. 365–6).

approved in 1987 and four in 1992–3 (Luo and Ning 1993, pp. 366–8). Although there were environmental components implicitly contained in some investment projects, the environmental portfolio in China indicates that the environment was clearly not a priority of the bank. Currently, the bank is in the process of vitalising its environmental policies, and considerable efforts have been made to strengthen the environmental sector. There have been efforts to increase research on pollution. However, results are not yet clear in the current condition of policy adjustment at the bank.

Energy represents the third-largest sector in the bank's lending (18.1 per cent). Efforts here have focused on increasing electricity generating capacity and improving transmission and distribution systems, with the aim of providing energy supply capacity for industrial development. Between 1982 and 1993, the bank provided $2.5 billion for 14 multi-million-dollar projects in the energy sector in China, including the development of 2 coal-burning power plants, 5 hydroelectric power stations, and 5 oil and natural gas projects. The bank has invested $500 million on coal-burning electric power plants. These loans were important catalysts in China's industrialisation.

Comparatively little attention has been paid to increasing energy end-use efficiency, industrial environmental management, pollution prevention, and cleaner coal technology R&D. In the past fifteen years or so, few World Bank projects have targeted energy conservation and end-use efficiency management, despite a number of pre-investment activities, such as the Energy Sector Management Assistance Programme (ESMAP) supported by the bank and the UNDP. These trends have been consistent with the overall policy of the bank in energy lending in the 1980s, in which only about one per cent of the energy loans aimed to improve end-use efficiency (Philips 1990, p. 59). It was not until 1992 that China started receiving soft loans from the International Development Association (IDA) for environmental projects. The bank also did little to encourage private sector investment in energy conservation and the environment.

Clearly, energy conservation and environmental protection were largely absent in world Bank policy in the 1980s, and it only increased its concern in the late 1980s and the early 1990s. Therefter several investigations were conducted, for instance in rural industrial development and environmental protection countermeasures (1991), energy conservation in industrial sectors (1992) and urban environmental management (1993). Arguably, these were important areas of concern already in obvious need of investment in the early 1980s, and the delay reflects an inadequate response from the bank. This may lead to larger marginal costs in future investments, since clean-up measures cost more than prevention. However, these attempts can be seen as part of the bank's policy shifts to reflect its new interest, in support of sustainable development in developing countries.

Traditionally, the World Bank believes that much energy can be saved by building up new power plants equipped with modern technologies. This has been the basic logic behind the bank's lending for the construction of new electric power plants. However, according to a report of the bank, important shifts should be made towards greater lending for end-use efficiency (World Bank 1992b). To what extent the bank has changed its behaviour and attitudes is not yet clear. The following case-study suggests that the bank can make changes and compromises, if the recipient country strongly insists on its own proposals with solid and reasonable arguments.

Beijing Environmental Project

The idea of supporting a project to improve Beijing's environment was proposed by Lin Chonggen (a former resident representative of the World Bank) in 1988. It was also a part of the bank's effort to improve the environmental situation in six megacities in Asia. The Chinese government submitted a proposal in 1989, but owing to the 1989 Tiananmen event the project was not approved by the bank until 1991. The bank provided $154 million in loans to the project, under

an agreement of 1.3 billion yuan ($277 million) of co-financing (64 per cent of the total investment) from the Beijing municipal government.[14] The project began in 1992, and was to be completed by 1997. It consists of 13 sub-projects, including air and water pollution control, urban waste disposal and industrial pollution treatment.

Grants were given to a number of sub-projects that will have little short-term economic return, but have potentially large social benefits. One of these is the Beijing District Heating Systems Development, the objective of which is to reduce air pollution in the form of particulates and sulphur dioxode. This sub-project also has an implicit objective of energy-saving by eliminating coal consumption from the thousands of small coal-burning boilers in the local area, by providing heating for 10.2 million square metres in western Beijing using a co-generation power plant and installing pipelines to residential areas. In place of this Chinese proposal, the Bank proposed to increase coal-washing capacities for the boilers. The rational for the bank's proposal was that the project was not economically feasible, owing to the high costs of installing the pipelines. However, the Beijing government environmental officials insisted on their proposal, pointing out that the project could replace more than a thousand small boilers, and would save 380,000 tons of coal annually. It could reach two objectives: reducing air pollution, and conserving energy by cutting coal consumption so that it would be economically feasible in the long run.

After prolonged debates and negotiations, the two sides reached a compromise, in which the bank accepted the Chinese proposal, but insisted on a number of conditions. The main condition was to let the Beijing Heating Power Corporation become an independent business body operating under market mechanisms with increased energy prices and an independent management structure. This company was heavily subsidised by the local government (more than 100 million yuan per year) and had a budget deficit for years. Another condition was that an environmental master plan for Beijing municipality be made. The bank proposed to hire foreign consultants to help make the plan, but the Chinese insisted on hiring local experts. The main concern of the governmental officials was, of course, the high cost of the foreign consultants.[15] This sub-project has now been completed, with positive results. Air quality has improved, and annual savings of some 380,000 tons of coal have been made. In accordance with the agreement, the Beijing Heating Power Corporation now operates as an independent business enterprise, with a potential to reduce its deficit in the near future. As a result, the project satisfied both the bank and China with a win–win situation.

Conditionality is a common feature of World Bank loans. When an energy project is proposed, the bank's general strategy is to negotiate for energy price reform. Deregulation and decentralisation are also big concerns of the bank. However, because of the political and economic sensitivity of the issue, the Chinese government often perceives energy price increase as a risky issue that has to be viewed in a wider context than the energy sector. The hesitation to introduce a radical energy price reform sometimes leads to prolonged negotiations, although eventually the Chinese take steps to make compromises. To many officials, however, conditionality has been a matter for complaints.[16]

The Beijing Environmental Project financial arrangements have strong support from the Beijing municipal government, so it is less risky for the bank. Its success depends on the pre-established institutional framework for management of this multi-sectoral project, which has involved some high-level governmental officials. The incentives and disincentives set up by the government ensure the successful operation of the project. It is considered a good example of cooperation that has benefited both sides.

United Nations Development Programme

The UNDP has been a major institution in areas of technical cooperation in China. It started providing assistance in 1979, and has substantially increased its support over the last fifteen years. China has been able to mobilise the UNDP's resources successfully, and has now become its second-largest recipient. In the early 1990s, the UNDP made an important policy adjustment to reflect the environmental concerns highlighted at UNCED. It has been cooperating with the Chinese government to assess production and use of energy resources with respect to environmental protection (UNDP 1990, p. 8).[17] It has influence through three channels: project financing, foreign consultation and training of domestic experts. There have been a number of successful cases in energy conservation.[18]

Assistance on the environment is seen as an increasing part of the UNDP's overall strategy and mandate on development in China. One example is the operation of the GEF as a mechanism to influence China's response to global environmental problems, in which more efficient use of energy is stated as an important component.

For many Chinese officials, the UNDP's reputation is different from that of the World Bank, as it provides grants rather than loans for its technical assistance projects. Because of its official policy of non-conditionality in project support, the UNDP has acquired a softer and more generous image among officials and project managers. Some researchers have complained about the complexity of project applications to the bank, and prefer to apply for grants from the UNDP, which also has simpler procedures.[19] However, this situation is changing, as the bank has started providing more grants for capacity-building and institutional reform. The bank has also committed itself to improving efficiency and cost-effectiveness in project approval.

In recent years, the UNDP's activity has been restricted by financial constraints that have already affected activities in China.[20] Between 1991 and 1995, about 25 per cent of the budget was cut. This caused the rejection of several projects, including a proposal for energy conservation, which UNDP insisted was too technical and poorly designed. Some Chinese officials believe the UNDP's main interest is how to use its limited resources to influence high-level governmental decision-making.[21] In order to adjust its widespread involvement in almost every area of development assistance, the UNDP has decided to focus on three priorities: poverty reduction, economic reform and environmental protection, with the top priority given to poverty.

Agenda 21

The government has been active in the development of the Agenda 21 plans and projects, which were financially supported by the UNDP. Pushed by the Earth Summit, the SSTC has been instrumental in setting up the organisation framework: the Administrative Centre for China's Agenda 21. The SSTC organised a group of experts in 1994 to select 62 key projects from within hundreds of proposals submitted by various ministries, in preparation for the first International Round-Table Conference (July 1994).[22] The objective was to mobilise foreign aid resources to make these projects operational in the next ten years. Among the proposals, energy conservation and environmental protection held a high status in the agenda. The proposals included the development of a number of key coal-combustion technologies to be used in power generation, such as the integrated gasification combined cycle (IGCC), and the coal-fired pressurized fluidized bed combustion combined cycle (PFBC). These generated positive responses from various institutions in China, and attracted considerable attention internationally, which created a high profile for China. The UNDP sent a number of foreign experts to help select and revise project proposals. This was a case of a close cooperation between the UNDP and the SSTC. However, some Chinese experts have complained that the foreign consultants had little experience in energy technologies and energy-related issues in general. There were also comments on the high cost of foreign consultants, in comparison with the low payments to the domestic ones.[23]

The Agenda 21 project can be considered a case of window-dressing . It did not increase national capacity directly, but rather helped to raise positive responses from line ministries in matters related to sustainable development. It produced a high profile for China, and so also the UNDP, which put China in a better bargain position for future international aid inputs.

Global Environment Facility

In the last few years, the World Bank and the UNDP have made policy adjustments in an environmentally responsive direction, demonstrated in part by the operation of the GEF (Gan 1993a). The GEF is the first international collective effort to provide a mechanism to help reduce the contribution to global environmental risks from developing countries. Both the bank and the UNDP have devoted considerable effort to formulating their policies, and field staff have made substantial attempts to coordinate the projects. As a World Bank field officer once commented, they had put so much energy into the GEF that it took up the time they should have devoted to other projects.[24]

China has been actively involved since the establishment of the GEF in November 1990. The preparation of projects for GEF support was supported by the government, with the expectation that the GEF might become a much bigger source of capital for national environmental schemes. The National Environmental Protection Agency (NEPA) therefore put considerable effort into project preparation. As a result, China was among the first countries to submit proposals, which received no major critical comments in the approval process of the first-tranche projects.[25]

Together with a number of other projects, a \$2 million technical assistance project, the Greenhouse Gas Emissions Strategy Study, was approved in 1992. With the Chinese government's inputs of \$92,000, this project initiated a systematic and quantitative analysis of the issues and options related to greenhouse gas (GHG) emissions control (particularly CO_2 emissions) across sectors of the economy. The project consists of three components: (1) assessment of GHG emissions, analysis of abatement strategies, and formation of least-cost reduction options and their implications for economic growth and development; (2) improving the quality of coal supply and the efficiency of coal use in the most important coal production base, Shanxi province; (3) improving the efficiency of 400,000 industrial boilers.

This project received financial support from the UNDP, and was executed by the World Bank. It has tested the ability of the government in its response to the risks of global climate change. It has involved a large number of institutions, including various ministries, the SSTC, the Academy of Sciences, research universities, and industry. The implementing agency for the project is NEPA, which coordinates with other governmental agencies in project management and implementation. The project was well designed, but there were operational difficulties owing to coordination problems among involved governmental agencies, particularly between the NEPA and the SSTC, as both sides wanted to play a leading role.

Even though global climate change became a concern for the Chinese government before the GEF was involved, the GEF has had positive effects on China's policies. It has improved understanding of the issue, and generated positive responses in government institutions. It can be argued that without GEF support it would be difficult to initiate actions on such a scale from within domestic institutions, owing to financial constraints. However, most government officials do not fully understand the CO_2 emissions problem and it is valued below other more pressing problems such as poverty reduction, land degradation and industrial pollution control. In particular, poverty reduction has become a top priority in the ninth five-year plan (1996–2000).

The GEF project is a compensation arrangement that leads to assessment of options. It has contributed to capacity-building both in organisations and in human resources development. The operation of the project could be more effective were coordination and communications to be improved among domestic institutions.

Energy Sector Management Assistance Program

The ESMAP was established in 1983 by the World Bank and the UNDP, in cooperation with more than ten bilateral aid agencies. It provides an institutional framework for energy assessment and capacity-building. From its establishment, ESMAP has assisted developing countries in conducting feasibility studies and pre-investment operations on a wide variety of energy projects. About 20 per cent of these projects have targeted improving energy end-use efficiency. In the 1980s, about 30 loans amounting to $1 billion were committed to promoting energy end-use efficiency.

ESMAP has provided technical, institutional and policy advice to energy decision-makers and managers in China. Table 8.2 lists a number of projects supported by ESMAP, focused on rural energy issues. Although the World bank and the UNDP worked closely to co-

Table 8.2   ESMAP Supported Energy Projects in China (in thousands of US dollars)

Year	Project	Amount
1988	Rural Energy Training and Technical Assistance	763.0
1988	Planning and Management of Small Power Companies	n.a.
1989	Fuelwood Forestry Pre-investment Study	354.0
1989	Training and Technical Assistance for Rural Energy Planning	245.0
1989	Country-level Rural Energy Assessment	n.a.
1989	Fuelwood Development and Conservation in Hunan	526.0
1992	Power Efficiency Pilot Study	n.a.
1992	Energy Conservation and Pollution Control	414.0
1994	Energy Efficiency and Pollution Control in Township Enterprises	142.0

n.a. = not available.

ordinate the ESMAP projects, the Bank has a larger institutional and financial capacity and this has made the UNDP subordinate. Lack of involvement from non-governmental organizations (NGOs) has been a problem.[26] Also the scientific community has been loosely involved and has received little support. With its pre-established relationship with the government, ESMAP adopted a top-down approach to projects, and this weakened its linkages to local participants and networks.

ESMAP's energy conservation effort in rural areas attemps to reduce energy shortage and local environmental problems. The Bank has shown an interest in increasing its lending for energy conservation, and it is currently in the stage of identifying areas for intervention. But it is still trapped by its traditional supply-oriented vision and cost-benefit analysis procedures. By contrast, the UNDP is limited by its budgetary constraints and extensive mandates. It is also handicapped by its lack of in-house capacity to appraise multi-sectoral projects.

These elements are important for understanding why the results of the ESMAP operation have had marginal effects in mobilising large-scale investment from both agencies. It is an intermediate arrangement in search of further solutions: to generate larger investment projects. It has been less successful in this regard, owing to institutional barriers in the bank and the UNDP, which either have less interest or else are unable to provide support (Gan 1993b).

Effects of project operation

There are several effects of international aid in China: changing norms and rules, helping establish new mechanisms, bringing structural change to institutions, mobilising domestic resources, assisting human resources development and capacity-building. In addition, aid has contributed to the development of an international tender system for new projects, which did not exist before the 1980s. It has also helped to establish a national tender system in project management, especially for projects supported by the World Bank. One obstacle to promoting energy conservation is the lack of proper regulatory mechanisms, such as the air pollution prevention law, and the emissions standards for industrial boilers. International aid has so far had little effect on this.

There is a knowledge barrier among foreign consultants working in China. Some economists frequently overestimate the development potential in China, without counting the costs of externalities. Many foreign consultants have limited knowledge of the country, or of the overlapping, sometimes conflicting, relationships of its institutions and governmental organisations. Some Chinese officials and energy experts commented that they had to 'teach' foreign consultants about the situation they were to work on before consultation started.[27] In addition, many officials within aid agencies still have limited knowledge about how to incorporate environmental accounting into cost–benefit analysis. This has led to their reluctance to finance projects that have indirect economic returns.

Cultural barriers mean that many aid agencies have difficulty understanding Chinese ways of thinking, reasoning, negotiating, and bargaining. Some also feel confused about the working of organisational structures, and the interest of their counterparts. One UNDP staff member commented that they (i.e., UNDP staff) felt puzzled having a dozen organisations claiming responsibilities for energy conservation and environmental protection. They also had difficulty figuring out which organisation was the most appropriate partner to work with.[28] A better understanding of the institutional discourse – culture, attitudes, interests and power relations – may contribute to a more effective utilisation of aid resources. It would also help to establish a better relationship between aid agencies and their governmental counterparts.

The problem of coordination is critical for ensuring effective project operation. The SSTC has wanted to establish a stronger relationship with the UNDP for a long time, but has been limited by the existing bureaucratic structure and the established rules. The China International Centre for Economic and Technical Exchange has acted as the main counterpart of the UNDP for more than a decade, but their relationship seems to have been overshadowed by dissatisfaction. The main question is how international aid agencies can avoid being affected by the power struggles between domestic institutions and at the same time be able to pursue their objectives effectively through establishing trusting relationships with their counterparts.

Time-lag is a critical factor affecting the effectiveness of project implementation. In the World Bank, it generally requires two to two and a half years to get a project approved and make it operational. According to some project officers in China, the bank's procedure is too complicated to allow a shorter time-span. This affects the entire project cycle, because of increased transaction costs (Picciotto and Weaving 1994, pp. 42–4).[29]

One characteristics of the aid operation in China is the lack of support for NGOs. However, their influence in decision-making as well as in grassroots movements has been increasing in recent years. One case is the China Energy Research Society; which has been influential in energy policy, particularly for energy conservation. Another example is the Friends of Nature, a new NGO devoted to environmental education in Beijing, which has been seeking financial support abroad for its activities. However, owing to the structural constraints and lack of information and proper channel, these NGOs have difficulties applying for funding from multilateral aid agencies.

Generally, international organisations tend to build up their operational capacity and governance in close collaboration with governmental organisations. It is not uncommon for them to ignore the need and importance of NGO's involvement, particularly at the local level where project operation often affects the everyday livelihood of local inhabitants. Traditional project operation is usually conducted in a top-down approach, which may not be successful, or cost-effective, because of the lack of local support.

Another issue is the cost of foreign consultation, which is some 13 times higher than that of employing Chinese nationals (US$13,000 as against US$1000 per person per month). There have been complaints from some senior managers and experts that international consultants absorb too large a share of project resources. They argue that China already has sufficient expertise. However, some field officers in the World Bank and the UNDP, including some international consultants, tend to disagree with such an argument. They insist that the lack of properly trained personnel is the main reason for hiring high-cost foreign consultants, which is part of the capacity-building process.[30] It is a fact that many officials and professionals in China have had difficulties writing qualified project proposals for international aid, owing to their lack of knowledge in application procedures and the language barrier, according to a senior officer from the SSTC.[31]

Conclusions

The World Bank has played a limited role through its portfolio policy in supporting energy conservation and the environment in China. It still favours development that is supply-oriented rather than end-use-efficient. Its behaviour is very much affected by the use of the established cost–benefit analyses that usually exclude environmental externalities in project appraisal. Although recent policy changes have given energy conservation and the environment a higher priority, much greater changes are still anticipated, because the bank has a strong capacity to adapt to new challenges. It is very likely that the contradictions between production and conservation in the bank's policy will continue in the foreseeable future.

Compared with the bank, the UNDP is less capable of giving energy conservation stronger support, as the issue is only considered as one component of its many areas of interest. The UNDP is also limited by its financial resources. To a large extent, the UNDP's ability to adapt to new development challenges depends largely on the improvement of the knowledge capacities of its staff members and of its operational efficiency. To reduce costs in project operation is also a key factor, as a lot of resources are wasted owing to management problems.[32] The same is true for environmental issuesl, where considerable changes are needed to strengthen UNDP's ability to manage cross-sectoral projects.

In national capacity-building, the World Bank and the UNDP each have a different emphasis. The UNDP tends to have a long-term perspective, based on training and institutional development, while the bank is more concerned with short to medium-term objectives (through three-year rolling plans). International aid has given inadequate attention to strengthening the lending capacity of major banks in China in the public-goods sector. This might be seen as an important area for future policy intervention, as the Chinese government has proposed. In addition, new mechanisms could be established to encourage the involvement of NGOs in energy conservation and environmental protection at the local level.

In the cases discussed in this chapter, financial resources were used as specified in project design and implementation. All transfer arrangements produced positive results (some sub-projects are still under operation). However, some projects have led to unexpected, or hidden, side-effects. The Fuelwood Development and Conservation Project (1989) generated a new set of problems, because increasing coal supply as a substitute for fuelwood might lead to increased air pollution. The Urban Waste Disposal sub-project within the Beijing Environment

Project may lead to increased methane (CH_4) emissions, and methane is an important greenhouse gas.

The degree of consensus between the aid agencies has been increasing, as project operation demands more cooperation and cross-sectoral arrangements. There is a need to improve the coordinating capacity of the organisations involved. Reducing the communication gap is crucial, not only between donor and recipient countries, but also among domestic organisations involved in project implementation. The standard appraisal criteria tend to exclude the potential environmental benefits of projects, such as health improvements and reduced property damage.

The Chinese experiences demonstrate that international transfer of resources cannot be cost-effective unless it is operated in a nation-state system with strong institutional frameworks and management competence. Cooperative and effective dialogue between agency and recipient is an important factor for ensuring project success. This requires future aid activities to strengthen institutional capacity-building and human resources development.

Official development assistance is currently in the state of transition, from a donor-centred to a demand-oriented approach. Financial flows for sustainable energy management and the environment are expected to increase in scale. Institutional inertia generated by a variety of constraints has resulted in a weakened support for energy conservation and environmental protection in developing countries. The traditional mode of aid flows, aiming to satisfy governmental demands, has inherent limitations in improving operational efficiency. In many instances, traditional project cycles are incapable of dealing with new challenges and societal demands. Therefore, efforts should be made to encourage reform in project design, selection, appraisal and implementation. Post-project evaluation also needs to be improved within international aid agencies, which should help build up more dialogue with local participants. More important, a cooperative approach should be undertaken to improve communications between aid agencies and recipient countries, which is vital for effectively implementing international agreements for environmentally sustainable development.

Notes

1. This research was performed under a grant from the Swedish Council for Planning and Coordination of Research (FRN) in 1994–96. Its support is gratefully acknowledged.

2. The World Bank refers to the combination of the International Bank for Reconstruction and Development (IBRD) and the International Development Association (IDA).
3. There had been different estimates between 1980s and 1990s, concerning the costs of environmental pollution. According to Dr Qu Geping, the economic costs due to environmental pollution accounted for 69 billion yuan and ecological deterioration accounted for 26 billion yuan annually which was about 14 per cent of the GNP in the early 1980s (see Qu 1989, p. 147). The economic damage caused by environmental pollution (air, water, industrial waster and pesticide pollution) was estimated at around 95 billion yuan ($11.5 billion) annually, which accounted for 6.8 per cent of the GNP in the early 1990s. See Qu (1992, p. 47).
4. Clean technology is conceived as a preventive measure for reducing the environmental risks of production processes and products at the source. According to a definition by the European Community, clean technology is: 'any technical measures taken in the various industries to reduce, or even eliminate at source, the production of any nuisance, pollution or waste, and to help save raw materials, natural resources and energy ... clean technology can be introduced either at the design stage with radical changes in the manufacturing process or into an existing process with separation and utilization of secondary products that would otherwise be lost.' (*Official Journal of the European Communities*, no. C100/2, 20 April 1985).
5. In 1988, the energy industry consumed 12 per cent of the total energy and emitted 25 per cent of the pollution nationwide.
6. The issue of energy price reform is more complicated, owing to historical and structural problems. For discussions on the energy price reform, see: World Bank (1993b, pp. 65–67); Ministry of Energy (1992, p. 373). Recently, some local governments such as Beijing is has increased fuel prices, mainly aiming at reducing the deficit of the envergy industry (*China Environmental Reporter*, vol. 1, no. 1, 1997)
7. See Chapter 7. The dam is expected to generate around 18,000 megawatts of electricity, enough to supply the power needs of 150 million Chinese. See *China Energy Digest*, 11 October 1992. There are currently two nuclear power stations under operation and more will be built up in the next 10 to 15 years. See *People's Daily*, 29 March 1991, p. 3.
8. The choice of the Chinese government has been in favour of huge supply-oriented projects, such as the Three Gorges Dam project.
9. In 1995, public investment in China was 1082 billion yuan ($130 billion). In comparison, the World Bank provides about $1.5 billion in loans to China per year.
10. A major study supported by the Earth Council has been undertaken to investigate why sustainable energy development (energy conservation, and new and renewable energy development) is not taking a faster pace in the developing world, and its relationship with multilateral and bilateral aid agencies.
11. 'End use' refers to the last device or group of devices in a chain of processes, aimed at delivering an energy service. 'Energy end-use technologies' are the set of technologies providing services at the final stage of energy use or consumption, such as motive power, lighting, process heat, water heating, refrigeration, air cooling, cooking, and so on.

12. The World Bank has completed a study to identify the potential for energy conservation in China, and the issues and options for the Bank's investment opportunities in the future. See World Bank (1993b); Siddayao (1993).

13. Of the total of $14.2 billion in loans from the International Bank for Reconstruction and Development (IBRD), China borrowed $2.2 billion. Out of the credits from the International Development Association (IDA) totaling $6.6 billion, China borrowed $0.93 billion.

14. This includes a grant of 709 million yuan from the Beijing Municipal Government, a loan of 187 million yuan from domestic banks, and 379 million yuan self-financed by corresponding companies and organisations.

15. The costs of foreign consultants are more than 10 times higher than that for local experts. Local experts are often inadequately paid for their work, as indicated in the preparation process for China's Agenda 21 projects supported by the UNDP, according to comments from a Chinese expert.

16. Interviews by the author with some officials and project managers in the Ministry of Finance in 1994.

17. An international workshop on 'The Control of Environmental Protection' was held in 1990, jointly organized by the SSTC and UNDP. Coal washing was recommended as a priority area for financial support.

18. An example is the 'Modernization of 200 MW Fossil Fuel Power Generating Unit' project (1987–94), which may lead to sizeable economic and environmental benefits. For this UNDP provided a grant of $1.9 million, together with a co-financing arrangement of $50,000 from the Chinese government.

19. Based on an informal discussion with a staff member from the National Research Centre for Science and Technology for Development (NRCSTD), at the SSTC in 1995.

20. This situation is further affected by the worsening budgetary situation in Official Development Assistance (*International Herald Tribune*, 9 February 1995). According to an OECD report, in 1993 aid from industrialised countries to the developing world fell to its lowest level in two decades. It was reported that stagnant aid budgets could trigger a 'vicious circle' of inadequate development aid.

21. Interview with a governmental official in Beijing in 1994.

22. The Second International Round-Table Conference for Agenda 21 was held in Beijing in July 1996. This is an effort to strengthen the operation of key national priority projects. The main objective of the conference was to attract more foreign aid and investment.

23. A Chinese consultant involved in project consultation received only about 400 yuan ($47) for a whole month of work. By contrast, foreign consultants received about $350 per day, excluding travelling and hotel expenses.

24. From a discussion with a World Bank officer in Beijing in early 1992.

25. Interview with a World Bank staff member in October, 1991.

26. The NGO sector is small but growing, involved with a wide range of activities. However, most are active in education, scientific, and leisure activities, with very few advocate-oriented NGOs, owing to the control of the totalitarian regime.

27. Interview conducted by the author in Beijing in April 1994.

28. From discussion with a UNDP staff member in Beijing in March 1994.

29. A new project cycle has been introduced in the bank which has simplified project procedure.

30. Based on interviews during a field trip to China in February 1992.
31. From discussion with a staff member of the SSTC in October 1995.
32. According to comments from a senior staff member from the National Research Institute for S&T for Development, at the SSTC.

References

China Foreign Economic Statistics: 1979–1991 (1993) (Beijing: China Statistical Information and Consultant Service Centre).

Gan, Lin (1990) 'Global Warming and Options for China: Energy and Environmental Policy Profile', WP-90-52 (Laxenburg: IIASA).

Gan, Lin (1993a) 'The Making of the Global Environment Facility: An Actor's Perspective', in *Global Environmental Change: Human and Policy Dimensions*, 3, (3).

Gan, Lin (1993b) 'Global Environmental Policy and the World Bank: A System in Transition?', in *Project Appraisal*, 8 (4), December.

Gan, Lin (1995) 'Energy Conservation as a Megapolicy: The Case of China', in: J. D. Montgomery and D. A. Rondinelli (eds.) *Great Policies: Strategic Innovation in Asia and the Pacific* (Westport, CT: Praeger).

Jia, Hao and Lin, Zhimin (eds) (1994), *The Changing Central–Local Relations in China: Reform and State Capacity* (New York: Westview).

Levine, Mark D. and Meyers, Stephen (1992) 'The Contribution of Energy Efficiency to Sustainable Development in Developing Countries', in *Natural Resources Forum*, 16, (1) February.

Liu, Xueyi, *et al.* (eds) (1993) *Collection of the Joint Research on Energy and Environmental: Japan and China* (Beijing: Geology Publishing Company).

Luo, Qing and Ning, Jinbiao (eds) (1993) *Operational Guidelines for the World Bank Lending* (Beijing: China Financial and Economic Press).

The Ministry of Energy (1992) *Collection of Energy Policy Research, vol. 2* (Beijing: Ministry of Energy).

NEPA (1992) *China Environment Yearbook, 1992* (Beijing: China Environmental Science Press).

Philips, Michael (1990) *Alternative Roles for the Energy Sector Management Assistance Program in End-Use Energy Efficiency* (Washington, DC: International Institute for Energy Conservation).

Picciotto, Robert and Weaving, Rachel (1994) 'A New Project Cycle for the World Bank?', in *Finance & Development*, 31 (4).

Qu Geping (1989) *Zhongguo de Huanjing Guanli* (Environmental Management in China) (Beijing: China Environmental Science Press).

Qu Geping (1992) *Environment and Development in China* (Beijing: China Environmental Science Press).

Schipper, Lee and Meyers, Stephen *et al.* (1992) *World Energy: Building A Sustainable Future* (Stockholm: Stockholm Environment Institute).

Siddayao, C. M. (1993) *Energy Investments and the Environment: Selected Topics* (Washington, DC: World Bank).

Sinton, Jonathan *et al.* (eds.) (1996) *China Energy Databook* (Berkeley: Ernest Orlando Lawrence Berkeley National Laboratory).

State Planning Commission (SPC) *et al.* (1993a) *Environmental Problems in Energy Development Project in China* (Beijing: China Construction Industry Press).

State Planning Commission (SPC) (1993b) *Energy Conservation in China* (Beijing: State Planning Commission).

SSTC (1993) *China Science and Technology Indicators, 1992,* S & T Yellow Book, No. 1 (Beijing: Science Press).

SSTC (1994) *China's Agenda 21: The White Paper of Population, Environment and Development in China in the 21st Century* (Beijing: China Environmental Science Press).

SSTC and SPC (1994) *China Environmental Protection Action Plan (1991–2000)* (Beijing: China Environmental Science Press).

State Statistics Bureau (1994) *China Development Report (1993)* (Beijing: China Statistics Press).

UNDP (1990) 'Prevention and Control of Environmental Pollution in China, 1990', Report of the International Workshop on the Control of Environmental Pollution in China (Beijing: UNDP).

Wang, Shaogang and Hu, Angang (1993) *China National Capacity Report* (Shenyang: Liaoning People's Press) (in Chinese).

World Bank (1992a) *World Development Report: Development and the Environment, 1992* (Washington, DC).

World Bank (1992b) *Energy Efficiency and Conservation in the Developing World: The World Bank's Role* (Washington, DC).

World Bank (1993) China: Energy Conservation Study, Report No. 10813-CHA (Washington, DC).

World Bank (1996) *World Development Report 1996: From Plan to Market* (Washington, DC).

Yan, Changle (ed.) (1994) *China Energy Development Report* (Beijing: Economic Management Press).

Zhao, Zongci *et al.* (1992) *Greenhouse Gas Effects and Global Climate Change: Impact to China* (Gland, Switzerland: WWF International).

9
Urban Transport in China: Whither the Bicycle?

Andrew Spencer

The bicycle is to China what the car is to America. For many visitors, that is part of the country's attraction; as compared with other Asian countries, Chinese cities appear to offer (almost literally) a breath of fresh air:

> Tianjin, a city of 8.5 million, devotes a meagre 4.8 per cent of its land area to streets and roads. It is experiencing explosive growth with industrial output, housing supply and the bus fleet all increasing by 70 per cent between 1980 and 1988. Most megacities experiencing such conditions would exhibit massive traffic congestion, major transport related air pollution problems, high traffic accident rates, and high transportation investment and operations costs ... Tianjin, which relies on non-motorised vehicles for four out of ten person-trips, instead has high mobility, few traffic congestion problems, very low traffic accident rates, very low public and personal cash expenditures with only modest time expenditures for transport. (Thornhill 1991, quoted by Replogle 1992, p. 20)

Replogle (1992, p. xiii) credits China with having developed 'the most resource efficient urban mobility systems in the world'.

All the same, motor traffic and congestion are growing and nobody who walks along Shanghai's Nanjing Road will be under any illusions about that city's transport problems. China stands not so much at a crossroads as at a T-junction: having approached by way of the bicycle, the diverging arms beckon to mass motorisation on one hand and mass transit on the other. How far down any of the roads must, or can, China travel? This chapter attempts to highlight some of the challenges.

Trends in bicycle and private vehicle ownership

Table 9.1 shows that in 1988 China had on average 272 bicycles per thousand population. While below the level for the industrialised countries shown here, it is well above those for other developing countries. Conversely, it lags behind other Asian countries in ownership of motor vehicles. An expansion of cycle production during the 1950s, the provision of travel allowances for workers in state enterprises even if they cycled (Wang 1989) and the creation of cycle lanes on many urban roads (Replogle 1992, p. 42) all encouraged its use. Policies of social equity and a drive to conserve oil supplies also encouraged its wider adoption.

The economic reforms and associated rising average incomes have been an additional spur to ownership, in both urban and rural areas. In 1978, every hundred urban households owned on average 102 cycles, and this had risen to 188 by 1990. The figures for rural areas was from only 30 per hundred households to 118 (Zhang 1992, table 2). Between 1980 and 1990 the number of bicycles in Guangzhou rose by 157 per cent; as a result three-quarters of the city's population have a bicycle. Similar trends can be seen in the municipalities of Beijing, Shanghai and Tianjin.

The changing demand for bicycles has been documented by Zhang (1992), who suggests three main determinants: employment, income levels and price. Employment status has changed rapidly, particularly in rural areas where the setting up of new township industries has increased the need to commute. Incomes have also risen rapidly and

Table 9.1   Bicycle and motor vehicle ownership in selected countries

Country	Year	Bicycles/000 pop.	Motors/000 pop.
China	1988	271.7	1.1
India	1985	58.8	2.0
Indonesia	1985	100.0	9.0[a]
South Korea	1982	153.8	14.0[a]
Thailand	1982	51.0	8.2
Malaysia	1982	178.6	64.3
Japan	1988	491.8	251.6
Netherlands	1985	785.7	350.0
USA	1988	420.4	567.3

[a] 1981 figure
Source: Computed from Replogle (1992, table 1.1); Sinha *et al.* (1990).

bicycles are readily affordable. Prices were for a long time around 160 yuan (currently US$19), and even before the urban reforms began a worker could save this sum over a year or two. The lifting of bicycle taxes in the 1970s also helped. Although average prices had climbed to 213 yuan (currently US$26) by 1987, the increase was well below the rise in incomes over the same period.

Zhang further describes how for a long time the supply of bicycles lagged behind demand; indeed, from 1973 they were rationed. From 1979, however, a new policy emphasis on light manufacturing and an easing of restrictions on raising capital made bicycle manufacture particularly attractive to local governments. It held out the prospect of high profits, and was labour-intensive. Numerous small factories sprang up, many of them producing poor-quality products. Despite rising demand, the shortage became a glut and between 1983 and 1986 the government ended rationing, relaxed price controls and took some steps to regulate quality. This led to a shakeout of producers, and ended a black market that could almost double the price of major brands. Greater exposure to competition required those remaining to promote their products more aggressively.

But at the same time as universal adult ownership of bicycles is approaching reality, a new yet familiar trend is becoming apparent. Table 9.2 makes it clear that in Guangzhou (Canton) motorcycle and car ownership, though still in their infancy, are rising fast. In the first half of 1996 production of bicycles fell by 24 per cent nationally compared with the previous year; much of this fall was attributed to the growing popularity of light motorcycles (Anon 1996a). A survey of cyclists in central Shanghai has suggested that 64 per cent of them would like to own a motorcycle despite the much higher cost (Yan and Zheng 1994). The drive for personal mechanised transport, whatever

Table 9.2   Bicycles and motor vehicles per 1000 population in Guangzhou, 1980–90

Year	Bicycles	Cars[a]	Motorcycles	Other motor vehicles
1980	346.5	2.0	1.2	5.0
1990	741.4	7.5	43.8	16.2
Percentage change, 1980–90	114.0	275.0	3550.0	224.0

[a] Includes cars, taxis, vans and minibuses.
Sources: Computed from Thomas *et al.* (1992, table 2 and p. 21).

its underlying cause, appears to all intents and purposes to be universal, and China's cities are unlikely to be any exception.

For the moment, institutional factors are holding these trends in check. Most city governments are restricting the issue of motorcycle licences because of concerns about fuel consumption and safety. Guangzhou allows 6000 new licences per year (Thomas *et al.* 1992), while Shanghai's annual quota is less than 1000 (Xu and Yu 1996). Cars, light vans and minibuses are usually owned by work units and access to them is a matter of privilege. A 1990 survey in Beijing suggested that only a quarter of motor vehicle movements involved cars and 80 per cent of these were based on work units, mostly for business trips (MVA Consultancy 1993, table 3.4). The typical car or van driver travels to work by cycle or bus and only then takes out the vehicle, incidentally spreading and flattening the morning traffic peak.

Pressure for change is coming, however. The China Automobile Industry Corporation expects demand for motor vehicles to rise by 8 to 9 per cent between 1996 and 2010, by which time China could be one of the world's three biggest markets. The government regards the development of a motor vehicle industry as a 'pillar' of its national economy and an automobile industry policy, set out in July 1994, stipulates that China should encourage private car ownership with the mass production of economy-class models. The strategic importance of this is shown by the intention to limit foreign investment to carefully designated sectors of the industry, and to establish technical and design centres (Huang 1995). It is the prospect of (government-sanctioned) mass private motoring that makes the need for appropriate urban transport policies all the more pressing.

Bicycle use

Table 9.3 gives an indication for various cities, with cycle use accounting for up to 53 per cent of all trips. By comparison, in Yogyakarta, Indonesia's 'bicycle city', 23.5 per cent of trips in 1976 were by bicycle and 15.5 per cent by motorcycle (Kartodirdjo 1981, p. 111). Only in Dalian and Chongqing (a very hilly city) is public transport more important than cycling.

Smaller cities might be expected to be more conducive to cycling than larger ones. But although the median figures bear this out the relationship is certainly not fixed. Just as significant as size is urban form: cities dependent on cycling tend to be compact, polycentric and with mixed land use (Replogle 1992, p. 42). Zibo fits into this category:

Table 9.3   Median modal splits in selected cities in China (percentages)

Population	Walk	Bicycle	Public transport	Other[a]
Over 2 million	37.40	35.20	19.20	4.10
1 to 2 million	35.90	45.50	14.70	3.45
Under 1 million	38.20	53.25	4.35	2.40

[a] Includes motor vehicles.
Note: The median percentages in a row do not add up to 100.
Source: Computed from cities tabulated by Mei *et al.* (1994, table 1).

it is a loose agglomeration of five towns spread up to 20 kilometres away from their geographical centre. Tianjin is of particular interest. On the one hand it is compact enough for most homes to be within 5.4 kilometres of workplaces: a comfortable 25 minutes' cycling time. On the other hand, central area redevelopment and the building of new housing further out have made walking to work less attractive. Buses are both infrequent and overcrowded. As a result, Tianjin has come to be regarded as the most cycle-dependent large city in China (Ren and Koike, 1993).

The bicycle is first and foremost a means of travelling to work. Sixty-two per cent of work trips by Beijing residents are by bicycle, compared with only 39 to 45 per cent of other home-based trips (MVA Consultancy 1993, table 3.1). In a smaller city like Changchun the proportions are 51 per cent for work and 8 to 28 per cent for other purposes (Yang *et al.* 1990, table 4). In both cities walking tends to dominate for non-work trips, either because they are shorter or because the main income earners appropriate the cycles for commuting and the rest of the household have to manage without. Despite what this may imply, women use bicycles almost as much as men do. Women form a substantial proportion of the workforce and China seems to be largely free of prejudices against women cycling. Nor is there any major social or class stigma; although the highest income groups tend not to cycle, a survey in the fairly small city of Baoding showed that whereas 14.7 per cent of respondents regarded cycling as a low status mode, 6.7 per cent saw it as high-status (Tanaboriboon and Ying 1994; Kubota and Kidokoro 1994).

As with ownership, bicycle use is rising. Not surprisingly, Shanghai and Guangzhou (Tables 9.4 and 9.5) also show a rise in the use of personal motorised modes (concealed in 'other' in Table 9.4). The trend in

Table 9.4   Trends in vehicular modal split, Shanghai urban area, 1981–91 (percentages)

Year	Bicycle	Bus	Other
1981	30.5	67.7	1.8
1986	40.3	58.2	1.5
1991	43.9	53.8	2.3

Source: *Cai* (1996, table 2).

public transport use is less clear, though Shanghai seems to be exhibiting a steady decline. Interestingly, figures for Beijing (MVA Consultancy 1993, tables 3.1, 3.2) suggest that bicycle use by 'floating' populations is far lower than among permanent residents, and that their use of public transport and taxis is correspondingly higher.

Bicycles represent an admirable solution to most people's travel needs, particularly in smaller cities (Shimazaki and Yang 1992). They can easily negotiate the often extensive narrow lanes or *hutong* that serve the older residential areas. Even in larger cities, the attraction of public transport is often reduced by congestion. A survey by Beijing Public Transport Corporation in 1986 found that door-to-door journey speeds by bicycle were almost double those by bus (16.3 kilometres per hour as against 8.7). Lack of investment and the poor traffic conditions have meant that many bus fleets are unable to keep pace with the growing demand for travel, leading to long boarding times, overcrowding and the familiar vicious circle of declining patronage and worsening service (Jones 1991).

Trends in travel demand

As economic transformation proceeds, so the demand for urban transport is evolving. The sheer physical growth of cities means a rise not only in the number of people travelling but also the length of their journeys. These impacts, daunting enough in themselves, are being accentuated by at least two further changes: in urban land use patterns and in personal lifestyles (see for instance the growth of motorcycle use in Guangzhou – Table 9.5). The first of these is worth considering more closely.

The traditional Chinese city was compact and displayed a mixed pattern of land uses. Following liberation in 1949, most businesses

Table 9.5   Trends in modal split, Guangzhou, 1984–92 (percentages)

Year	Walk	Bicycle	Bus	Car/taxi	Motor cycle
1984	40.9	30.6	21.2	6.9	0.4
1989	36.5	30.6	21.0	10.6	1.3
1992	30.6	33.8	21.8	7.5	6.3

Note: Based on origin–destination surveys in 1984 and 1992 and estimates for 1989 based on vehicle registration data. Trips by ferryboat are excluded.
Source: Computed from Thomas *et al.* (1992, table 1); Zhou and Frame (1994).

were transferred to public ownership. This often meant their removal from shopfronts lining the streets to office or factory complexes. As Leeming (1993, p.136) remarks, this meant that city streets became purely arteries of movement, rather than locales for petty trading as in other developing countries. Much of the responsibility for providing housing was borne by work units, particularly from the early 1970s onward. While it was commonly built within the unit's own compound this was not always possible and a suburban location might be used instead (MVA Consultancy 1993, paragraph 2.4.2). It was always intended that residential areas should provide a range of communal facilities such as schools, health centres, markets and shops (Wang 1992; Chiu 1994). Although some workers might have to commute, the idea (however hard to realise in practice) was that residential areas should be more or less self-contained.

Since the reforms three factors in particular have been at work. One has been the wider range of opportunities for businesses and commerce. A second has been the more or less planned creation of satellite cities such as Pudong, across the Huangpu River from Shanghai, and Henan/Panyu, across the Pearl River from Guangzhou. A third, more long-term in its impacts, is the fostering of an urban land market. In the past, urban land was allocated to work units in perpetuity, at no charge. Since 1990, most land use rights have been made transferable for payment, and over the next 20 to 30 years it is envisaged that all eligible urban land will have been transferred to 'paid land use' (Zhou *et al.* 1993). The result is likely to be a gradual sorting of land uses, with inner-city manufacturing premises cashing in on their assets and moving to peripheral zones where more modern factories can be built, their place being taken by the conventional gamut of high-rent-paying central-business-district activities.

In Beijing, for instance, it is proposed to develop several perpheral residential areas, to remove manufacturing industries to the suburbs, to

Table 9.6 Projected population and employment change in Beijing, 1992–2010 (percentages)

	Population	Employment
Four inner districts	–20.3	+0.4
Four outer districts	+34.5	+46.3
Whole urban area (eight districts)	+14.9	+26.7
(including floating population)	+24.2	—

Source: Computed from MVA Consultancy (1993, tables 2.3, 2.4, 2.6).

redevelop several areas in the central city for commercial, shopping and entertainment uses, and to create separate business nodes both to the east and around the new railway station in the west (MVA Consultancy 1993, paragraph 2.4.4). Table 9.6 summarises the projected changes in the distribution of population and jobs up to 2010 and underlines how the city is increasingly reflecting worldwide trends. In the much smaller city of Ningbo (population 430,000) a similar process can be observed:

> [s]ingle-function zones are apparently being adopted ... Ningbo plans to redevelop existing central commercial space (after this function's relocation to less-travelled streets) into a financial and administrative centre along the lines of 'downtowns' in Western cities. (Jamieson and Naylor 1992, p. 35)

Some estimates of how these changes may affect travel patterns have been offered by the Beijing Transport Planning Study (MVA Consultancy 1993). Travel is forecast to rise from 1.19 trips daily per capita in 1992 to 1.68 in 2010. Most of this increase will consist of non-work trips fuelled by rising incomes and growing opportunities for private consumption, whether of housing, consumer goods or leisure and cultural activities. It must be stressed that the study was a modelling exercise, not a detailed behavioural analysis, but the projected trip rates are similar to past trends in Hong Kong. Interestingly, Beijing's forecast trip rate for 2010 will still be below the current rate in Hong Kong, implying that there is still enormous potential for further growth. Although the report gives no estimates for overall trip lengths, the average length of public transport trips is forecast to grow from 10.6 kilometres in 1992 to 11.5 in 2010 (ibid., table 4.8).

Table 9.7 shows the projected change in transport modes over the same period. Note that the study modelled only the effect on modal

Table 9.7   Daily vehicular trips in Beijing by mode, 1992 and 2010

	1992		2010	
	Trips (000)	*%*	*Trips (000)*	*%*
Bicycle	3 921	47.7	5 331	40.9
Public transport	3 334	40.6	5 210	40.0
Other motor vehicles	965	11.7	2 488	19.1
All modes	8 220	100.0	13 029	100.0

Source: Computed from MVA Consultancy (1993, table 4.2).

split of changes in vehicle ownership (whether bicycles or motorised); it took no account of whether public transport improvements, such as new subway lines, might themselves be able to attract passengers away from private modes. Although this imparts a slightly conservative bias, it is significant that the proportion of trips by public transport is expected to change very little. Motor vehicle trips, on the other hand, are forecast to gain ground at the expense of the bicycle (even though in absolute terms the number of bicycle trips will increase by over a third).

The implications are clear. Even in Beijing, a city with many wide streets, considerable lengths of road will be carrying volumes above their capacities in peak periods by the year 2000, while the average speeds of motor vehicles will fall from 30.5 to an estimated 22.5 kilometres per hour between 1992 and 2010. Already long tailbacks are occurring at many junctions. Some of the most severe impacts will be on local access and distributor roads, particularly in the central area (ibid., paragraphs 4.3.7–10). Hamer (1993) asserts that in most cities the land area currently occupied by roads will need to be doubled. In the foreseeable future this will be almost impossible to achieve, leading to the prospect of development running ahead of transport infrastructure and overloading it, increasing the difficulties of travel. Some of the difficulties, and some associated environmental problems, are described in the next section.

Bicycles and urban transport problems

China's urban transport problems follow an oft-repeated litany. Congestion is all-pervasive. Buses in central Shanghai average 10 kilometres per hour compared with 25 in the suburbs (Armstrong-Wright 1993). On one of Beijing's widest streets, Chang'an Avenue, the average speed of motor vehicles has fallen from 35 kilometres per hour in 1959 to 25 in 1980 (Yang 1985). It is easy to blame much of this on the bicycles: after all, they occupy a great deal of roadspace. A World Bank study of non-motorised transport in ten Asian cities estimated that whereas buses could carry 2700 passengers per hour per lane in mixed traffic, bicycles could carry only 1330 (Kuranami *et al.* 1994). At junctions bicycles can cause obstructions, either as they start away from the green light in massed formation or as they make left turns across the lines of traffic, commonly waiting in the middle of the junction for a clear path (Wang and Wei 1993). On the sections between junctions on a road with two lanes in each direction, as the volume of cyclists increases they overflow out of the nearside lane, which they usually occupy, and come into conflict with motorised vehicles. A regression analysis suggested that a volume of 1750 bicycles per hour would reduce motor vehicle speeds by about 6 kilometres per hour (Zhou and Akatsuka 1994).

But arguably this is a very modest impact for a flow of nearly thirty bicycles per minute! Research by Guo (1996) suggests that cycles similarly cause very little obstruction or or delay to buses, even though buses constantly have to 'break into' the bicycle stream at stops as they make way for a stopping or departing bus. Extrapolating to the future, it is not the bicycle that appears as the great consumer of roadspace but its potential successor – the private car.

Accidents are a serious problem in China. In 1985 there were 48 deaths per 10,000 motor vehicles. This rate is similar to India's, almost double that of Indonesia or Thailand, and about 19 times the UK or USA rate (Navin *et al.* 1994; Spencer 1989). It is quite easy to show how cyclists form a large proportion of the casualties. Wang (1989) argues that 60 per cent of traffic accidents in urban areas involve bicycles, while Xu and Li (1994) point out that Shanghai sees 300 cyclist fatalities a year (half of the city's total road deaths). Yet neither of these studies takes into account the degree of exposure to accident. If there is a large number of cyclists, it is only to be expected that a large proportion of accidents will involve them. Figures for causes of accidents – assuming that these have been correctly attributed – present a fairer picture. In Beijing and Changchun motor vehicles, despite their smaller numbers, take the largest share of responsibility. Nor do bicycles generally do much damage. Although in Xian they were responsible for just over a quarter of all accidents, they caused no more than 16 per cent of fatalities. Were the cyclists to change to other modes then accidents, and certainly injuries, could by no means be guaranteed to fall.

As has been seen in Chapter 8, energy consumption is a significant environmental challenge. It is reassuring to see that China's transport sector accounts for a remarkably low consumption of energy compared with other parts of the world. The question is how long this can last. It is a feature of developing countries, particularly the more dynamic ones, that income demand elasticities for motor fuel are well above those in developed countries, and price demand elasticities generally lower (Birol and Guerer 1993). Rising incomes in China will be more than reflected in rising demand for both vehicles and their fuel. The Automobile Industry Policy, mentioned earlier, is calling for the annual production of motor vehicles to rise by over 300 per cent between 1994 and 2010, and that of private cars ('sedans') by no less than 1500 per cent (Huang 1995). A rise in fuel prices from their current low level will do very little to offset this. It takes little imagination to picture the pollution and energy implications. It needs hardly be said that very little pollution or fuel consumption can be blamed on bicycles – and most of what does occur will be during their manufacture, not when they are on the streets.

Development of urban transport policies

How are the urban policy-makers responding to these challenges? Until the late 1970s traffic was light and urban transport was not seen as a productive activity; hence transport planning was given a low priority. It was only with the reforms and the consequent growth of congestion that research into urban transport received significant official support. Perhaps inevitably, Chinese transport planners have drawn upon methods developed in the cities of Western Europe and North America. In these countries planning for bicycles was barely taken seriously; the emphasis was on the problems posed by the private car and on means for attracting its users onto public transport.

This had two implications. First, China imported techniques and software which were based on Western experience: algorithms for modelling modal splits and the effect of congestion on speeds had been designed around cars and were quite inappropriate for handling bicycles. Second, and in spite of this, the bicycle found itself treated as cars might be treated. Thus a joint research agenda, sponsored by the Ministry of Construction and supported by other government bodies, referred to 'The development prospect of bicycles *and other private transportation means* in our cities and the relative policies' (Xu 1992 p. 36, emphasis added). A 1986 symposium on traffic policy concluded that: 'We should ... give priority to the development of public transport. Its development should be ensured in policy-making, urban planning construction and financing. Otherwise, private transportation means will continue to grow' (ibid., p. 39).

More explicit still were the proceedings of a conference on the role of bicycles, held in Beijing in 1983. These recommended restrictions on private motorised vehicles and 'controls' on non-motorised vehicles in order to achieve a modal split based on city size. Bicycles would only be the major mode in cities with less than 100,000 population; in larger cities they would progressively yield their modal share to public transport, which would play the dominant role in cities with over half a million inhabitants (Jamieson and Naylor 1992). It would be wrong to infer that transport planners automatically see the bicycle as a problem. Yet most appear to be sceptical as to its virtues. The general opinion was apparent at a 1994 conference on non-motorised transport in Beijing when some Westerners, enthusing about the city's apparently 'green' transport system, provoked a response from Chinese delegates who argued that retaining the *status quo* was simply not feasible. The reasoning behind this view should by now be fairly clear. If today's cyclist is potentially tomorrow's motorist, it is essential to pre-empt the trend by fostering a public transport culture.

This does not mean that urban roads are not being built – far from it. Undoubtedly there are some who hold that this is the 'infrastructure' needed to create a 'modern' image and attract foreign investment. There have been suspicions that Beijing is following this line and it may be no coincidence that a series of postage stamps for 1995 featured motorway interchanges in that city. Its extensive, almost monumental layout makes it something of an exception, and it has been possible to build three orbital motorways and to widen several radial roads without wholesale destruction of buildings. Shanghai is also, with World Bank support, building a series of bi-level motorways.

At the same time, many cities are planning to expand public transport. The Ministry of Construction has called for the number of buses per 10,000 inhabitants to rise by a quarter in cities of over 2 million people and to be more than doubled in smaller cities. Beijing's main bus operator has found it necessary to enter into a joint venture with the Austrian manufacturer Steyr in order to modernise and expand its fleet. Beijing, Shanghai and Guangzhou all have new metro lines under construction, and there have been proposals for Chongqing, Shenyang, Nanjing, Tianjin and Qingdao (Anon 1993). Inevitably, attracting the investment funds has been difficult. In mid-1996 it was announced that the last three of these schemes had been put on hold; Guangzhou has gone ahead, relying on a mixture of bond issues and sales of development rights close to stations (Anon 1995, 1996b).

Regarding bicycles themselves, Wang Z. H. (1989) identifies two bodies of opinion. One group, taking a fairly critical line, would attempt to divert as many cyclists as possible onto public transport in order to release precious road space. Those taking such a view would seek to limit their production, introduce licensing with the proceeds earmarked to public transport improvments, and regulate bicycle parking more strictly. Others feel that the investment needed to soak up the required number of cyclists would be prohibitively expensive and that its ability to make public transport attractive enough is questionable in any case. Western transport planners will not need to be reminded that many hugely expensive bus and rail improvements have drawn only a disappointingly small proportion of riders away from private transport.

In fact, there is a considerable overlap between the two views. Both acknowledge that much could be achieved by segregating traffic types and reducing conflicting movements at junctions. The World Bank study referred to earlier has claimed that providing segregated lanes for both buses and bicycles could raise passenger capacities by 93 per cent and 35 per cent respectively, compared with letting the vehicles fend for themselves in mixed traffic (Kuranami *et al.* 1994). Shanghai has begun to implement a plan for a complex classification of streets, open to different traffic types, and with a number of them restricted to buses only, or bicycles only. Even its elevated motorways will have physically segregated cycle lanes on their lower levels. The aim is to preserve a role for the bicycle, particularly for short journeys of up to 5 kilometres (Cai 1994). A combination of priority measures and a generally conservative policy towards providing road space for cars may yet be the most feasible way of achieving a 'sustainable' urban transport system.

Conclusion: pressures for change

China's urban transport dilemmas may be distinctive in their details, but in their underlying nature they are familiar enough. National ambitions for a car industry must be reconciled with accommodating the vehicles which it produces (Spencer and Madhavan 1989). Its people's aspirations to a 'developed' lifestyle must be reconciled with that lifestyle's costs in terms of paying for the roads and enduring the ensuing congestion, noise, severance and pollution. At the same time, pleas for respecting the ozone layer, coming as they do from countries whose own environmental records are far from impeccable, appear rather hollow. Vice Premier Zou Jiahua stated in 1994 that China could not put environmental protection ahead of economic development, and that developed countries would need to back up their strictures with aid (Anon 1994). (General Motors responded by donating an electric car to China for trials!)

Impressive though mass cycling may seem to the advocate of sustainability, one cannot expect the *nouveau-riche* urbanite to live in an ecological museum. All the same, the opportunity for preventive action is there. The cities have not yet reached the motorised mayhem that is Bangkok. Press reports in mid-1996 suggested that some policy-makers are beginning to acknowledge the need to make economic development subject to what is environmentally feasible (Anon 1996c). Beijing itself plans to implement a scheme that will allow cars to travel in the city only on alternate days, according to their number plates. There is still time to take a hard look at urban land use policies. The next few years could be critical for the emergence of a sustainable urban transport policy.

References

Anon (1993) 'China Will Make Great Efforts for Development of Public Transportation', *China City Planning Review,* 9 (1) 54–5.

Anon (1994) 'GM Gives Electric Car', *Far Eastern Economic Review,* 157 (29) 75.

Anon (1995) 'Subway Fare', *Far Eastern Economic Review,* 158 (34) 59.

Anon (1996a) 'Sales of Bicycles Start to Yield Way to Motorcycles in What Has Been Dubbed the "Bicycle Kingdom"', *Far Eastern Economic Review,* 159, (33), 25.

Anon (1996b) 'State Councillor Puts Environmental Protection Above Development', *Far Eastern Economic Review,* 159(34) 23.

Anon (1996c) 'Global Transport News: Road: China', *Global Transport,* 6, 15.

Armstrong-Wright, A. (1993) *Public Transport in Third World Cities* (London: HMSO).

Birol, F. and Guerer, N. (1993) 'Modelling the Transport Sector Fuel Demand for Developing Countries', *Energy Policy,* 21, 1163–72.

Cai, J. X. (1996) 'Bicycle Transport in Shanghai: Status and Prospects', *Transportation Research Record,* 1563, 8–15.

Chiu, R. L. H. (1994) 'Housing', in Yeung, Y. M. and Chu, D. K. Y. (eds) *Guangdong: Survey of a Province Undergoing Rapid Change* (Hong Kong: Chinese University Press) 277–300.

Guo, J. (1996) 'A Study of Traffic Behviour in Bus Stop Areas with Mixed Traffic', unpublished PhD thesis, Transport Studies Group, University of Westminster.

Hamer, A. (1993) 'China Urban Land management: Options for an Emerging Market Economy', World Bank, Washington DC. Executive summary reprinted in *China City Planning Review,* 9(1) 17–26.

Huang, W. (1995) 'Auto Industry Faces Challenges and Opportunities', *Beijing Review* 38(45) 15–18.

Jamieson, W. and Naylor, B. (1992) 'Planning for Low-cost Travel Modes in Ningbo, China', *Transportation Research Record,* 1372, 31–9.

Jones, T. S. M. (1991) 'Urban Public Transport in Beijing (PRC) Present and Future', paper presented at the London–Beijing Symposium on Transport and Tourism, Middlesex Polytechnic.

Kartodirdjo, S. (1981), *The Pedicab in Yogyakarta: A Study of Low Cost Transportation and Poverty Problems* (Yogyakarta: Gadjah Mada University Press).

Kubota, H. and Kidokoro, T. (1994) 'Analysis of Bicycle-Dependent Transport Systems in China: Case Study in a Medium-Sized City', *Transportation Research Record,* 1441, 11–15.

Kuranami, C., Winston, B. P. and Guitink, P. A. (1994) 'Nonmotorized Vehicles in Asian Cities: Issues and Policies', *Transportation Research Record,* 1441, 61–70.

Leeming, F. (1993) *The Changing Geography of China* (Oxford: Blackwell).

Mei B., Wang, X. and Xu, J. Q. (1994) 'Study on the Development Trends of Urban Bicycle Traffic', in Ren, F. T. and Liu, X. M. (eds) *Proceedings of the International Symposium on Non-motorised Transportation,* Beijing Polytechnic University, 52–7 (in Chinese).

MVA Consultancy (1993) *Beijing Transport Planning Study: Draft Final Report.* For Beijing Academy for City Planning and Design and Great Britain Overseas Development Administration.

Navin, F., Bergan, A., Qi, J. S. and Li, J. (1994) 'Road Safety in China', *Transportation Research Record,* 1441, 3–10.

Ren, N. and Koike, H. (1993) 'Bicycle: A Vital Transportation Means in Tianjin, China', *Transportation Research Record,* 1396, 5–10.

Replogle, M. (1992) *Non-Motorised Vehicles in Asian Cities,* Technical Paper 162 (Washington, DC: World Bank).

Shimazaki, T. and Yang, D. Y. (1992) 'Bicycle Use in Urban Areas in China', *Transportation Research Record,* 1372, 26–9.

Sinha, K. C., Varma, A. and Faiz, A. (1990) 'Environmental Issues in Developing Countries', Seminar N, PTRC Summer Annual Meeting, University of Sussex, 37–46.

Spencer, A. H. (1989) 'Urban transport', in T. R. Leinbach and Chia L. S. (eds) *Southeast Asian Transport: Issues in Development* (Singapore: Oxford University Press) 190–231.

Spencer, A. H. and S. Madhavan (1989) 'The Car in Southeast Asia', *Transportation Research A,* 23A, 425–37.

Tanaboriboon, Y. and Ying, G. (1993) 'Characteristics of Bicycle Users in Shanghai, China', *Transportation Research Record,* 1396, 22–9.

Thomas, C., Ferguson, E., Feng, D. and DePriest, J. (1992) 'Policy Implications of Increasing Motorization in Developing Countries: Guangzhou, People's Republic of China', *Transportation Research Record,* 1372, 18–25.

Thornhill, W. (1991) 'Non-Motorised Transport in China', paper presented at the Transportation Research Board Annual Meeting, Washington DC.

Wang, D. H. (1992) 'A Review on the Development of Planning and Design of China's Urban Residential Areas', *China City Planning Review,* 8/1, 46–55.

Wang, Z. H. (1989) 'Bicycles in Large Cities in China', *Transport Reviews*, 9, 171–82.

Wang, J. and Wei, H. (1993) 'Traffic Segregation on Spatial and Temporal Basis: the Experience of Bicycle Traffic Operations in China', *Transportation Research Record*, 1396, 11-7.

Xu, P. and Li, B. (1994) 'The Study of Strategy for Bicycle Safety in Shanghai', in Ren F. T. and Liu X. M. (eds) *Proceedings of the International Symposium on Non-Motorised Transportation*, Beijing Polytechnic University, 378–87 (in Chinese).

Xu, K. W. and Yu, T. W. (1996) 'Macro-Management of Shanghai Public Transport', *Public Transport International*, 1996/2, 28–32.

Xu, X. C. (1992) 'Ten Years of Urban Traffic Planning Development in China', *China City Planning Review*, 8/2, 32–41.

Yan, K. F. and Zheng, J. L. (1994) 'Study of Bicycle Parking in Central Business District in Shanghai', *Transportation Research Record*, 1441, 27–35.

Yang, J. M. (1985) 'Bicycle Traffic in China', *Transportation Quarterly*, 39, 93–107.

Yang, Z. S., Paaswell, R. E. and Rouphail, N. M. (1990) 'Growth of urban transportation in the People's Republic of China', *Proceedings of CODATU 5*, São Paulo, pp. 919–30.

Zhang, X. H. (1992) 'Enterprise Response to Market Reforms: The case of the Chinese Bicycle Industry', *Australian Journal of Chinese Affairs*, 28, 111–39.

Zhou, G. Z. and Study Group (1993) 'Policy Framework for the Development of Real Estate and the Real Estate Industry in China', *China City Planning Review*, 9/1, 2–16.

Zhou, H. L. and Frame , G. (1994) 'Study on Guangzhou's Bicycle Policy', in Ren, F. T. and Liu, X. M. (eds) *Proceedings of the International Symposium on Non-Motorised Transportation*, Beijing Polytechnic University, pp. 90–5 (in Chinese).

Zhou, Y. Q. and Akatsuka, Y. (1994) 'A Study on Characteristics of Bicycle Traffic Under Mixed Traffic on a Road Segment in Beijing, China', in Ren, F. T. and Liu, X. M. (eds) *Proceedings of the International Symposium on Non-motorised Transportation*, Beijing Polytechnic University, pp. 195–200.

10
Is Ecological Agriculture Sustainable in China?

Richard Sanders[1]

'Take grain as the key link ...'

Mao Zedong

The advent of family farming in the 1980s

The initial impetus away from the collective and towards more privat-ised forms of agriculture in the countryside in the late 1970s came from below, from discontented elements in Anhui and Sichuan, two of China's poorest provinces. After some initial prevarication, the reforms were taken up and pushed through by the central government with such aggression and alacrity that by 1982 almost all collective property, including land, had been distributed on a household-by-household basis, and responsibility for agricultural production transferred from the brigade *(dadui)* and work team *(xiaodui)* to the family *(jiating)*. The new era of family farming had begun.

The land, though still nominally owned by the state, was leased to households, usually for a period of fifteen years. In return the family was contracted to produce a certain amount of grain (or other farm products) to be sold to the state at preordained prices. The family could farm as it wished, with as much or as little human and capital input as it could muster. Once the state contract was fulfilled, the household could use its land and dispose of its output in any way it chose, nor-mally for its own consumption or for sale in local markets. The initial plots of land distributed were small by any standards, and in most vil-lages households rarely came away with much more than one to two *mu* per person. The division was on such an egalitarian basis that fam-ilies were often allocated two or three plots of differing qualities and locations to ensure each would have its fair share of good and bad land. The size of the resulting fields was thus further reduced: in many of the old collectives, the land was divided to resemble patchwork quilts, and most families found themselves farming fields no bigger than 'noodle strips' (Hinton 1990, p. 14).

Despite the fragmentation of the land and resulting small scale of farming operations, agricultural output rose in leaps and bounds in the early 1980s. The grain harvest, for example, which was only a little over 300 million tonnes in 1978, climbed above 400 million tonnes in 1984. The output of oil-bearing crops more than doubled in the same period (*China Statistical Yearbook* 1996, p. 371). It is not surprising that land reform, coupled with price liberalisation, was credited by Chinese and Western observers alike with having 'unleashed the enthusiasm of the farmers' (a commonly heard explanation of events of that time), providing the material incentives for significant increases in production and productivity (World Bank 1991, p. 38). For the reformers in the Chinese government, the huge increases in agricultural output in the early 1980s justified the massive policy shifts they had embraced. The problem of maintaining food security in a country with such a large and rapidly rising population seemed nearer a solution than at any time in the previous twenty years.

However, that initial increase in production in the early part of the decade was not immediately sustained. Grain output fell in the mid-1980s and did not reach 1984 levels again until 1989. And while subsequently the grain harvest has risen once more, reaching a record 466 million tonnes in 1995, it has done so in fits and starts. Nor has the rate of harvest growth matched that of population growth, resulting in lower outputs of grain per capita. Thus, while the countryside produced 0.39 tonnes of grain per head in 1984, it produced only 0.385 tonnes in the harvest of 1995 (*China Statistical Yearbook* 1995, p. 59 and p. 347; and China Statistical Yearbook, 1996, p. 69 and p. 371). There has been a significant increase in the output of animal products, fish and vegetables to satisfy the increasing variety of foods demanded by an ever-richer domestic population. But the uneven grain crop, coupled with a significant decline in the cotton crop, has once more become a cause for concern. Even if the doom-laden forecasts like those of Lester Brown (1995) can be discounted (Johnson 1995), any complacency there might have been within the Chinese government over food security has been dissipated.

The inability to sustain the post-reform farm output growth in the short run is not difficult to explain. To begin with, the high growth rates in the early 1980s took place from a very low base. And while the farmers' enthusiasm was increased by the advent of family farming, the incentive to produce was certainly sharpened by an increase of approximately 50 per cent in the state procurement prices in 1980. The cutting of those prices in 1985 had a predictable impact on the output of that year. But, faced with generous state procurement prices, farmers did not raise farm output and profitability merely by working harder. They also increased farm inputs, particularly of chemical fertilisers. The consumption of such fertilisers (predominantly nitrogen, phosphate and potash) in the countryside, for example, increased from 8.84 million tonnes in 1978 to 17.39 million tonnes in 1984, doubling within a six-year period (*China Statistical Yearbook* 1995, p. 337). Given the diminishing impacts of chemical fertiliser application upon soil productivity (see below), the initially rapid increase in output was based on conditions that could not be indefinitely sustained.

Industrialisation and family farming in the 1990s

Since the early 1980s, price controls have been progressively (though unevenly) abandoned, and the influence of the market has expanded. But the forms of landholding and the responsibility for (and scale of) farming in most parts of China have remained almost unchanged. In most villages (previously brigades, or *dadui*, now renamed *cun*), farming remains the responsibility of the family and is performed with high labour and low capital intensity. The scale of its operations remains remarkably small. In many cases the holdings are even smaller than in the early 1980s, as arable land has been gobbled up for construction and other purposes. In 1995 the area of cultivable land per household averaged only 2.17 mu per capita, but was lower than 1 mu per capita in Fujian and Zhejiang provinces and less than 1.5 mu per capita in another 11 provinces, mostly in the south and east (*China Statistical Yearbook* 1996, p. 367). Meanwhile, in many parts of the countryside, particularly in the poorest provinces in the centre and west, traditional wooden ploughs are still pulled by donkeys or water buffaloes when not pulled by hand. In 1995, across the whole country, there were 560 draught animals per 1000 rural households, and 403 handcarts with rubber tyres, but only 99 mini and walking tractors, 77 large and medium tractors and a mere 5 motor vehicles (*China Statistical Yearbook* 1996, p. 366).

Despite the slow pace of technical change in farming practices, however, the face of the post-reform Chinese countryside has been revolutionised as a result of burgeoning industrialisation caused by the mushrooming of township and village enterprises (TVEs). During the period of collective agriculture, communes for the most part eschewed 'sideline' activities and proscribed any form of private initiative. Even peasants making cakes from traditional local recipes or straw hats for sale were condemned as 'capitalist tails'. But the reforms led to such a surge of industrial activity of all shapes and descriptions, mostly owned collectively *(jiti)* but some privately *(geti hu)*, that well before the end of the 1980s industry was generating far more income in the countryside than was agriculture. By 1995, the value of gross industrial output of TVEs was 6891 billion yuan. This was more than treble the gross output value of the agricultural sector (including farming, forestry, animal husbandry and fishery) at 2034 billion yuan (*China Statistical Yearbook* 1996, pp. 356, 365). With greater income came greater employment prospects.

By the mid–1990s, villagers working mostly in the fields had become a minority. While many families still farmed their small plots of land and kept livestock, usually a few chickens or a pig, most household income was generated by other family members, mainly young and frequently male, labouring in village enterprises. The work in the fields was increasingly left to the elderly and to women. As Li Wenjuan observes, there has been an increasing feminisation of Chinese agriculture:

> According to the statistical data of 1993 ... these female labour forces [are] engaged in about 60 per cent of farming jobs. In some cotton-growing areas, tea growing areas and silkworm raising areas, more than 90 per cent [of the] labour force are women. (1995, p. 9)

At the end of the 1970s, almost all peasants, young and old, male and female, collectively worked on the fields in teams, producing almost exclusively grain, earning work-points, living mostly in mud and straw huts, without running water, electricity or consumer durables, and relying for cooking, heating and sleeping on the traditional stove or *kang*. By the mid--1990s a snapshot of a typical village would produce a very different picture. The female and older members of the household would be farming small plots of land still mostly by hand (but with increasing amounts of chemicals) to produce food for the family's own consumption to fulfil contracts and, if possible, for sale in markets as well. The rest of the household would be working (if they had not already migrated to the town) in local factories (mostly collectively owned) producing bricks, or padded jackets, or chemicals or motor vehicle parts or whatever, earning the greater part of the growing family income, increasingly spent on modern consumer goods (colour televisions, video-recorders, hi-fi, refrigerators, even air-conditioning) produced in other parts of China or abroad and enjoyed in their brick-built, often two-storey homes.

Farm productivity and sustainability in the 1990s

Many observers both inside and outside China take a fairly sanguine view of the picture described above. For example, on the basis of fieldwork in relatively poor rural areas, Aubert (1995) and Pennarz (1995) recognise limitations on farmers' abilities to increase or maintain output, but accept that solutions can largely be found within current policy, technology and scale. Aubert argues:

> Rather than authoritarian measures aiming at creating 'economies of scale' ... it seems that the problem can only be solved progressively by the development of outside job opportunities, with the temporary expansion of part-time farming. Future programmes should therefore take into account this multiple activities dimension of the farms ... In that respect, establishment of monitoring networks, providing economic information and accounting advice to the farmers should be a priority. (Aubert 1995, pp. 55–6)

Meanwhile Pennarz argues for the positive encouragement of the present system:

> For sustainable solutions to agricultural development, the diversified land-use systems of smallholders should receive more support in order to allow small-scale economic systems to become an economically viable alternative to the labour-division type of agriculture. Since the greatest portion of the population will have to live in rural areas also in the future, smallholder agriculture is an important model. (Pennarz 1995, p. 19)

Indeed, relatively complacent views about the present state of agriculture are not surprising, given the fact that the output of grain and other farm products has continued to grow. *Beijing Review* (8 April 1996) took a very optimistic view of the state of agriculture, a view seemingly borne out by the record grain harvest declared for 1996 of 490 million tonnes (*Statistical Survey of China* 1997, p. 85). But despite the apparently satisfactory gross output levels posted recently, questions remain about the sustainability of agricultural production in the longer term.

It is not the intention here to dwell on the meaning of agricultural sustainability, given the extensive literature on the subject (for a concise review, see Cai and Smit 1994). For the terms of the present debate, any form of production that cannot somehow be sustained in the short term without threatening the survival of life or livelihood in the longer term will be regarded as unsustainable. Moreover, it will be accepted, following Cai and Smit (1994), that agricultural sustainability has at least three key and interrelated components: techno-economic, socio-political and biophysical-environmental. I will argue that the current performance of Chinese agriculture, given the changes in the country-side described above, is becoming increasingly unsustainable. The low material rewards from agriculture reduce the willingness of villagers to engage in agriculture at all, so undermining the techno-economic and socio-political sustainability of agriculture. And where farmers do continue to work the fields, they have been encouraged to use methods that increasingly undermine its environmental sustainability.

The roots of the problem

Economic and social unsustainability

Deng Xiaoping's agricultural reforms unleashed the enthusiasm of the peasants, it is true. But it has been the enthusiasm for making money that has been unleashed, rather than the enthusiasm for beneficial agricultural practices *per se*. Where the two have coincided, well and good, but where they have not, the first impulse has taken priority. This has led to a widespread exodus from and consequent neglect of the land in some areas. In others it has generated a desire to maximise short-term output, with little concern for long-run productivity. The reforms gave to all households their own plots of land, but plots so small that mechanised forms of production are still largely ruled out and the simplest economies of scale unobtainable. Without wishing either to exaggerate scale economies or to disregard environmental costs of large-scale production, it is surely difficult to sustain an argument that the ideal farm size is 0.145 hectares per capita of household, the average farm size across China as a whole (Li 1995, p. 10). As Li Wenjuan suggests:

> Because of the large population and limited land resources, the household scale of crop farming in China is very small. The small scale of crop production has resulted in low productivity, especially

in East China where the economic level is much higher than other regions ... The small farming scale also affects the use of agro-machinery, especially the large-scale machines. (Li 1995, p. 9)

Li adds that

low economic profit of crops farming activity is the most restrictive factor blocking the sustainable development of crops production in China. The reasons for low profits [include] ... small production scale. (Li 1995, p. 7)

Hinton, who has studied Chinese agriculture at first hand for fifty years pulls no punches:

The heart of the matter remains: mechanisation, to be successful, must have some scale. To go all out at the 15 horsepower level is to condemn China to a chronically backward agriculture. (Hinton 1990, p. 116)

There are, of course plenty of other reasons advanced for low farming productivity and associated low profitability. Li (1995, p. 7) adds high agro-material prices, the low quality of agro-products and the low educational level of the farmers, accentuated by the feminisation of agriculture already referred to. Others (Wehrfritz 1995; Zhou 1996; White 1993; Lin 1990) stress low state grain procurement prices. But whatever the reasons, there is clear evidence from all over China that agriculture, particularly cereal growing, is not the route to material prosperity. As George Wehrfritz writes:

Losses are starting to mount. Farmland is built over as factories sprout like weeds. Farmland is lost to erosion. Peasants switch crops or move to the cities ... This much is certain: China's 800 m. peasants are tired of hauling in enormous grain harvests ... The result: 110 million rural refugees have flocked to the cities since Deng took power and the equivalent of all the cropland of Sichuan province has fallen out of production. Last year, the cumulative neglect finally produced the predictable result: farmers turned in a disappointing harvest. (Wehrfritz 1995, p. 9)

In the words of Xiao Xingji, 'if farmers earn 5 kuai a day in the fields and 25 kuai in the factory, they'll work in the factory'.[2] Accordingly, where agriculture is not a route to material prosperity, where it operates with low profitability, it is not sustainable in economic or social terms.

Environmental unsustainability

While a record grain harvest was recorded in 1995, farming has become increasingly dependent upon techniques which undermine long-run environmental sustainability. The disturbing trends in the application of chemical fertilisers and pesticides, begun in the Maoist period of collective farming and continued in the early post-reform years, have gone on unabated. While the period 1978–84 saw a doubling of the application of chemical fertilisers, the period 1984–95 saw a further doubling, up from 17.4 million tonnes to 35.9 million tonnes (*China Statistical Yearbook*, 1996, p. 361). This is coupled with much more extensive use of chemical pesticides and increases in the area of irrigated land, up by nearly 5 million hectares between 1988 and 1995. So despite an overall reduction of 0.8 million hectares in the total area of cultivated land, agriculture has (despite low levels of mechanisation) become ever more dependent on energy imported into the countryside. According to Cheng, Han and Taylor:

> During 1965–88, the total industrial energy used in China's agriculture increased by over 9 times. The dominant energy use, for manufacturing inorganic fertiliser, increased by nearly 12 times ... In 1988, the [latter] accounted for 83 per cent of the total industrial energy used in China's agriculture ... In planning for the future, there are real concerns about China's capacity to increase fossil fuel energy supplies at a pace adequate to sustain continued grain yield increases required for feeding the country's immense and increasingly well-to-do population. (Cheng *et al.* 1992, p. 1127)

Moreover, the fossil fuel constraint is not the only problem caused by use of chemical fertilisers. More direct environmental problems result, including the leaching of nitrates into groundwater and runoff into streams and surface water. Other potential problems include the eutrophication of lakes and the hardening or crusting of soil. Meanwhile, the increased use of chemical fertilisers has been accompanied by a levelling-off in the use of organic fertilisers, with implications for the long-run productivity of the soil. Plants' ability to use nutrients efficiently is reduced and crop yields decline, and to maintain those yields, the application of chemical fertilisers has to be accelerated, the textbook case of diminishing returns. As Cheng *et al.* argue:

> There is a real concern that a further erosion in the relative import- ance of organic fertilisers will (militate against) realization of the increased yields otherwise possible from intensive inorganic fer- tiliser use (1992, p. 1130).

The increased use of chemical pesticides also results in toxicity to the humans directly involved in their application, toxic residues in water, soil and food, and the increased resistance of pests to pesticides. According to Karen Janz:

> China uses the highest amount of agrochemicals in the world. When I stayed in a normal village in Hebei last year, the farmers told us that every year several female farmers die because of chem- ical pesticides application in cotton fields. The amount is so high that a simple reduction would not be enough.[3]

It is clear that the small scale of family farming has negative implica- tions for agricultural sustainability. On the one hand, many farmers, offered better opportunities in the towns and enterprises, have simply neglected the land, while others, unable to increase the productivity of the land through mechanisation or scale economies, have had to resort to the increased application of chemical inputs to maximise short-run returns.

It is also clear that another aspect of the reforms has further encour- aged farmers to take the short view: the (relatively) short time period of 15 years over which the leases were initially granted. Farmers have had little reason to suppose that their plots would remain their own to farm for long. Indeed,they had every reason to believe that contra- dictory shifts in government policy would take them away at any moment. So they have had particular incentives to maximise short-run gain, without any regard to the long term. It is hardly surprising, in these circumstances, that the input of chemical fertilisers and pesti- cides has increased so fast.

But it has not only been the dramatic increase in chemical inputs that has threatened the environmental sustainability of the post- reform rural economy. The rural industrial enterprises have been and still are frequently highly polluting. Villagers have shown little hesit- ation in running chemical works, or paper factories or brickworks if they can make a profit, whatever their impact on the local natural environment. Meanwhile, the breakup of the communes involved an equal distribution of all collective property. This included trees which were, in many cases, immediately chopped down for firewood, construction or sale, provoking, according to Pu Mao Sen, 'a level of deforestation not seen since the Great Leap Forward 30 years before'.[4]

Marginal land, unsuitable for intensive production, was also brought into play. Hinton in characteristically colourful vein summarises:

> [The] reform unleashed … a wholesale attack on an already muchabused and enervated environment, on mountain slopes, on trees, on water resources, on grasslands, on fishing grounds, on wildlife, on minerals underground, on anything that could be cut down, plowed up, pumped over, dug out, shot dead or carried away. (1990, p. 21)

And the breakup of the collective has had one further negative impact on the environment: it has become that much more difficult for village leaders to mobilise large gangs of villagers to build dams, or ditches or engage in reforestation or repair roads, or indeed, collectively to deal with environmental damage from whatever source.

Thus the productivity of the land has increased since the reforms as grain output has risen despite declining cultivated acreage. But this has occurred as a result of a steep increase in the application of ecologically damaging chemicals and the energy-intensity of agriculture. This is despite a chronic shortage of energy resources, in a rural environment increasingly degraded and polluted, with its arable land decimated by non-agricultural activities. Muldavin argues that the increases in grain production and yields in the last decade or so consequent to the reforms have resulted from the simultaneous mining of 'ecological capital' (1996a, p. 229) and 'communal capital' (1996b, p. 289). In this light, it is surprising how many Western scholars still discuss Chinese agriculture without reference to its sustainability in environmental terms. But it is because many Chinese scholars have recognised the unsustainability of the rural political economy that the government has been increasingly drawn to the promotion of practices that are more environmentally sensitive, and specifically to the promotion of 'ecological agriculture' (*shengtai nongye*).

Chinese ecological agriculture

According to Qu Geping (1991, p. 13), Chinese ecological agriculture (CEA) has been adopted since the early 1980s as a direct result of the environmental problems posed by 'high input, high output' production, with its Western-style reliance on fossil fuel energy. That reliance, he suggests, poses considerable difficulties, including the waste of mineral energy, intensification of the energy crisis, exhaustion of natural resources and the pollution of the environment.

In contrast, CEA is an attempt to develop farming in a sustainable way. There is no single word in Mandarin that directly translates as 'sustainable' and the expression for sustainable development (*chixu fazhan*) would more usually be translated as meaning sustained rather than sustainable development. In any event, CEA, according to Qu Geping (1991, p. 13), is a 'mode of sustainable development with Chinese characteristics' (*you Zhongguo de tese chixu fazhan*).[5] CEA recognises the problems of food security and economic strength and the need to increase absolute levels of agricultural output. But it attempts to do this without a crisis of energy generation, while at the same time dealing with the increasingly manifest environmental problems in the countryside. It has emphasized farming based on sound ecological principles in order to construct a local rural economy based on a series of environmentally benign cycles at minimal economic cost.

Organic systems of agriculture are, of course, not new to China. F. H. King (1926) explains in great detail the centuries-old practices such as crop rotation, inter-planting and the application of organic manures. These allowed farmers, albeit at enormous cost of human time and labour, to maximise land productivity while maintaining soil fertility. But those benign practices (performed in a Daoist spirit of working in harmony with the natural environment) were almost entirely neglected for thirty years after liberation. During much of that period, Mao Zedong encouraged grain monoculture ('take grain as the key link') amidst a form of socialist ideology that emphasised mankind's domination of nature by means of technical innovations.

CEA has been a more recent attempt to develop modern scientific agricultural techniques based largely on traditional, organic principles to promote a farming system enjoying the best of both worlds. As such, it not only emphasises not only those traditional practices mentioned above, but also encourages practices of direct benefit to the environment, including the prevention of soil erosion, afforestation, energy conservation, a reduced dependence on fossil fuels and the utilisation of waste. However, CEA attempts to go a great deal further than merely applying environmentally friendly principles to agricultural practices. Rather, it attempts a comprehensive response to the problems of the rural economy. It addresses not merely the problem of environmental degradation, but others, such as satisfying the peoples' increasing material expectations and maintaining employment opportunities in the countryside. It is thereby designed to reduce the already very substantial levels of internal migration from rural to urban areas, indeed to maintain the very fabric of rural communities. As a result, CEA puts a great deal of emphasis on the all-round development of the rural economy and specifically on rural sideline industrial employment and income-generating activities. The completed version of Mao's famous quote runs 'take grain as the key link, pay attention to animal husbandry, forestry, fish-raising and sideline occupations, and develop an all-round rural economy' (Hinton 1990, p. 25), but in practice, the latter four activities were honoured more in the breach than the observance. For Qu Geping, CEA is not to be so confined:

> [E]cological agriculture is a kind of 'macro agriculture' based on the integrated planning and reasonable arrangement of cultivation, breeding occupations and processing trades. Emphasis is laid on the all-round development of agriculture, forestry, livestock, side-line occupations, fishery and so on, the integrated operation of agriculture, industry and commerce, the coordination of the links among various departments of [the] agricultural sector and the practice of [a] diversified economy. (1991, p. 17, emphasis added)

As Cheng *et al.* (1992, p. 1135) observe, the conceptual underpinnings of CEA are fivefold:

- First, there is a holistic approach to resource use involving attempts to take into account all the natural resources in any locality and both the production and environmental implications of their use.
- Second, 'stereo' agriculture is promoted, involving a multidimensional use of space and time, a common example being the cultivation of rice, azolla (a nitrogen-fixing, moss-like aquatic plant) and fish in the paddy fields.
- A third component is the promotion of integrated production systems whereby outputs or by-products of one system are used as inputs of another. Examples of this include the use of organic wastes, such as rice or wheat stalks or animal excrement as inputs to biogas digesters (see below), which in turn produce not only 'clean' energy but also slurry that can be fed to fish or returned as organic fertiliser to the fields. Indeed, biogas digestion is at the heart of the

archetypal ecological agricultural system, being the key component in a virtuous circle of material recycling.

- Fourthly, ecological agriculture involves environmental management, which attempts to reduce the use of chemical fertilisers and pesticides, to increase afforestation and to generate power, as far as possible from renewable or continuing resources, e.g. from biogas, sun or wind.

- Fifthly, it involves diversification of production, combining grain cultivation with animal husbandry, fishing, forestry and other processes with agricultural and non-agricultural industries.

As Li Zheng Fang (1994, p. 16) emphasises, CEA is distinguished from Western organic agriculture (and indeed from Chinese organic agriculture, promoted in China since 1994) largely by a more explicit role for government agencies, more complicated and diversified methods of production, higher inputs of labour, higher yields and profit, more intensive enterprise integration and material recycling and, crucially, a more relaxed view on the partial use of chemical inputs. As a result, for those observers of agricultural practices who have faith only in the purest organic methods promoted by IFOAM (the International Federation of Organic Agriculture), CEA is a disappointment. Though an improvement perhaps on the more obviously environmentally degrading and polluting agriculture practised in most of China, it is a long way short of what they consider to be required. However, other observers may be concerned to encourage any environmentally friendly processes in an increasingly degraded and polluted rural environment. To the extent that CEA does so and at the same time helps to solve pressing economic problems in the countryside such as employment generation, it may appear to them a more politically and socially acceptable, realistic and thus sustainable project than IFOAM purism. And if so, they would, like me, wish to encourage its dissemination across China.

Biogas in China

Biogas is produced when organic matter decays (biologically digested) under anaerobic conditions. It is about 60 to 70 per cent methane, the rest consisting of carbon dioxide, nitrogen, carbon monoxide, hydrogen and hydrogen sulphide. According to Foley, 'in the late 1960s, biogas production was very much in vogue. It was even referred to as the fuel of the future' (1987, p. 187). The Chinese government initiated the first ever large-scale biogas programme in the 1970s when reportedly some seven million biogas digesters were built, five million in Sichuan province alone. The construction of a biogas digester can, at its most minimal, involve covering a pit full of rotting organic matter of a few cubic metres capacity with a fixed brick cover. The pressure rises as the gas builds up inside the pit and the gas is recovered in pipes and distributed to household kitchens for cooking and lighting. The huge extension of the biogas programme in the 1970s was based on minimalist digesters of this type, with fixed brick-built domes, normally of less than 8 cubic metres capacity, built, run and utilised by individual households. Larger biogas digesters, with a capacity of 40 to 100 cubic metres, and supplying gas at a community level, are possible, but this requires the coordinated input of substantial amounts of organic matter and the initial construction is complex and expensive.

The ready adoption of biogas was made easier by the longstanding traditions of fermenting animal and human excrement to break the faecel pathogen cycle in areas where fish farming and irrigated agriculture were carried out (Foley 1992, p. 359). The Chinese government were well disposed towards biogas digestion in the 1970s because of its potential for solving the rural energy problem. It was thus initially encouraged primarily on economic grounds: it promised a cheap source of fuel where there were few alternatives. The fact that the fuel was 'cleaner' than burning wood, stalks, kerosene or coal was a secondary issue. That the slurry produced could be used as feed for the fish or as enriched fertiliser on the fields was a further bonus.

The 1980s saw a severe retrenchment of the programme, however, largely because of the evident difficulties and technical failures associated with the household-level digesters. They need to be built to good standards to avoid leaks; the digestion process is also highly susceptible to changes in the ambient temperature and in the quantity and quality of input material. Considerable quantities of water need to be available if the digester is to operate throughout the year, while dry spells can cause problems with the cracking of structures (Foley 1992, p. 360). Taken as a whole, biogas digestion is most successful in areas with a moist, uniform climate that avoids extremes of temperature, a regular supply of animal excrement and other inputs and skilled labour in the construction and maintenance of the digesters. That these conditions were rarely found together in the Chinese countryside of the early 1980s explains why the household-level biogas digestion programme lost its momentum. As a result, the government became more concerned to promote community-level biogas digesters within a comprehensive ecological agricultural system.

The popularisation of ecological agriculture

The government has encouraged the promotion of ecological agriculture since 1982, primarily by encouraging environmental protection and research institutes and agencies to set up demonstration sites for extension and training work. In 1982 the first was established in Liu Min Ying, a small village in Daxing County, in the suburbs of Beijing. Others quickly followed, so that by the end of the decade the National Environmental Protection Agency (NEPA 1991, p. 9) claimed the existence of more than 1300 pilot projects at different administrative levels, 29 at county (*xian*) level, 138 at the township *(xiang)* and 1200 at the village *(zhuang* or *cun)* level. In the 1980s NEPA's emphasis was on model ecological agricultural villages, but in 1993 a new programme was initiated involving the promotion of 50 new model ecological counties.

My research has taken me to seven of these model ecological agricultural villages as well as to four eco-counties.[6] All of the villages are perceived to be 'successful' to the extent that they have received provincial, national or international honours for environmental achievement, four having won the UNEP Global 500 award within the last ten years. While there are significant differences amongst them, they all exhibit impressive environmental and economic gains. (This is not surprising, given the difficulty of being permitted to research freely, and in particular the difficulty of researching bad news in China.) In each of the seven villages, agriculture depends primarily on organic rather than chemical fertilisers (normally in proportions of roughly 70:30), a range of ecologically sound 'stereo' techniques such as intercropping and multi-layer cropping are used, animal husbandry (frequently with large stocks of pigs, cattle, chickens and ducks, providing enormous quantities of excrement) is well developed, recycling of wastes takes place and some attempts have been made to reduce fossil fuel energy consumption through the introduction of biogas and solar energy (with varying success).

In all villages, significant afforestation has occurred, normally up to at least 25 per cent of the land area. Some of the villages have developed particular specialist activities, such as the rearing of turtles, the farming of oysters, the raising of rare fish, or the growing of mushrooms. Meanwhile, all have developed a range of (largely unpolluting) industries, often linked to farming activities, such as abattoirs and factories for the production of animal fodder, processed foods such as Beijing duck, porridge and canned drinks, bamboo furniture and dried flowers, padded jackets and handmade quilts, providing income and employment for all villagers. More recently, some have developed forms of ecologically-sensitive tourism. Incomes per head are uniformly higher than the average for their regions, and the villages have built houses, schools and other amenities to high standards, well above the norm for the countryside.

Four of the villages (Liu Min Ying and Dou Dian, both in Beijing municipality, Tou Teng, in northern Jiangsu province, and Qian Wei, in the municipality of Shanghai) exhibit archetypal CEA systems, with community-level biogas digesters of between 60 and 100 cubic metres capacity at their core. Stalks from the fields combined with excrement from households and the animal farms (pig farms and cattle farms, for example, set up primarily for the purpose) are used as inputs to the biogas digesters, 'clean' energy is provided to households for cooking and lighting, the liquid slurry is used to irrigate the fields while the solid slurry is either used for fish feed in the fishponds (the mud from the bottom of the ponds eventually being dredged for fertiliser) or used directly as rich, organic fertiliser back on the fields. These four villages are those where CEA is most developed and appears to have most staying power.

Each village is a 'model' (and hence not typical), having received at least some financial help and/or technical assistance from outside and been promoted positively by the authorities at different levels. Yet each is a functioning, 'real' village where the adoption of an ecological agricultural system was an important, conscious political decision and where that adoption seems to have benefited the villagers and remains popular with them. Environmentally-friendly farming has been accepted and polluting industry rejected, while at the same time the rapidly-rising material expectations of the villagers have, in the main, been more than fulfilled. There may thus be some grounds for optimism that CEA is a sustainable alternative, technically, socially and environmentally, to the 'high-input, high-output' agriculture practised in most other parts of the countryside once it has been adopted.

However, therein lies the problem. Despite the examples set by model villages and other demonstration sites, government propaganda and financial encouragement, and technical assistance from environmental agencies and institutes, ecological agriculture remains difficult to popularise and its adoption is all too painfully rare. About three thousand or so ecological agricultural sites are claimed to exist, but these represent only a tiny proportion of villages. So what is the difficulty in the extension of CEA?

My research suggests that the villages that have successfully adopted ecological agriculture may be atypical in all too many respects and not merely because they have been beneficiaries of initial outside assistance. Indeed, despite the very substantial differences in size, location, proximity to markets, levels and types of industrialisation and other factors exhibited by the seven villages, some key factors unite them. All, by the time they consciously adopted ecological agriculture, were relatively rich villages and all had leaders who were well trusted, clearly able, imaginative and powerful. Most had been around a very long time; indeed all but one had first become leader either before or during the Cultural Revolution (1966–76).

The relative wealth of a village and able leadership are, of course, likely to be related. Villagers who have little knowledge of the potential benefits of new, apparently environmentally beneficial practices are clearly more easily persuaded to adopt them by leaders to whom they are grateful for past successes and whom they respect. All the villages had become relatively rich before the reforms, and although the majority decollectivised and divided the fields, none did so without some reluctance, particularly within the leadership. Significantly, two of the seven never divided the fields, while a further two, having done so, have put them back together again. Thus, in a majority of the villages researched, the factories and the fields are run by the collective, while in each of the others, the leadership (particularly that of the Communist Party branch) remains a powerful force and a high degree of collective control exists. But what is particularly noteworthy is that those four villages that manage agriculture wholly-collectively (Liu Min Ying, Dou Dian, Tou Teng and Qian Wei) are the very four with a community-level biogas digester at the core of their ecological agricultural systems.

The research tentatively suggests that CEA has been most easily and successfully adopted and maintained where the collective still continues to play a strong role. This applies not only in developing and managing factories and other local enterprises, where it is fairly commonplace everywhere, but also in agricultural production and animal husbandry, where it is not. And it is not too difficult to understand why this is so. On the one hand, in villages where fields have been put back together and where agriculture (ecological or otherwise) is collectively organised, it is simply more efficient, more productive and profitable. But more importantly, CEA emphasises material recycling and a comprehensive approach to the local economy, integrating agriculture with animal husbandry and other local enterprises. It is therefore unsurprising that ecological agriculture is most easily and successfully adopted where farming, animal husbandry and local enterprises are, by the very nature of things, run in an integrated fashion by the collective.

It is clearly not by accident that the four villages that have most successfully developed biogas digestion at the community level are the wholly collectively-run villages. The coordination of the collection of literally tonnes of excrement per day to provide the input to the digester, to keep the digester well maintained and efficiently run, to manage the distribution of the biogas to every household for cooking and lighting and coordinate the return of the digester's slurry to the fields and fishponds demands collective resources, their commitment and mobilisation far beyond what is available in the average village where the land has been privatised. Indeed, the expense entailed in the initial construction of a community-level biogas plant (apart from the expertise needed for its efficient running and maintenance) is beyond the resources of individual households. Recent studies of energy generation in developing countries suggest that the latter is best not left to the private sector, and biogas digestion is no exception. And therein lies a contradiction. The privatisation of farming has, at least in part, led to the present unsustainability of agriculture, yet it is that same privatisation that presents the greatest obstacle to the adoption of a more ecologically sound alternative in the form of CEA.

Of course, the privatisation of farming *per se* does not stop individual farmers from raising a few animals and using the manure to provide organic fertiliser for their fields, as they have done for centuries. It does not stop individual farmers using human and animal excrement as input to a household biogas pit and emptying the slurry on their fields. Indeed, the poorer the village, the more attractive such propositions are likely to be (particularly when chemical fertiliser is expensive). But they are both messy businesses, associated with poverty and backwardness, and unattractive when money can be earned in the enterprise or town. An ecological agricultural system, particularly involving the successful generation of biogas, has to be a collective operation if it is to generate benefits on a sufficient scale for it to be socially sustainable over time.

The land question

There are therefore very real political questions to be considered concerning the future of the landholding system if CEA is to be popularised. In one critical respect, there has been a change: since 1994 the government has (although this has not been uniformly implemented across the country) encouraged the extension of household leases over the land for another thirty years, and in some cases fifty. To the extent that villagers have a long-term interest in the land they farm, they are that much more likely to use methods, such as the application of organic fertiliser, designed to maintain the fertility of the soil over time. But while this change has been welcomed by farmers and indeed does address one source of unsustainability, it has the negative effect of cementing the *status quo* into the second quarter of the twenty-first century.

Li Bingkun, an official of the State Council, is quoted under the headline 'RURAL LAND SYSTEM NEEDS CHANGING' as saying:

> China has to encourage systems that facilitate scaled and efficient development of agriculture ... the transfer of land rights is encouraged. In actual practice, several new patterns have been developed. The most [popular] one is the so-called 'dual-land system' under which every farmer has his ration of land for food. The rest of the land, *connected and smooth,* is to be leased to people who are capable of scaled farming ... In some areas, farmers [have] got the rights to dispose of the land they rent. They may, except for selling, lease the land again, join partnerships or shareholding collectives with it, *and even lease it back to the land collective owner.* (*China Daily*, 15 June 1995, p. 4, emphasis added)

Li Bingkun is clear that change should be based on the 'free will of farmers' but suggests that central and local government 'do their best to help perfect the systems' and adds:

> Right now, the key point is to allow transfer of the land use rights so all production resources can be distributed economically and efficiently. *And to put as much land back into scaled use, favourable conditions should be created for farmers so [that] many will give up their land thoroughly and willingly.* (*China Daily*, ibid., emphasis added)

This is not an isolated view. Shao Ning argues that:

> A micro-economic mechanism for rural China must ... be able to solve the problems of agricultural operations *on an appropriate scale* ... A central issue in China's agricultural transformation is the transfer of surplus labour, yet if labour is transferred and land is not concentrated, labour transfer will not serve agriculture itself. (1992, p. 20, emphasis added)

Conclusion

An authoritarian return to collectivisation is clearly unthinkable and not an option, but the *status quo* for the next 30 to 50 years is not sustainable either. That *status quo*, where the rural economy is frequently, through TVEs, dependent on collective industry and services, on the one hand, yet on *privatized* agriculture on the other, creates an anomaly that offers no encouragement to the prospect of sustainable agriculture. When Mao Zedong exhorted the collectives to 'take grain as the key link, pay attention to animal husbandry, forestry, fish-raising and sideline occupations, and develop an all-round rural economy', the latter was frequently forgotten in an orgy of grain monoculture. It is surely paradoxical that today, many villages and townships in the post-reform countryside are collectively going ahead with sideline occupations and the all-round economy, whilst leaving the planting of grain ('the key link') to a privatised, precarious and increasingly unsustainable system. This rules out the spread of ecological agriculture, and the promise of a more sustainable future.

Notes

1. This chapter was based on periodic research in China from 1992 to 1997 funded by Nene College Centre For Research and the British Council. I am grateful for their generosity. I am also grateful to a large number of Chinese scholars, researchers, leaders and farmers who gave of their time and expertise. I am particularly indebted to Zhou Shengkun at the Centre for Integrated Agricultural Development at Beijing Agricultural University, Professor Bian Yousheng at the Beijing Institute for Environmental Protection and Research and Xiao Xingji at the Nanjing Research Institute of Environmental Science for their ideas on the substantive questions raised in this work. I am solely responsible for the views contained herein, however.
2. Xiao Xingji is currently Deputy Director of the NEPA Organic Food Centre, Nanjing Research Institute of Environmental Science. Information was provided in interview in the summer of 1996. '*Kuai*' is Chinese slang for yuan, the unit of currency.
3. Karen Janz is currently a rural development consultant in Berlin. She recently worked at the Centre for Integrated Agricultural Development at Beijing Agricultural University and was responsible, with Ye Jingzhong, for editing the report on the proceedings of the First International Symposium on Organic Farming in China in May, 1994. Information from private correspondence in the spring of 1996.
4. Pu Maosen is an official in the Environmental Protection Bureau in Simao county, Yunnan province. Information from private interview in the summer of 1995.

246   *Ecological Agriculture*

5. To label a particularly favoured social process as being 'with Chinese characteristics' is common in China. The present reform-and-open economic policy (*gaige kaifeng*) (which to all intents and purposes is ushering in capitalism and free market allocation) is popularly referred to as 'socialism with Chinese characteristics' (*you Zhongguo de tese shehui zhuyi*).
6. The seven villages in which the research fieldwork took place were Liu Minying (in Daxing county, Beijing municipality), Xiao Zhangzhuang (in Yingshang county, Anhui province), He Heng (in Tai county, Jiangsu province), Qian Wei (in Chongming Dao, Shanghai municipality), Teng Tou (in Fenghua county, Zhejiang province), Tie Xi (in Mishan county, Heilongjiang province) and Dou Dian (in Fangshan district, Beijing municipality). I also visited the county environmental protection bureaux in Daxing county (Beijing), Chongming Dao (Shanghai), Simao (Yunnan) and Dazu (Sichuan). I am extremely grateful to all the leaders, officials and villagers who helped me carry out this research and to Xiong Ying for her interpreting skills.
7. The quilts are made in Xiao Zhangzhuang, in northern Anhui province. They are bought for a few yuan by a Shanghai export agency and sold in shops in the UK for upwards of £100.

References

Aubert, Claud (1995) 'Grain and Meat Production in China', paper to the Fourth European Conference on Agricultural and Rural Development of China, Manchester Business School, UK.

Brown, Lester (1995) *Who Will Feed China? Wake-up Call for a Small Planet*, (London: Earthscan).

Cai, Y. and Smit, B. (1994) 'Sustainability in Agriculture: a General Review', *Agriculture, Ecosystems and Environment*, 49, 199–307.

Cheng, Han and Taylor (1992) 'Sustainable Agricultural Development in China', *World Development*, 20, (8) 1127–44.

China Statistical Yearbook (1995) State Statistical Bureau, People's Republic of China, English ed (Beijing: China Statistical Publishing House).

China Statistical Yearbook (1996) State Statistical Bureau, People's Republic of China, English ed, (Beijing: China Statistical Publishing House).

Foley, G. (1987) *The Energy Question*, 3rd edn (Harmondsworth: Penguin).

Foley, G. (1992) 'Renewable Energy in Third World Development Assistance – Learning from Experience', *Energy Policy*, 20 (4) 355–64.

Hinton, William (1990) *The Great Reversal, The Privatization of China 1978–89* (New York: Monthly Review Press and London: Earthscan).

Johnson, D. Gale (1995) 'China Poses No Threat to the World's Food Supply', *China Daily*, July 11.

King, F. H. (1926) *Farmers of Forty Centuries* (London: Jonathan Cape; Rodale Press, Emmaus, PA).

Li Zhengfang (1994) 'Chinese Organic Agriculture, Ecological Agriculture and Prospect of Organic Food Development', paper to the First International Symposium on Organic Farming in China, Janz and Ye (eds), CIAD, Beijing Agricultural University.

Li Wenjuan (1995) 'An Analysis on Sustainable Development of Crops Production in China', paper for the Fourth European Conference on Agricultural and Rural Development of China, Manchester Business School, November.

Lin, J. Y. (1990) 'Institutional Reforms in Chinese agriculture: Retrospect and Prospect', in Dorn, J. and Wang, X. (eds) *Economic Reform in China, Problems and Prospects* (University of Chicago Press).

Muldavin, J.S.S (1996a) 'Agrarian Reform in China', in Peet, R. and Watts, M. (eds) *Liberation Ecologies* (London and New York: Routledge).

Muldavin J. S. S. (1996b) 'Impact of reform on environmental sustainability in rural China', *Journal of Contemporary Asia*, 6 (3) 289–331.

NEPA (1991) *China's Eco-Farming* (Beijing: China Environmental Science Press).

Pennarz, Johanna (1995) 'Adaptive land-use strategies of Sichuan smallholders: subsistence production and agricultural intensification in a land-scarce poverty area', paper for the Fourth European Conference on Agricultural and Rural Development of China, Manchester Business School, UK.

Qu Geping (1991) *The Review and Prospect of Eco-Farming Construction in China* (Beijing: China Environmental Science Press).

Shao Ning (1992) 'Development and Reform: China's Agriculture in the 1990s', *Social Sciences in China*, 2, 16–22.

Statistical Survey of China (1997) State Statistical Bureau (Beijing: Chinese Statistical Publishing House) (in Chinese).

Wehrfritz, George (1995) 'Grain Drain', *Newsweek*, 15 May.

White G. (1993) *Riding the Tiger, The Politics of Economic Reform in Post-Mao China* (London: Macmillan).

World Bank (1991)*The Challenge of Development: World Development Report*, (Oxford University Press).

Zhou, Q. R. (1996) 'Agricultural Reform: Property Rights and New Organization', paper to the Annual Conference of the Chinese Economics Association, London School of Economics.

Part III
Erosion Problems and Policies

11
Assessing and Managing the Soil Erosion Problem in Southern China

David Higgitt

Introduction: evidence for an emerging soil erosion problem

Soil erosion constitutes a major environmental issue in China. Traditionally focused on the semi-arid environments of the north, degradation has now emerged as a significant topic in the humid south in recent decades. Inventories of land affected by erosion show a dramatic increase in the extent of degradation, which has led to speculation about future food security (Smil 1993).

On a journey through the countryside, the evidence of degradation is clear to see. As the train from Shanghai rumbles west into Jiangxi province, the frequency with which patches of abandoned land is encountered increases. Scrub vegetation partially covers the indurated dark-red badlands. This is the so-called 'red desert', where the Quaternary Red Clay is exposed as the soil cover has been stripped away: a desert despite the mean annual rainfall in excess of 1000 milimetres. Almost 2000 kilometres away, a bus winds precariously through the mountains of western Yunnan on the backpackers' trail to ancient Dali, and past newly claimed fields clinging to the slopes on extreme gradients. Back east 800 kilometres, a short ride away from the bustling tourist hordes in Guilin, grey knuckles of limestone poke through the surface of former arable land like an exhumed skeleton.

Examples of erosion-induced damage are not difficult to find, but degradation is not ubiquitous. Further north in Guangxi, isolated in the mountains bordering Hunan, are the breathtaking terraces of the Yao and Zhuang minority nationalities. They remain well maintained as they have for seven centuries since these ethnic groups were driven away from the lowlands by the colonial expansionism of the Han majority. The picture from southern China is therefore one where soil erosion can be severe but is sporadic in occurrence. This is indicative of a delicate balance between the natural conditions that control the production, detachment and transport of sediment on one hand, and the utilisation and management of the land surface that exacerbates or impedes sediment redistribution on the other. That the soil erosion problem of southern China has largely emerged in the last few decades suggests that environmental stress is at a critical level.

Although the impact of severe soil erosion can be recognised at particular locations, estimating its extent and magnitude over larger units of land (catchments, counties, regions) is not straightforward. China has one of the world's most comprehensive schemes of land resource inventory, and it provides much information about the relative extent of the erosion problem. Estimates of the total land area affected by erosion vary between sources (Table 11.1), but a figure between 150 and 200 million hectares (around 15 to 20 per cent of all territory) seems consistent. About 40 per cent of arable land is considered to be affected by erosion (Wen Dazhong 1993).

Several Chinese rivers are near the top of the world league table of sediment discharges. The Huang He (Yellow River) lies second only to the Amazon, although its water discharge is two orders of magnitude smaller. The Yangtze River is fourth, the Zhu Jiang (Pearl River) sixteenth and the Liaohe twenty-third (Meade 1996). The Brahmaputra, Hong He (Red River), Mekong and Heiliong Jiang (Amur), which have part of their catchment areas within Chinese territory, also feature in the top twenty. The export of sediment from Chinese rivers to the oceans amounts to about 2000 million tonnes annually. Not all eroded soil reaches the sea. The dramatic shrinkage of natural lakes in recent years provides further evidence for the scale of contemporary sediment transfer. Dongting Lake, linked to the lower course of the Chang Jiang in Hunan, experienced a 37 per cent reduction in surface area and 40 per cent shrinkage in capacity in the three decades up to 1977. Current sedimentation rates in the lake are 3.5 centimetres per year.

Across the nation, soil erosion varies in magnitude and according to the controlling processes. Wen Dazhong (1993) identifies four main regions:

- the Loess Plateau;
- the northern mountains spanning Hebei, Shandong and Liaoning;
- the north-eastern rolling hills of Jilin and Heilongjiang;

Table 11.1   Estimates of extent and gross rate of erosion

	Causation [information source]	Area affected (Mha)	Percent
All China	China Daily [1]	367	38.2
	1991 Official [1]	162	16.9
	[2]	183	19
All cultivated land	[2]	56.7	43.6
	by desertification	6.7	
	by salinisation	8	
	by 'serious' wind and water erosion	42	
		Annual loss (mt)	
Soil loss	[2]	5500	(20% world total)
	[3]	5000	(8% world total)
Sediment discharge to oceans	[3]	2000	(8% world total)
N, P, K loss	[4]	1913	(10 to 15% world total)
	[2]	6.06 Mt	

Sources: [1] cited in Edmonds (1994); [2] Wen Dazhong (1993); [3] Shi Deming and Yang Yansheng (1992); [4] Meade (1996) – based on sum of Chang Jiang, Huang He, Liao He, Zhu Jiang, Hong He and Heilong Jiang.

- the southern erosion region, encompassing land south of the Chang Jiang plus eastern Sichuan, but excluding the Sichuan Basin, the lower Yangtze lake plains and the deltas of the Yangtze and Zhu Jiang.

Of these erosion regions, the Loess Plateau is the most celebrated and has drawn most attention and investment in erosion control. By comparison, soil erosion in southern China is neither as severe nor as widespread as on the Loess Plateau, but has become more critical in recent years. Estimates of the extent of erosion show dramatically the increase in affected area in provinces along the Middle and Lower Yangtze Valley since the 1950s (Figure 11.1). The most sensational increases have affected Sichuan and Guizhou. The extent of erosion in every province of the south is given in Table 11.2. Wen Dazhong (1993) suggests that more than a third of arable land south of the Chang Jiang has been adversely affected by soil erosion.

The estimates of national erosion provide stark reading. Like most resource inventory estimates, they are based upon criteria that need to

Table 11.2 Estimates of extent and gross rate of erosion in southern China by province

Province	Source	Area affected (mid-late 1980s) (million ha)	% of province
Sichuan	[2, 3]	38.2	67.3
Guizhou	[2]	3.53	31.2
Anhui	[2]	1.93	30
Jiangxi	[1]	3.79	22.7
Hunan	[1]	4.41	20.9
Zhejiang	[1]	1.48	18.7
Guangxi	[1]	3.8	16.1
Guangdong and Hainan	[1]	2.53	14.2
Jiangsu	[2]	0.61	12.3
Fujian	[1]	1.34	11
Yunnan	[3]	3.55	9.3
Hubei	[3]	0.87	4.6
Southern China	[4]	69	43
of which cropland:		6	36

Sources: [1] Xu Daping and Yang Minquan (1991); [2] CAS (1988) appear to refer to parts of province within Chang Jiang catchment only; [3] Yang Yansheng and Shi Deming (1994); [4] Wen Dazhong (1993).

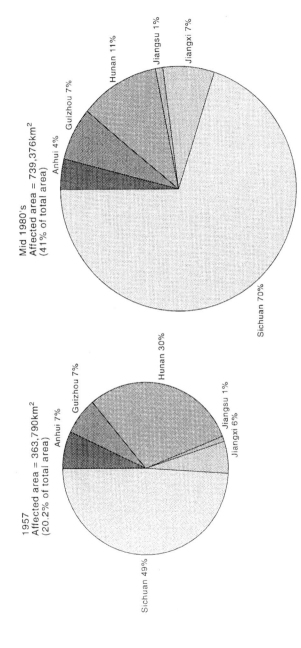

Figure 11.1 Changes in land area affected by erosion between the 1950s and mid-1980s, in selected provinces of the Chang Jiang Valley

1957
Affected area = 363,790km²
(20.2% of total area)

Mid 1980's
Affected area = 739,376km²
(41% of total area)

Sichuan 49%

Guizhou 7%
Anhui 7%
Hunan 30%
Jiangxi 6%
Jiangsu 1%

Sichuan 70%

Anhui 4%
Guizhou 7%
Hunan 11%
Jiangsu 1%
Jiangxi 7%

be treated with caution. The figures draw attention to the enormity of the erosion problem and engender mechanisms for the distribution of anti-erosion funding. Stating the dimensions of degradation, however, does little to solve the problems that lead to and result from accelerated soil erosion. Invited to address a conference of experimental geomorphologists, Stocking (1995) delivered an entertainingly provocative critique of the disjunct objectives of researchers and administrators relative to the requirements for the solution of erosion-inducing conditions. Obsession with announcing the severity and scale of degradation is a long way removed from positive action to improve the situation.

The routes towards solving erosion problems lie in both technical and political-economic issues. Though the factors controlling erosion are well known in a general sense, identification of process dynamics, rates of soil loss and the pathways by which soil is transported into the fluvial system present scientific challenges. Understanding the social, economic and political context that gives rise to unsustainable land uses, or compromises the likelihood of adoption of sympathetic land husbandry techniques, presents further and more significant challenges. Nevertheless, improved understanding of the soil-formation–sediment-transfer system has a part to play in environmental management. In this chapter, two examples of research concerned with assessment of erosion and sediment delivery are discussed. The first case-study is from the mountainous subtropical environment of Fujian province. The second explores the sedimentation issue at the Three Gorges Reservoir in the light of evidence for increasing erosion within the Upper Yangtze Basin. Before the case studies are introduced, consideration is given to the context of the emerging soil erosion problem in southern China and to the technical difficulties in assessing its magnitude and extent.

Context, causes and consequences

Soil erosion arises from a web of environmental and political-economic factors. It is worth emphasising, as many have before, that the detachment and removal of soil material is a natural process that is accelerated by certain human activities. The focus on 'southern China' involves a region that is rather extensive, demarcated largely by the limits of dominant rice production (Map 11.1). While the characteristics of soils, landscape and erosion processes in this area are distinct from other erosion-affected areas further north, southern China is very diverse. It corresponds roughly with the 1000 milimetre isohyet,

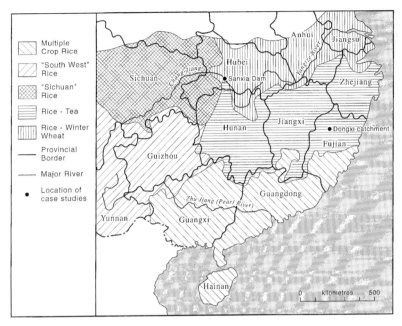

Map 11.1 Distribution of provinces and traditional agricultural areas of southern China (based on Vermeer 1979)

though the Sichuan basin and the northern edges of Guizhou and Yunnan may have slightly less average precipitation than this. Rainfall generally decreases from south-east to north-west, with a rainy season influenced by summer monsoons between May and October but likely to be wettest in May and June.

The physical and chemical properties of the soils, coupled with the region's rainfall characteristics and abundance of steep land indicate an environment where sustainable use of soils requires careful management. As the erosion problem of southern China appears to have become acute in recent years (Shi Deming and Yang Yansheng 1992; Edmonds 1994), attention is now turned towards human impact. Consideration is given to deforestation, impact of population growth and land reform policies.

Population and land use factors

It is clear that soil erosion has been a threat to agricultural activity since farming began, but this chapter will deal only with recent issues.

Despite ambitious afforestation plans and ebullient claims in the 1950s and 1960s, forest cover has continued to decline. Three phases of rapid deforestation in southern China have been associated with changes in national policy:

- the Great Leap Forward (1958–61), when charcoal was needed for small-scale iron production;
- a removal of harvesting restrictions during the early part of the Cultural Revolution;
- Rural Responsibility System policies after 1978, which ended collectives and encouraged extraction of minerals and timber in hilly and mountainous environments.

Smil (1992) estimates a continuing loss of 10 per cent during the 1980s, the majority of which was of mature stands. According to Zhou Guangyi (1995), the average rate of destruction of tropical forest on Hainan Island has exceeded 2 per cent per year since 1949 and has considerably harmed environmental quality, with among other things serious erosion and increased flood frequency. Ni Shaoxiang (1993) reports a more than twenty-fold increase in sediment load and runoff following clearance and cultivation of forest land in Hainan, while erosion rates exceeding 3000 tonnes per square kilometre per year on shifting cultivation land have been estimated (Xu Deying 1993).

Pressures on forest resources result from the expansion of agricultural land, commercial plantations and demand for timber. Relationships between growing population and demand versus environmental quality continue to provoke controversy. Demographic models project that population will continue to expand until the third decade of the twenty-first century (Edmonds 1994). Given the shortage of cultivated land (and despite the now acknowledged underestimate of the official figure of 96 million hectares) (Smil 1992), available land per capita is extremely limited and in decline. In many parts of southern China it is already below 1 mu (0.067 ha) per person. Encroachment of urbanisation and abandonment of severely degraded land must be matched by increased productivity of existing land or expansion of arable production. In the hilly topography of southern China, the latter involves the clearing of slopes. Despite the outlawing of agricultural production on slopes steeper than 25 degrees, there is frequent use of steep land, which is unlikely to halt, given the threat of food shortages. Some studies have found clear relationships between population density and environmental degradation reminiscent of Malthusian limits (Xu and Zeng

1992; Hill 1993; Li and Li 1993), although counter-examples can be found elsewhere in the world (Tiffin *et al.* 1993; *Ecologist* 1993). The issue is the extent to which environmental degradation threatens food security. The impact of soil erosion on fertility and productivity is often overlooked, because year-to-year variations in yield associated with the vagaries of weather, improving strains, fertiliser inputs, etc., tend to mask any impact of a worsening trend in soil quality. A decomposition analysis of grain yields for the whole of China for the period 1976–89 (Huang Jikun and Rozelle 1995) shows that yields increased by nearly 1300 kilograms per hectare during the period but that environmental stress, including soil erosion, reduced potential growth by 56 kilograms per hectare. The impact is small but does indicate that environmental degradation is contributing to the decline in the rate of yield increase.

The accentuation of soil erosion in southern China over the last four decades has coincided with profound changes in agricultural practices (Smil 1987). Technological developments have dramatically increased productivity, which has supported rapid growth in population. Increasing inputs of fertilisers and herbicides have replaced the need for some agricultural labour. There has been upheaval in the organisation of agricultural labour, land ownership and the market value of particular crops. Such changes have exerted influences on land utilisation, which, in turn, have implications for soil erosion. Untangling the relationships between cause and effect is complex.

Assessment of erosion

Collecting information on the rates of erosion is an expensive and time-consuming activity. Investigations of degradation in tropical and subtropical environments are frequently hampered by limited data, but in this respect southern China is an exception. An administrative structure has been developed that permits complete coverage of land area for erosion evaluation. The provincial governments are required to fulfil the obligations of rules laid down by the State Council in August 1993, based on the National Legislative Committee's 1991 directive on soil and water conservation. At each level of the local government hierarchy (town, county, city-region and province) there are soil and water conservation committees or agents. At the grass roots, most town local governments will have an individual or small group of officers charged with compiling the erosion status inventory to be reported to the county government, usually via an agricultural committee.

Procedures for evaluating and reporting erosion status are based on criteria devised at provincial level through interpretation of the State Council's requirements. The approach to erosion zoning concentrates on extent, and attempts to attribute magnitude qualitatively. Although the coverage of zoning is impressive, there is likely to be considerable operator variance in declaring the erosion status category. Experience of compiling inventories of forestry resources in China, for example, has often resulted in large discrepancies between survey and reality, depending on the way in which criteria are interpreted (Richardson 1990). The use of the inventory for targeting resources for remedial action opens the system to some distortion. Much of the provincial-scale information about the degree of affected area, such as that reported in Table 11.2, derives from a nationwide erosion audit under-taken in the period 1984–6, and a decadal survey is presently in progress. While the information portrays something of the extent of degradation, a physical basis for conservation and land use planning depends on information regarding the extent, magnitude and fre-quency relationships of detachment and transport processes.

Aside from plot experiments, predictive equations and qualitative survey, what methods exist for the determination of soil loss dynamics? Measurements of actual soil movement, whether conducted in plots experiments, by means of collections in sediment traps or through the exposure of survey markers, are very time-consuming. Methods that allow rapid appraisal of erosion status are particularly sought. These might be based on the analysis of soil profile properties (comparing eroded and uneroded phases) or on depositional sediments (Olson *et al.* 1994). The amount of sediment exported from a catchment provides another means of estimating erosion. Unfortunately, sediment yields provide spatially and temporally integrated information, in situations where identification of key source areas may be required. Furthermore, only a fraction of the soil eroded is delivered to the catchment outlet. The estimates for gross sediment transfer in China (Table 11.1) suggest that 30 to 40 per cent of eroded material reaches the oceans. These issues – the sediment delivery problem (Walling 1983) – hamper the use of sediment yields in erosion surveys.

Detailed field techniques may prove valuable in the investigation of particular management problems and provide a means of validating erosion prediction models or interpretations made from air photo-graphs or satellite images. Moving beyond the quantification of soil loss, there is little research into rates of soil formation and the impact of soil loss on productivity. Shi Deming and Yang Yansheng (1992)

report that the ratio between contemporary erosion and soil loss tolerance is 6–16 in the hilly regions of southern China, although the basis
for the calculation is not divulged. Significantly, this imbalance
exceeds the ratio for the Loess Plateau, where weathering and soil formation processes are more rapid. Relationships between the distribution of erosion and other soil properties have been examined in a
case-study in Fujian province.

Fujian: distribution of erosion in a mountainous subtropical environment

Fujian province lies in the humid subtropics (Map 11.2). The coastal
zone of Fujian has a long history of trading, and the ports of Xiamen
and Fuzhou have flourished. Separated by mountainous terrain occupying some four-fifths of the land area, the hinterland has remained
largely peripheral to the economic prosperity of the coast, although
some industrial development has infiltrated along the main river
valleys. The industrial city of Sanming in the Shaxi valley, for example,
increased dramatically in size as a result of the transfer of workers from
Shanghai who came to steel production plants during the Cultural
Revolution. It is now the third largest city in Fujian and the emergent
industrial economy imposes change on the functioning of the local
agricultural economy.

With average annual temperature of 17 to 21°C and average annual
precipitation of 1100 to 2000 milimetres (Zhu Hejian 1990), Fujian agriculture has traditionally been geared to multiple rice cropping in the
south and rice–tea production in the north. Agricultural expansion into
the Fujian area is likely to have begun around 3000 years ago (Zhu
Hejian 1990) and the mountainous topography dictated a characteristic
pattern of land utilisation in relation to altitude. The scarcity of land
suitable for agriculture combined with a growing population (now in
excess of 30 million) continues to place pressure on land resources.
Available land has declined from 2.4 mu (0.160 ha) per capita in 1949
to around 1 mu (0.067 ha) at present. There has been a loss of existing
agricultural land to urbanisation and an expansion of agriculture onto
steep, unsuitable slopes. In Datian, for example, 100,000 mu of land has
been converted to fields during the period on slopes up to 40 degrees.

Fujian continues to be a major source of forest resources in southern
China. Liu Chungchu and Lin Cang (1991) report that forest cover
amounted to 43.2 per cent of the provincial land area in 1988, but had
declined from 47.4 per cent three years before. More than two-thirds of

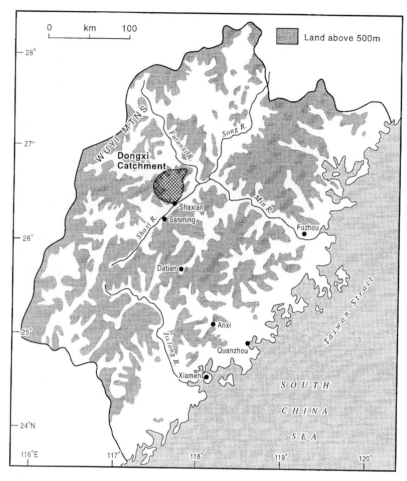

Map 11.2 Fujian Province. The location of Dongxi catchment is indicated

the forest is used for commercial forest production, particularly for Chinese fir and pine and very few areas of primary subtropical forest remain. Population growth not only increases deforestation from the expansion of marginal agricultural land, but also increases demand for fuelwood. Each year Sanming city region (23,058 square kilometres) supplies 1.8 million cubic metres of fuelwood for local consumption and a further 1 million cubic metres to the government to assist national demand. The 1984–6 inventory of erosion damage across the province estimated that 4.8 per cent of Sanming was affected by erosion and a little over half of this occurred in forested upland.

Shaxian county is one of twelve under the jurisdiction of Sanming city region. Fieldwork was undertaken in 1993–4 in the Dongxi River catchment, which comprises the northern half of Shaxian county. The project was evaluating the geomorphological controls on the distribution of soil erosion, land degradation and sediment sources, conducted in conjunction with Nanjing University. Dongxi catchment was selected for two main reasons. First, it is typical of the rolling topography of the southern China Red Earth region. Much of the investigation of soil erosion has focused on localities where rates are spectacular. The 4.8 per cent of land area affected by erosion in Sanming city region is well below the 11.0 per cent provincial average, although it should be noted that forest exploitation and population have risen dramatically in Sanming since the time of the inventory. Conditions are therefore not biased towards extreme rates of erosion. Second, the catchment had been selected for a pilot land evaluation scheme (Ni Shaoxiang *et al.* 1987), which provided good background information on land use.

The Dongxi River is a left-bank tributary of the Shaxi River, which in turn is a tributary of the Min Jiang (Map 11.2). The catchment of the Dongxi comprises 942 square kilometres, most of which lies within Shaxian county, although the administrative borders do not exactly match the physical watershed. The county town of Shaxian located at the confluence of the Dongxi and Shaxi rivers is about 100 metres above sea level. The topography of the catchment is rugged with mountains rising to over 1000 metres.

Geologically, the upland areas are dominated by Palaeozoic plutonic granites and metamorphic rocks. Tectonic activity during the Cretaceous, associated with the marginal influence of a subducting plate boundary to the east, resulted in a series of down-faulted basins, up to 20 kilometres in length. The majority of these were infilled by sediments derived from the surrounding uplands creating a formation known as the Cretaceous Red Beds, a succession of red or purple shales and sandstones. These sediments have been subject to intense weathering throughout the Tertiary and are largely capped by Quaternary river terrace deposits. Within Dongxi catchment, deeply weathered red soils are developed over Cretaceous sediments or Quaternary fluvial sediments in the fault basins of Shaxian, Gaoqiao and Fukou. Little infilling of the Xiamo fault basin took place and the soils are developed over granite regolith. Rapid fluvial incision during the Quaternary resulted in the dissection of the basins forming a topography of low relief hills, typically around 100 metres in length and 30 metres relative relief. While the Holocene terraces and contemporary floodplains are used for grain production, the hills are largely dominated by terraced arable cultivation and form a focus for degradation. Mapping the extent of degraded soils from aerial photographs (Map 11.3) reveals

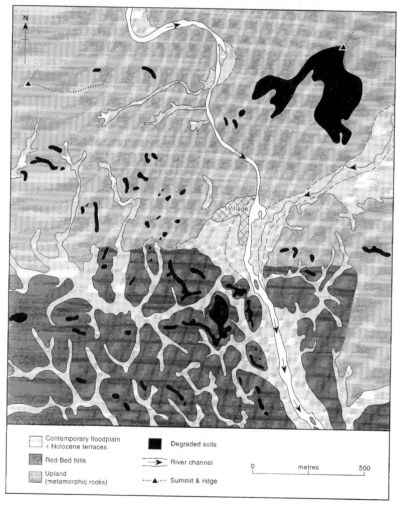

Map 11.3   Distribution of degraded soils on the north-eastern edge of Shaxian red bed area, Dongxi catchment (based on Higgitt and Rowan 1996)

erosional damage in upland areas subsequent to deforestation and on Red Bed hills, particularly those closest to settlement.

Traditionally the region produced rice and tea, then tea prices declined in the 1960s and many tea gardens switched to tea oil production. As the economic viability of tea oil (used in food and herbal medicine) has also declined in recent years, many of the hillsides are now being converted to citrus fruit production or replaced by further arable crops. In part, the introduction of citrus fruit is being promoted as a conservation measure. The criteria for assessing soil erosion status in oil tea gardens are based on slope gradient, presence of inter-row buffer strips and orientation of cultivation with respect to slope. During the establishment of tea gardens ground protection is poor and soils are susceptible to erosion, but once the plants have matured (after 4–5 years) they form an effective barrier to runoff as long as they have been planted parallel to the contour. The removal of mature tea gardens under the guise of improved soil conservation may be misleading and soil erosion is likely to be higher in the intervening period before orchards are established. Encouragement of fruit production by conservation agencies might be regarded as 'pork barrel politics', as the current market price of fruit is persuading farmers to change land use in any event.

Although the Red Bed hills have limited relative relief, careful management is required to prevent surface runoff. Slope profiles are typically convex such that the steepest parts of the slope usually occur just above the valley terrace level. Frequently the base of a slope has been artificially excavated as a source of clay for brick-making and is often occupied by farm buildings. Slope profiles surveyed during a soil sampling programme have a mean slope angle of 17 degrees, and those used for arable cultivation have been extensively terraced. In a few locations, such as Xiamo, terraces have been poorly maintained and are severely degraded, such that some land has been abandoned. Processes leading to land abandonment are complex. Terrace maintenance is a labour-intensive activity and the increased rural-to-urban migration may account for a lack of labour at key times of the year. Ironically, it is advances in agricultural technology, such as the use of herbicides, that have enabled many operations in the farming calendar to be undertaken by fewer people. Traditional, labour-intensive conservation measures, which would have been part of the normal cycle of farming activity, have been reduced. Alternatively, the abandonment of land may be related to the breakdown of commune land management following the 1978 land reforms. What is clear is that on the most vulnerable red soils, which in Fujian are particularly those developed on granite, the cessation of management for even a short period may enable degradation to occur to such an extent that rehabilitation of that land cannot be accomplished without major effort.

A number of sites were sampled on arable land in the fault basins of Xiamo, Fukou Gaoqiao and Shaxian as well as on a smaller area of arable land at Gaizou, a mountain village south-west of Fukou (Map 11.4). In each basin, slope profiles were surveyed and soil pits were excavated at slope crest, mid slope and lower slope locations. Soil profile details were noted and incremented samples collected at 5-centimetre increments to a depth of 25 centimetres, in addition to a depth-integrated bulk sample. To enable the examination of variations in soil properties in relation to land use types, the site characteristics were grouped into four categories: undisturbed, tea plantation, arable slope crest, and arable slope. The latter two categories distinguish between sites on low-gradient slopes near the crest of small hills and down-transect sites that are on steeper gradients.

The number of samples collected during the programme is somewhat restricted, but the results indicate that arable cultivation on sloping sites results in depletion of soil nutrient status and is coincident with

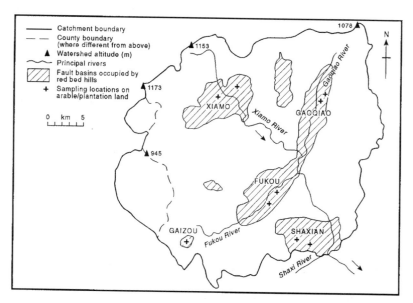

Map 11.4   Distribution of main agricultural areas within Dongxi catchment

indicators of enhanced erosion. Using a simple model for converting caesium-137 redistribution into soil loss, mean rates of soil removal of 1.6, 8.0 and 10.4 milimetres per year were obtained for slope crest, tea garden and arable slope locations, respectively. Estimation of the baseline fallout to the catchment is fraught with difficulty, so the erosion estimates should be treated with large error estimates of at least ± 50 per cent. But the inventories encountered do correspond with other indicators of nutrient depletion and degradation.

Analysis of depositional sediment profiles offers an alternative means of assessing erosion rates. From the point of view of the investigation, the location of the four reservoirs in Dongxi catchment is unfortunate, each being positioned in headwater reaches upstream of agricultural land where the majority of the catchment areas are under forest cover. The previous existence of rice paddies along valley floors provides a convenient marker horizon in reservoir sediment cores. Examination of pits dug through sediments exposed during the dry season in the floor of Yan Bang Reservoir, upstream of Xiamo, were used to infer a sediment yield of 110 tonnes per square kilometre per year from a largely pristine forested sub-catchment, which probably represents the long-term geologic erosion rate from steep slopes on granitic terrain, most likely derived from channel erosion.

Attempts to examine sediment profiles downstream of agricultural areas are thwarted by the widespread interference of sediment profiles through various human activities such as the construction of paddy fields or the mining of fluvial sediments for construction materials. Furthermore, the obstacles to the transmission of sediment through the fluvial system raise a number of issues concerning the extent to which sediment yields reflect the magnitude of soil erosion processes. A preliminary description of the Dongxi sediment delivery system (Higgitt 1995) attempts to represent the difficulties facing the analysis of sediment delivery processes and hence the problems of predicting the implications of headwater soil erosion on downstream activities (Figure 11.2). If the study of sediment dynamics on a relatively modest scale is fraught with complications, consider the issues invoked by the construction of the world's largest dam on the Chang Jiang (Yangzi River).

Erosion and sedimentation in the Three Gorges

The proposal to go ahead with the Three Gorges Project (TGP) has generated enormous debate within and outside China (see Chapter 7 in

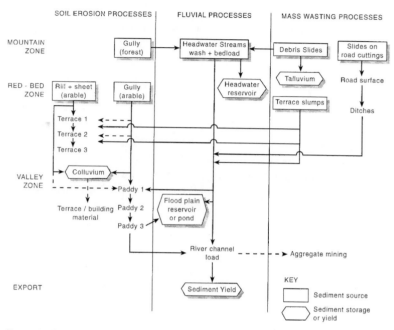

Figure 11.2   Schematic model of the sediment delivery system in a mountain-ous subtropical environment

this volume). International opinion has not often been favourable, and the complexities of the arguments of proponents and opponents have been evaluated elsewhere (see e.g. Edmonds 1992; Luk and Whitney 1993).

The impact of sedimentation on the operational life of the Three Gorges Reservoir is one of many environmental issues under scrutiny. Rapid reduction of storage capacity has compromised the objectives of many previous large dam schemes, including the Sanmenxia Dam built on the Huang He in 1961. Proponents of the scheme to dam the Chang Jiang have recognised the problem of high sediment loads, but have argued that flow regulation procedures will permit the mainte-nance of long-term storage capacity by discharging sediment-laden waters. The approach requires a low reservoir level during the flood season from June to September, enabling flood events and their associ-ated sediment pulses to be discharged through specially designed sluices. Such an operation is slightly at odds with the reservoir's flood protection and water storage functions, but it is claimed that impoundment of water from October onwards will attain sufficient water storage to supply throughout the dry season. Much of the sediment deposited during the impoundment phase would be scoured during the following flood season, when the operating level is lowered once more. In this respect, the canyon-like cross-section of the reservoir is beneficial in promoting the remobilisation of sediments, and it is claimed that after a period of infilling of dead storage the reservoir will eventually become self-flushing.

Much of the debate surrounding the regulation procedures has focused on the assumptions of hydraulic models of reservoir sedimentation (Qian Ning *et al.* 1993; Williams 1993), and there has been relatively little consideration of potential sediment input. Despite the frequently cited data on the increasing extent of soil erosion within the Upper Yangtze Basin, particularly within Sichuan, no clear trend in sediment yield in the main channel is apparent over the last 40 years. The long-term average of around 530 million tonnes per year forms the basis for most hydraulic engineering scenarios. Scientists engaged in the investigation of soil erosion and sedimentation would wish to seek explanation of the discrepancy between the apparent trends on the hill slopes and those in the main river.

In many ways the sedimentation management debate is reminiscent of the development of the Huang He Basin in the middle of this century, where emphasis was given to dealing with the symptoms of the problem – high sediment load – rather than the cause. Analysis of regional patterns of sediment yields is complicated by the difficulty of comparing data collected by hydrographic stations over different periods, as sediment loads are greatly influenced by hydrological conditions. Second, only a fraction of the soil removed from slopes reaches the river network, and is a function of basin area. This means that comparison of sediment yields from different-sized catchment areas requires caution.

Over the years there have been numerous attempts by geomorphologists to explain global and regional patterns of sediment yield in terms of climate (Langbein and Schumm 1958; Jansson 1988) and topography (Milliman and Syvitski 1992; Summerfield and Hulton 1994). The celebrated Langbein and Schumm model explains sediment yield in terms of interaction between the erosive energy of rainfall and the protective function of vegetation density. It suggests that maximum sediment yields occur at the transition of arid and grassland environments, where annual effective precipitation is around 300 milimetres. This model has gained favour with Xu Jiongxin (1994) as a means of explaining sediment yield across China, by implication suggesting that high sediment loads are essentially a geological phenomenon rather than a shortcoming of environmental management.

Within the Upper Chang Jiang catchment, which stretches slightly over 1 million square kilometres above the dam site, the pattern of sediment yield is highly complex, reflecting a diverse combination of climatic, topographic, lithological and land use controls. A plot of mean annual sediment load against catchment area for all stations with at least five years of measurements (Figure 11.3) indicates a significant relationship between load and catchment area, but one in which specific sediment yields (load per unit area) decline with catchment area and in which individual tributaries exhibit manifestly different sediment delivery characteristics.

Data compiled from county soil conservation units by the Chinese Academy of Sciences (CAS 1988, Figure 1), show that the land area classified as affected by soil erosion within the provinces along the Chang Jiang Valley has doubled since the 1950s. Sichuan and Guizhou have exceeded other provinces in the extent of affected area, the

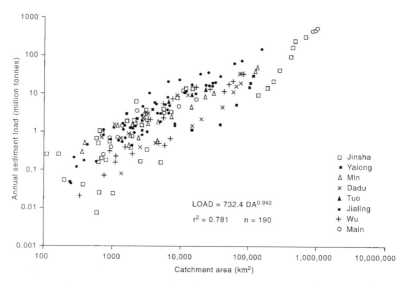

Figure 11.3   Plot of mean annual sediment load against catchment area for all stations in the Upper Chang Jiang catchment with at least five years of measurements. (Symbols represent different tributaries – 'Main' refers to the main Chang Jiang channel and its smaller tributaries in the Three Gorges area.)

former experiencing a quadrupling of degradation. Although the rivers draining these areas contribute much of the total sediment load to the Chang Jiang, immediately above the Three Gorges, a clear trend in sediment yields is not coincident (Gu Hengyue and Douglas 1989: Luk and Whitney 1993).

Higgitt and Lu Xixi (1996) have analysed data collected by 255 hydrographic stations upstream of Yichang (the dam site) between 1956 and 1987. Filtering the database to extract comparable records and applying an empirically derived correction for sediment delivery ratio, it is possible to demonstrate the relative importance of particular tributaries over time. The relative annual contribution of the Jialing River from the 1950s onwards has been 2 to 3 times that to be expected if sediment yields were uniform across the basin, on average supplying more than 30 per cent of the catchment sediment load from just 15 per cent of the land area. Closer inspection shows that the relative contribution declined from more than 3.5 times its expected value in the late 1950s to early 1960s, to about double its expected level in the 1970s, before increasing slightly once more. Of the tributaries to the greater Jialing, the Fu followed a similar but less dramatic pattern, but the Qu has risen from obscurity to supply more than twice its expected load from the mid-1970s onwards. The Wu, draining the Guizhou plateau, shows the opposite trend from the Jialing, with its highest years of relative production occurring in the 1970s. Relative contribution declines steadily in a westward direction consistent with a lower proportion of agricultural land.

Attempts to map the spatial diversity of sediment yields are also made problematic by the sediment delivery ratio effect and the representation of nested catchment areas in a hierarchy of hydrographic stations. One approach (adopted by Higgitt and Lu Xixi 1996) is to map the distribution of standardised residuals from a specific sediment yield-catchment area regression. In Map 11.5, the proportional squares indicate greater than expected contributions of sediment. The largest magnitude of positive residuals clusters around the northern margins of the Sichuan basin, and other positive residuals occur throughout the rolling topography of eastern Sichuan, most of the Sichuan Basin and the border area of south-western Sichuan and Yunnan. Negative residuals (circles) plot throughout the western part of the catchment draining the increasingly arid interior of Qinghai and northern Tibet, the Kunming area of Yunnan and the eastern part of Guizhou. The agricultural areas are clearly the largest providers of sediment but often exhibit a high degree of variability in annual sediment yields. The

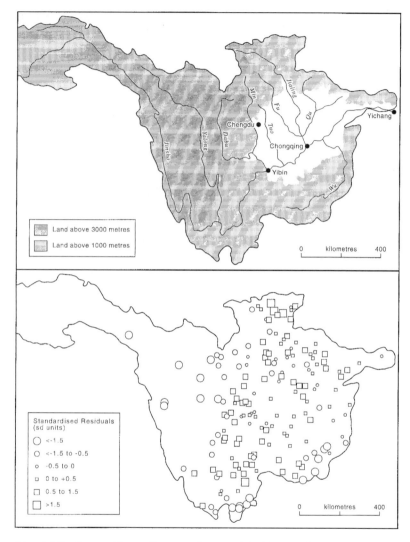

Map 11.5 Upper Chang Jiang catchment. (a) Topography and tributaries. (b) Plot of standardised residuals of annual sediment yield (based on Higgitt and Lu Xixi 1996)

pattern is consistent with the large increase in reported soil erosion since the 1950s and yet a trend in the overall sediment export at Yichang is not apparent. Where is the sediment going?

There are several possible reasons for the mismatch between apparent erosion rates and sediment yields. First, year-to-year hydrological variability in the Chang Jiang is large and it may be masking an underlying pattern in sediment trends. Second, it is possible that much of the sediment generated by extensifying erosion has been trapped in temporary storage, particularly in the reservoirs of water conservancy projects initiated in the 1960s. It has been estimated that the combined reservoir storage above the dam site is over 16,000 million cubic metres (Gu Hengyue *et al.* 1987), which is roughly equivalent to 30 years of total sediment export. Many of the smaller reservoirs are already experiencing chronic siltation problems, and as the capacity continues to decline so the relative throughput of sediment will increase. Third, the period over which sediment yield data have been analysed includes dramatic episodes of deforestation, which may have generated high initial sediment yields but then declined as vegetation cover re-established.

Hence, the increased extent of erosion noted by audits may not necessarily equate with an increase in magnitude. Geomorphological studies in the eastern USA have demonstrated that sediment derived from erosion induced by colonial settlement is now being remobilised from upland valley floors (Trimble 1993). The time-lag between soil loss on the slope and delivery to the Three Gorges Reservoir may involve centuries. Regulation of sediment-laden water has never been attempted on such a scale and it is clear that the linkage between soil erosion and sediment load in large catchments is still poorly understood.

Prospects for controlling the erosion problem

The case studies illustrate some interpretations of soil loss and sediment transport in southern China. Experimental research, principally coordinated by the Institute of Soil Science, Academia Sinica, provides explanations of various degradation-related processes in soils. Applied research provides models of rational land use. Meanwhile, the momentum of the erosion problem shows no sign of subsiding. Why does the threat of further degradation remain?

The lack of progress in halting erosional destruction, beyond small-scale initiatives, involves the discourses of political ecology (Blaikie 1985; Bryant 1992). It is difficult to make general comments about the situation without belittling the considerable effort of individuals and organisations devoted to the limitation of erosion problems. But fundamentally the continuation of unsustainable land use is about a lack of participation and a lack of alternatives. In a compilation of research papers from southern China, Parham *et al.* (1993) paint an optimistic appraisal of the technical ability to solve problems imposed by degradation. In particular, the development of vertical ecology (Ni Shaoxiang *et al.* 1987; Luo Shiming and Li Huashou 1993) has proved apposite for the rugged topography of the region. Encouraging results are also forthcoming from the experimental demonstration zones established by the Institute of Soil Science, where integrated production systems of agriculture, forestry, fruit, animal husbandry and fisheries are promoted. However, few papers outlining technical developments address the issues of adoption.

The comprehensive nationwide erosion auditing, and the number of people employed in soil and water conservation agencies, is unrivalled among other countries in tropical and subtropical environments. The administration of erosion monitoring raises two main concerns. First, the information collected for erosion hazard zoning, with its emphasis on reporting percentages belonging to particular categories rather than information on process controls or rates, may not provide sufficient or appropriate detail for implementing conservation measures (Higgitt and Rowan 1996). Second, the bureaucracy is extremely hierarchical, such that the grass roots conservation officer has rigid guidelines about what to do and what to report. Information flow is dominantly to the centre and there is limited opportunity for the diffusion of research results and ideas. Prospects for integrated catchment management towards the solution of erosion–sedimentation issues also appear limited. The jurisdiction of sediment-related problems lies with the administrative committees for river basins, whereas on-site problems are discussed by agricultural committees of local government, with little evidence of lines of communication.

In reviewing the status of soil erosion in southern China and the prospects for its future control, a number of issues have resonance. The research framework exists for developing and testing conservation strategies, although methods for assessing the rates of soil loss, quality deterioration and pathways of sediment transport could be augmented. The step from the design of conservation strategies to their implementation is crucial. For those of us involved in the research of environmental processes, soil erosion is a big issue. For those attempting to maintain a livelihood on the soils of southern China there are more pressing issues.

References

Blaikie, P. (1985) *The Political Economy of Soil Erosion* (Harlow: Longman).

Bryant, R. L. (1992) 'Political Ecology: An Emerging Research Agenda in Third World Studies', *Political Geography*, 11, 12–36.

CAS (Leading Group of the Three Gorges Project Ecology and Environment Research Project, Chinese Academy of Sciences) (1988) *Ecological and Environmental Impact of the Three Gorges Project and Countermeasures* (Beijing: Science Press) (in Chinese).

Ecologist, (1993) '"Carrying Capacity", "Over Population" and Environmental Degradation', reproduced in Kirkby, J., O'Keefe, P. and Timberlake, L. (eds) (1996) *The Earthscan Reader in Sustainable Development* (London: Earthscan) 101–3.

Edmonds, R. L. (1992) 'The Sanxia (Three Gorges) Project: The Environmental Argument Surrounding China's Super Dam', *Global Ecology and Biogeography Letters*, 2, 105–25.

Edmonds, R. L. (1994) *Patterns of China's Lost Harmony: A Survey of the Country's Environmental Degradation and Protection* (London: Routledge).

Gu Hengyue, Ai Nanshan and Ma Hongliang (1987) 'Sediment sources and trends in the TGP reservoir area' (in Chinese), in: Leading Group of the Three Gorges Project Ecology and Environment Research Project, Chinese Academy of Sciences (ed.) *Collected Papers on Ecological and Environmental Impact of the Three Gorges Project and Countermeasures* (Beijing: Science Press) 522–541.

Gu Hengyue and Douglas, I. (1989) 'Spatial and Temporal Dynamics of Land Degradation and Fluvial Erosion in the Middle and Upper Yangtze River Basin', *Land Degradation and Rehabilitation*, 1, 217–35.

Higgitt, D. L. (1995) 'Assessment of Erosion and Sediment Delivery in a Mountainous Subtropical Catchment, Fujian province, China', in: Singh, R. B. and Haigh, M. J. (eds) *Sustainable Reconstruction of Highland and Headwater Regions* (Rotterdam: Balkema) 299–306.

Higgitt, D. L. and Lu Xixi (1996) 'Patterns of Sediment Yield in the Upper Yangtze Basin, China', in *Erosion and Sediment Yield: Global and Regional Perspectives* (Proceedings of the Exeter Symposium, July 1996), IAHS Publication no. 236 (Wallingford: International Association of Hydrological Sciences) 205–214.

Higgitt, D. L. and Rowan, J. S. (1996) 'Erosion Assessment and Administration in Subtropical China: A Case Study from Fujian Province', *Land Degradation and Development*, 7, 1–10.

Hill, R. D. (1993) 'Land, People and an Equilibrium Trap: Guizhou Province, PRC', *Pacific Viewpoint*, 34 (3), 1–22.

Huang Jikun and Rozelle, S. (1995) 'Environmental Stress and Grain Yields in China', *American Journal of Agricultural Economics*, 77, 853–64.

Jansson, M. B. (1988) 'A Global Survey of Sediment Yield' *Geografiska Annaler*, 70A, 81–98.

Langbein, W. B. and Schumm, S. A. (1958) 'Yield of Sediment in Relation to Mean Annual Precipitation', *Transactions of the American Geophysical Union*, 39, 1076–84.

Li, J. and Li, C. (1993) 'The Gradation and Assessment of the Damage Degree of the Natural Landscape in the Hilly Region of South China: Taking Xing'an

County of Zhuang Autonomous Region of Guangxi as the Example', in Parham, W. E., Durana, P. J. and Hess, A. L. (eds) *Improving Degraded Lands: Promising Experiences from South China* (Honolulu: Bishop Museum Press) 117–21.

Liu Chungchu and Lin Cang (1991) 'The Present Status and Potential Use of Hill Land in Fujian Province', in Horne, P. M., Macleod, D. A. and Scott, J. M., (eds), *Forages on Red Soils in China, ACIAR Proceedings No. 38* (Canberra: Australian Centre for International Agricultural Research) 106–9.

Lu Xixi and Shi Deming (1991) 'Soil Erosion and Revegetation in the Hilly Area of South China', in Horne, P. M., Macleod, D. A. and Scott, J. M. (eds), *Forages on Red Soils in China, ACIAR Proceedings No. 38* (Canberra: Australian Centre for International Agricultural Research) 31–4.

Lu Xixi, Shi Deming, Yang Yansheng and Liang Yin (1991) 'Evaluation on the Water Retention Properties of Eroded Soil Developed from Quaternary Red Clay Region', *Acta Conservationis Soli et Aquae Sinica*, 5(3) 88–96 (in Chinese).

Luk, S.-H. and Whitney, J. B. (eds.) (1993) *Megaproject: A Case Study of China's Three Gorges Project* (Armonk, New York: M. E. Sharpe).

Luo Shiming and Li Huashou (1993) 'Agroecosytem Models to Prevent Land Degradation and to Improve Land Productivity in the Jian River Watershed', in Parham, W. E., Durana, P. J. and Hess, A. L. (eds) *Improving Degraded Lands: Promising Experiences from South China* (Honolulu: Bishop Museum Press) 91–102.

Meade, R. H. (1996) 'River-Sediment Inputs to Major Deltas', in Milliman, J. D. and Haq, B. U. (eds) *Sea-Level Rise and Coastal Subsidence* (Dordrechdt: Kluwer) 63–85.

Milliman, J. D. and Syvitski, J. P. M. (1992) 'Geomorphic/Tectonic Control of Sediment Discharge to the Ocean: The Importance of Small Mountainous Rivers', *Journal of Geology*, 100, 525–44.

Ni Shaoxiang (1993) 'Soil Erosion in Tropical Southern China: Problems and Countermeasures', in Parham, W. E., Durana, P. J. and Hess, A. L. (eds) *Improving Degraded Lands: Promising Experiences from South China* (Honolulu: Bishop Museum Press) 151–4.

Ni Shaoxiang, Bao Haosheng, Peng Buzhou and Li Chunhua (1987) 'A Preliminary Study on Land Classification and Evaluation in the Dongxi River Basin of Shaxian County, Fujian Province', *Journal of Nanjing University*, 8, 83–92.

Olson, K. R., Norton, L. D., Fenton, T. E. and Lal, R. (1994) 'Quantification of Soil Loss from Eroded Soil Phases', *Journal of Soil and Water Conservation*, 49, 591–96.

Parham, W. E., Durana, P. J. and Hess, A. L (eds) (1993) *Improving Degraded Lands: Promising Experiences from South China* (Honolulu: Bishop Museum Press).

Qian Ning, Zhang Ren and Chen Zhicong (1993) 'Some Aspects of Sedimentation at the Three Gorges Project', in Luk, S.- H. and. Whitney, J. B. (eds) *Megaproject A Case Study of China's Three Gorges Project* (Armonk, NY: M. E. Sharpe) 121–160.

Richardson, S. D. 1990 *'Forests and Forestry in China'* (Washington, DC: Island Press).

Shi Deming and Yang Yansheng (1992) 'Effects of Soil Erosion on Land Degradation and its Control in China', in Gong Zitong (ed.) *Proceedings of an*

International Symposium on the Management and Development of Red Soils in Asia and the Pacific Region (Beijing: Science Press) 117–24.

Smil, V. (1987) 'Land Degradation in China: An Ancient problem getting worse', in P. Blaikie and H. Brookfield (eds), *Land Degradation and Society* (London: Methuen) 214–22.

Smil, V. (1992) 'China's Environment in the 1980s: Some Critical Changes', *Ambio*, 21, 431–36.

Smil, V. (1993) *China's Environmental Crisis: An Inquiry into the Limits of National Development* (Armonk, New York: M. E. Sharpe).

Stocking, M. (1995) 'Soil Erosion in Developing Countries: Where Geomorphology Fears to Tread!', *Catena*, 25, 253–67.

Summerfield, M. A. and Hulton, N. J. (1994) 'Natural Controls of Fluvial Denudation Rates in Major World Drainage Basins', *Journal of Geophysical Research*, 99, 13871–83.

Tiffin, M., Mortimore, M. and Gichuki, F. (1993) *More People, Less Erosion: Environmental Recovery in Kenya* (Chichester: Wiley).

Trimble, S. W. (1993) 'The Distributed Sediment Budget Model and Watershed Management in the Palaeozoic Plateau of the Upper Midwestern United States', *Physical Geography*, 14, 285–303.

Vermeer, E. B. (1977) *Water Conservancy and Irrigation in China* (The Hague: Leiden University Press).

Walling, D. E. (1983) 'The Sediment Delivery Problem', *Journal of Hydrology*, 65, 209–37.

Wen Dazhong (1993) 'Soil Erosion and Conservation in China', in Pimental, D. (ed.) *World Soil Erosion and Conservation* (Cambridge University Press) 63–85.

Williams, P. B. (1993) 'Sedimentation Analysis', in Barber, M. and Ryder, G. (eds), *Damming the Three Gorges* (London: Earthscan) 126–132.

Xu Daping and Yang Minquan (1991) 'Soil Erosion in the Red Soil area of Southern China', in Horne, P. M., Macleod, D. A. and Scott, J. M. (eds) *Forages on RedSoils in China, ACIAR Proceedings no. 38* (Canberra: Australian Centre for International Agricultural Research) 82–5.

Xu Deying (1993) 'A Comparison of Potential Productivity and Actual Productivity in the Context of Land Degradation on Hainan Island, China', in Parham, W. E., Durana, P. J. and Hess, A. L. (eds) *Improving Degraded Lands: Promising Experiences from South China* (Honolulu: Bishop Museum Press) 69–72.

Xu Jiongxin (1994) 'Zonal distribution of River Basin Erosion and Sediment Yield in China', *China Science Bulletin*, 39, 1356–61.

Xu, J. and Zeng, G. (1992) 'Bengang Erosion in Sub-tropical Granite Weathering Crust Geoecosystems: An Example from Guangdong Province', in *Erosion, Debris Flows and Environment in Mountain Regions (Proceedings of the Chengdu Symposium)*, IAHS Publication 209 (Wallingford: International Association of Hydrological Sciences) 455–63.

Yang Yansheng and Shi Deming (1994) *Study on Soil Erosion in the Three Gorge Region of the Yangtze River* (Nanjing: South East Universities Press) (in Chinese).

Zhao Qigao (1992) 'Ecological Environment and Integrated Exploitation of the Red Soil Hilly Region of China', in Gong Zitong (ed), *Proceedings of an International Symposium on the Management and Development of Red Soils in Asia and the Pacific region* (Beijing: Science Press) 2–7.

Zhao Qigao (1993) 'Ecological Environment and Integrated Exploitation of the Red Soil Hilly Region of China', in Parham, W. E., Durana, P. J. and. Hess, A. L (eds) *Improving Degraded Lands: Promising Experiences from South China* (Honolulu: Bishop Museum Press) 177–180.

Zhou Guangyi (1995) 'Influences of Tropical Forest Changes on Environmental Quality in Hainan Province, P.R. of China', *Ecological Engineering*, 4, 223–9.

Zhu Hejian (1990) 'The Present State and Developmental Orientation of Land Utilization in Mountainous Red Earth Regions in China', *GeoJournal*, 20, 375–9.

12

Soil Erosion and Conservation on Subtropical Arable in Yunnan Province, South-west China

Mike Fullen, David J. Mitchell, Andrew P. Barton, Trevor J. Hocking, Liu Liguang, Wu Bo Zhi, Zheng Yi and Xia Zheng Yuan

> 'Once the skin is gone, where can the hair grow?'
> Ancient Chinese proverb, quoted in T. Min Tieh (1941)

Introduction

China has one of the world's most severe soil erosion problems, extensively reviewed by Wen (1993) and Edmonds (1994) (see also this volume, Chapters 11 and 13). The population is putting severe pressures on the soil resource, which supports 22 per cent of the global population on 7 per cent of the world's cropland (Brown 1984). The productive soil resource is severely restrained by climate. Much of western China, particularly Xinjiang, Gansu, Ningxia and Inner Mongolia provinces, is too arid, while the Qinghai–Tibetan Plateau of the west is also too cold for extensive crop production (Zhao 1986). Hence, most crops are grown in the humid east. Only about 13.5 per cent (130 million hectares) of total land area is cultivated (Wen 1993). Whilst government policy prohibits cultivation of slopes steeper than 28 per cent (Barrows *et al.* 1982), this limit is often breached to extend crop production. Land resource pressures exerted by 1200 million people are superimposed on diverse environments, which are often geologically and geomorphologically unstable. Therefore, physical factors, such as slope steepness and stability, tectonic activity, rainfall erosivity and soil erodibility interact with anthropogenic activities, producing the complicated erosion problem. Thus, erosion is produced by a complex interplay of environmental and anthropogenic factors.

It is estimated that 15 to 20 per cent of the world's water erosion occurs in China (Brown 1984, Wen 1993), although the database is limited (Dregne 1992). Total erosion is estimated at 5500 million tonnes (Mt) of soil per year, with associated loss of 27.5 Mt of organic matter, 5.5 Mt of nitrogen (N), 0.5 Mt of available potassium (K) and 0.06 Mt of available phosphorus (P) (Wen 1993). These losses account respectively for 63, 46 and 2 per cent of the total K, N and P applied annually to cropland in China. Therefore, soil erosion increases the dependence of agriculture on artificial fertilisers, with subsequent increases in production costs. However, erosion rates, patterns and processes are spatially highly variable, which can be illustrated by comparing and contrasting soil erosion in the basins of the Yellow and Yangtze rivers. The Yellow River flows through the arid north, which is the main area of wheat production. The Yangtze River flows through the humid south, an area dominated by a rice cultivation.

The Yellow River (Huang He) is 5464 kilometres long; it rises in the uplands of the Qinghai–Tibet Plateau and flows eastward through arid Qinghai, Gansu, Ningxia and Inner Mongolia provinces. Vast amounts of sediment are entrained in the Loess Plateau, especially in Shanxi and Shaanxi provinces (Cao and Coote 1993, Douglas *et al.* 1994). Loess is fine, silty material, mainly transported as dust during the Pleistocene glacials of the last two million years. The Loess Plateau of north central China forms the most extensive loess area in the world, mantling 530,000 square kilometres and reaching depths of more than 300 metres. The deepest known section is 318 metres thick, at Jiouzhoutai near Lanzhou.

The unconsolidated silty material is easily eroded by wind and water, with an estimated soil loss from the Loess Plateau of about 2200 million tonnes annually, equivalent to 51 tonnes per hectare (Wen 1993). Maximum sediment concentrations in the middle reaches of the Yellow River approach 700 kilogrammmes per cubic metre, about 50 per cent by weight (Robinson 1981). Water erosion has resulted in a highly dissected, gullied landscape, which requires an elaborate system of terraces for successful cultivation (Fu 1989, Dregne 1992). Most of the estimated 1600 million tonnes transported by the Yellow River to the Bohai Sea originate in the Loess Plateau; hence its name, as the river is actually yellow (Fu 1989; Wen 1993). Wind erosion is also a major problem, to the extent that scientists at the Mauna Loa Observatory in Hawaii, some 5000 kilometres away, can detect the onset of the Chinese spring ploughing season by an increase in atmospheric dust fallout (Parrington *et al.* 1983).

On the low coastal plains of northern China, the Yellow River has been notorious throughout historic times for catastrophic floods, hence its nickname as 'China's sorrow'. High sediment loads encourage aggradation on the river bed of about 10 centimetres per year. Currently it is generally 6 to 10 metres and up to 12 metres above the floodplain, thus posing a serious threat of levee bank failure and floods (Robinson 1981; Fu 1989; UNEP 1990; Wen 1993). About 1500 floods have resulted from the river breaking its dykes over the past 2000 years. Thus, severe erosion brings considerable problems, to areas of both soil export and soil import.

The Yangtze River also rises in the western uplands of the Qinghai–Tibet Plateau, but its 6300 kilometres length traverses a more humid landscape, through southern and central China (Map 12.1). The headwaters are in tectonically active and geologically unstable uplands. Furthermore, the basin is generally under intensive agricultural use, mainly for rice cultivation. Hence, erosion rates are high, estimated at 2400 million tonnes per year (Wen 1993). These high rates are of increasing concern, especially considering the construction of the Three Gorges (Sanxia) Dam in the middle section (Douglas *et al.* 1994). Sedimentation within the reservoir could impair its efficiency and therefore soil conservation must be an integral component of basin management (Edmonds 1994).

The soil erosion problems of Yunnan province

Much of the upper Yangtze basin lies in Yunnan, south-west China (Map 12.1). The province borders Myanmar (Burma), Laos and Vietnam, and covers 383,278 square kilometres. It encompasses a wide range of environments, including subtropical rainforest, temperate uplands and cool highlands of the Hengduan and Gaoligong Mountains, part of the Himalayan range. Altitude varies from 6740 metres at Mount Kagebo to 76.4 metres on the Honghe River, averaging between 1000 and 3000 metres. About 95 per cent of land is moderately to steeply sloping, thus only 6.8 per cent of Yunnan's land area can be used for agricultural activities (Thomas 1992). Field erosion surveys have been carried out by the authors both in cool montane environments of the Upper Yangtze basin (Dongchuan and Huize counties) and in arable subtropical uplands (Kunming district, Lunan, Xundian and Yuanmou counties).

The montane areas are tectonically active and unstable and are thus prone to earthquakes, which often trigger landslides, debris avalanches and mudflows. Plate 12.1 shows a landslide in the Huize uplands, which occurred rapidly because of intense rains. Voluminous and intense seasonal rains, produced by moist maritime airstreams penetrating from the south, cause high erosion rates, which can result in

282

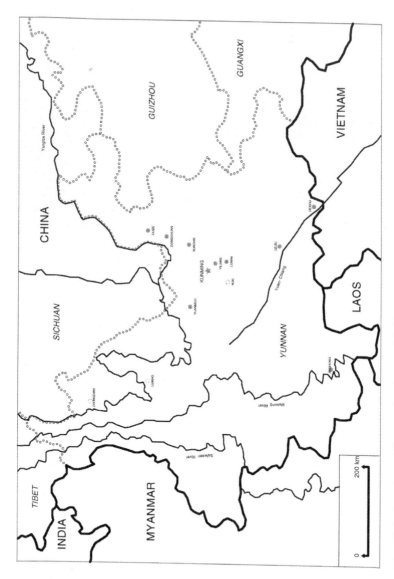

Map 12.1 Location of Yunnan Province and field sites

Plate 12.1 Landslide in the uplands of Huize county, August 1993; it occurred on 12 July 1991 and caused six deaths

extreme gully erosion. Slope runoff rapidly transports sediments into the Yangtze River, and at confluences in the Upper Yangtze the red water colour from sediments derived from areas draining sandstone rocks and the grey water from shale and mudstone areas are clearly distinguishable. Intense rains also alter the geotechnical properties of slope materials, increasing regolith contents beyond both the plastic and liquid limits and so inducing material failure, slumping and mudflows.

Most of Yunnan's croplands are located on the central plateau. The main cash crops are tobacco and tea, while maize, rice, wheat and potatoes are the main food crops. Soils are typically Ultisols (US taxonomy) – deep, highly leached, weathered and acidic soils common in the humid tropics and subtropics. Ultisols are distinctive for their deep red colour (produced by intense oxidation of iron oxides) and so are denoted as Red Soils in Chinese soil classification. Agriculture relies on the summer monsoon rains, usually with over 80 per cent of the annual rainfall falling between May and September. Annual rainfall varies between about 600 mm in dry valleys to 1700 milimetres in the mountains (Thomas 1993). The monsoon rains are highly variable in terms of their amount, reliability and erosivity. Intense convectional

Plate 12.2   Severe gully erosion, Yuanmou county, August 1994

storms, embedded within the general southerly summer monsoonal airflow, are particularly erosive. Erosion episodes are rather brief, often lasting less than an hour. However, their cumulative effects can be very damaging; for instance, Plate 12.2 shows severe gully erosion on Ultisols in Yuanmou County.

Superimposed upon the geologically and geomorphologically unstable environment of Yunnan Province are anthropogenic influences. The Yunnan Plateau has been inhabited since 4000 BP. The province's population (40 million in 1996) and increased population pressure has encouraged the intensification and extension of agriculture. This has led to deforestation, cultivation of steep erodible slopes, overcultivation and adoption of unsustainable farming practices. About 10 per cent of land (38,209 square kilometres) is categorised as severely eroded (Chen 1989). On the basis of studies of lake sedimentation rates, Whitmore *et al.* (1994) suggested that erosion rates have increased fifteen-fold over the last few centuries. Poor land management, cultivation on steep slopes, deforestation and lack of conservation have contributed to soil erosion and decreased soil fertility (UNEP 1990). The forest cover of Yunnan declined from about 60 per cent in the 1950s to 24.2 per cent in 1990 (UNEP 1990).

Strategies for soil conservation on cultivated land in Yunnan

Regional policies

It is evident that rapid, effective and low-cost solutions to erosion problems are necessary for the maintenance of sustainable agriculture. Efforts to combat erosion are underway. The Yunnan Soil Conservation Service, at its headquarters in the provincial capital of Kunming, attempts to formulate soil conservation programmes. These are usually planned at a local scale, with agricultural advisors and soil conservation technicians implementing conservation in the province's counties (of which there are 127).

The local-scale, planned approach to soil conservation can be illustrated using Dongchuan as a case study. Plate 12.3 shows the characteristic environment of the area. Instead of adopting a broad plan, specific areas are targeted for conservation. A conservation plan is devised and land use zoned on the basis of ecological principles. Thus, upland areas above 1800 metres in altitude are planted with pines, particularly Yunnan pine (*Pinus yunnanensis*), while lower slopes are stabilised with eucalyptus trees. Middle sections are planted with flax, which is harvested to make rope. The flax harvest is limited with the consent of the

Plate 12.3   General view of uplands at Dongchuan, August 1993

local population, thus allowing them to gain an economic stake and interest in conservation activities whilst ensuring agricultural sustainability. The provincial government then funds engineering structures, such as diversion channels, to control and regulate storm torrents. Adjacent to the flood diversion structure in Plate 12.4 is a pomegranate orchard, located on a stabilised slope. Some of the funds from the orchard are used to pay for conservation work. A similar approach is adopted in Xundian county, where provincial government finance assists in the afforestation of eroded lands with chestnut trees. The local population benefits from the chestnut harvest and pays 8 per cent of income in tax, and this revenue is then used for further agricultural and social development within the County.

Dongchuan and Xundian illustrate some important principles. Soil conservationists have been accused of regarding conservation simply as an engineering problem. Engineering is a crucial component of a conservation plan, but economic and social factors must also be considered. It is essential that an effective dialogue develops between the conservationists and local people. The involvement, support and participatory agreement of the local population are crucial. Coupled with economic incentives, rewards and benefits by the implementation of

Plate 12.4 Diversion channel for mountain runoff and adjacent orchard, Dongchuan, August 1993

conservation strategies, sustainable agriculture and effective conservation are achievable. Thus, soil conservation and economic development can work together as mutually beneficial aims. Successful soil conservation strategies consist of a complex amalgam of engineering, technical, social, economic and political considerations.

Soil conservation and runoff plot studies

To contribute to the development of appropriate soil conservation strategies, a runoff plot study at Yunnan Agricultural University (Kunming) is evaluating the effectiveness of various soil conservation measures. Maize (*Zea mays*) is one of the most common food crops in the province, occupying 23 per cent of the total cropping area (Thomas 1992). Cropping treatments typically employed in local agronomic practices are used and have been applied to erosion plots on three different slopes, cultivated both parallel and perpendicular to the contour, thus simulating a range of agricultural conditions on arable slopes in Yunnan. The aim of the project is to identify treatments that conserve soil and soil fertility, while maintaining or enhancing crop yields.

The plot study is a joint research project between Yunnan Agricultural University and the University of Wolverhampton (Fullen *et al.* 1996). The network of thirty runoff plots was established on arable Ultisols on the experimental farm of Yunnan Agricultural University, 12 kilometres north of Kunming. The farm is located at an elevation of 1930 metres and so climatic conditions are moderate, with mean monthly temperatures ranging between 22.1 °C and 9.1 °C. Rainfall is monsoonal, with an annual average of 1035 milimetres. The plots have been established on the silty clay soils since April 1993, with 10 plots on slope facets of approximately 3 (Class I), 13 (Class II) and 31 degrees (Class III). The plots are planted with maize and five separate cropping practices employed (Figure 12.1). A common treatment in Yunnan is the covering of part of the soil surface with clear polythene sheeting, to increase crop productivity by conserving moisture and increasing soil temperatures. Therefore, one treatment is polythene mulch (i.e. a clear polythene sheet covering approximately 80 to 90 per cent of the soil surface). Other treatments include wheat straw mulch (applied at 0.4 kilograms per square metre), conventional tillage with no mulch, intercropping with soya beans and zero tillage. Each treatment is repeated with planting parallel and perpendicular to the contour. Reported erosion rates include the 1993, 1994 and 1995 cropping seasons.

Plot results have shown that erosion rates are temporally highly variable and closely related to rainfall erosivity. For instance, precipitation

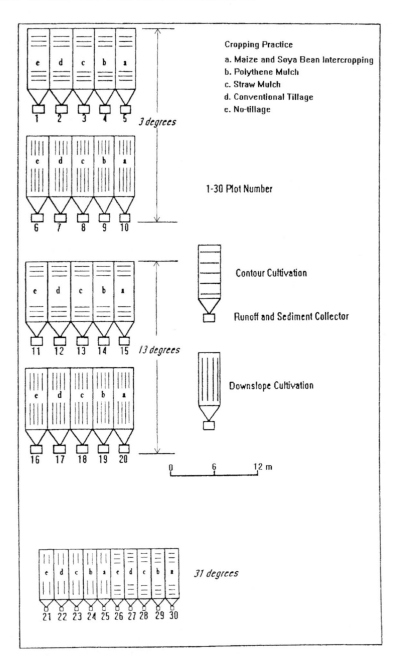

Figure 12.1   Plan of the Kunming runoff plots

Table 12.1   Erosion rates on the Kunming plots for the 1993, 1994 and 1995 cropping seasons (tonnes per hectare)

Treatment	1993	1994	1995	Mean
Intercropping	0.70	3.24	7.65	3.86
Polythene mulch	0.83	6.98	8.72	5.51
Straw mulch	0.59	1.36	1.66	1.20
Conventional tillage	0.73	4.02	11.81	5.52
No tillage	0.78	4.39	7.95	4.37
Total	3.63	19.99	37.79	
Growing season rainfall total (mm)	576.3	768.3	817.8	

Note
Values are means of six plot values.

amounts increased by 33.3 per cent from the 1993 to the 1994 growing season (Table 12.1). Total plot erosion rates increased by 550.7 per cent from 1993 to 1994. Comparing the 1993 and 1995 seasons, rainfall amounts were 41.9 per cent greater in 1995, but erosion rates increased by 1041.0 per cent (Table 12.2). Both the 1994 and 1995 seasons, especially 1995, were particularly notable for erosive convectional storms, embedded within the summer monsoonal airflow

Conservation treatment, direction of cultivation and slope all influenced erosion rates. The average rank order of treatment effectiveness in diminishing erosion rates was: 1 straw mulch, 2 intercropping, 3 no tillage, 4 conventional tillage and 5 polythene mulch (Table 12.1). Erosion rates were generally less on plots where contour cultivation was used (Table 12.2). From these data, it can be suggested that straw mulch and contour cultivation are particularly appropriate for soil conservation. Straw mulching is not widely practised in Yunnan and plot data suggest its adoption is advisable. Polythene mulch produced greater above-ground biomass, probably by retaining moisture and increasing soil temperatures, but these beneficial effects were offset by adverse effects on erosion rates. The impermeable plastic mulch surface prevented infiltration and erosive runoff then flowed over the adjacent bare soil between the sheets, causing higher erosion rates. Therefore, on balance, results suggest polythene mulch is inappropriate for long-term soil conservation, especially on steep slopes and particularly when treatment is perpendicular to the contour. Plot erosion rates increased markedly with slope, which indicates that the use of steep upland slopes for arable cropping is unsustainable. The use of contour

Table 12.2 Effect of slope and direction of cropping on mean erosion rates (mean of 1993, 1994 and 1995) (tonnes per hectare)

Surface treatment	Inter-cropping	Polythene mulch	Straw mulch	Conventional tillage	No tillage	Total
Cultivation across slope						
3 degrees	0.89	1.5	0.57	1.27	0.90	5.13
13 degrees	1.80	3.25	1.24	5.25	4.41	15.95
31 degrees	5.03	9.51	1.63	5.73	7.91	29.81
Cultivation downslope						
3 degrees	1.29	3.01	0.61	0.93	1.03	6.87
13 degrees	5.93	6.23	1.13	5.80	3.64	22.73
31 degrees	8.75	10.06	2.02	14.16	8.34	42.83

cultivation on moderate to steep slopes helped decrease erosion rates, and it appears the effectiveness of contour cultivation was positively related to slope angle.

Conclusions

Soil erosion is produced by a complex interplay of environmental and anthropogenic factors. In Yunnan it is seriously depleting the soil resource and poses a threat to sustainable agriculture. Soil conservation is essential, but its implementation requires consideration of a range of engineering, technical, social, economic and political issues. To some extent, demands for increasing crop production and soil conservation are conflicting, and measures must be found to establish an acceptable balance. Runoff plot studies indicate a number of simple, inexpensive conservation measures are very effective, especially straw mulch. Polythene mulch appears to increase erosion rates compared with conventional tillage and does not seem appropriate for sustainable agriculture on steep slopes. Generally, contour cultivation decreased erosion rates, especially on steeper slopes.

Acknowledgements

The joint research project between the University of Wolverhampton and Yunnan Agricultural University was funded by the British Council (Hong Kong), Yunnan Provincial Science and Technology Commission, the University of Wolverhampton and Dr Han Suyin. We thank the students of Yunnan Agricultural University for their assistance with plot studies.

References

Barrows, H. L., McCracken, R. J., Miller, R. J., Oschwald, W. R., Shiflet, T. N. and Willis, R. R. (1982) 'Report on China: An American View of How that Nation Manages its Soil Resources'. *Journal of Soil and Water Conservation*, 37(6), 315–18.
Brown, L. R. (1984) 'The Global Loss of Topsoil', *Journal of Soil and Water Conservation*, 39(3), 162–65.
Cao, Y. Z. and Coote, D. R. (1993) 'Topography and Water Erosion in Northern Shaanxi Province, China', *Geoderma*, 59, 249–62.
Chen Yongzhong (1989) 'New Progress of Study on Soil Erosion in China' (in Chinese), *Soil and Water Conservation in China*, September, 7–11.
Douglas, I., Gu Hengyue and He Min (1994) 'Water Resources and Environmental problems of China's Great Rivers', in D. Dwyer (ed.) *China: The Next Decades* (Harlow: Longman) 186–202.
Dregne, H. E. (1992) 'Erosion and Soil Productivity in Asia', *Journal of Soil and Water Conservation*, 47(1), 8–13.

Edmonds, R. L. (1994) *Patterns of China's Lost Harmony. A Survey of the Country's Environmental Degradation and Protection*. (London: Routledge).

Fu Bojie (1989) Soil Erosion and Its Control in the Loess Plateau of China, *Soil Use and Management* 5, 76–82.

Fullen, M. A., Mitchell, D. J., Barton, A. P., Hocking, T. J., Liu Liguang, Wu Bo Zhi, Zheng Yi and Xia Zheng Yuan (1996) 'Soil Erosion and Conservation on Subtropical Arable Ultisols in Yunnan Province, China', *International Erosion Control Association, Proceedings of Conference XXVII*, Seattle, March, 315–24.

Min Tieh, T. (1941) 'Soil Erosion in China', *Geographical Review*, 31, 570–90.

Parrington, J. R., Zoller, W. H. and Aras, N. K. (1983) 'Asian Dust: Seasonal Transport to the Hawaiian Islands', *Science*, 8 April, 195–97.

Robinson, A. R. (1981) 'Erosion and Sediment Control in China's Yellow River Basin'. *Journal of Soil and Water Conservation*, 36(3), 125–27.

Thomas, A. (1992) 'Agricultural Water Balance of Yunnan Province, PR China: Agroclimatic Zoning with a Geographical Information System', *Agricultural Water Management*, 21, 249–63.

Thomas, A. (1993) 'The Onset of the Rainy Season in Yunnan Province, P. R. China and Its Significance for Agricultural Operations', *International Journal of Biometeorology* 37, 170–76.

UNEP (United Nations Environment Programme) (1990) *China Conservation Strategy* (Beijing: UNEP and China Environmental Science Press).

Wen Dazhong (1993) 'Soil Erosion and Conservation in China', in: D. Pimental (ed.) *World Soil Erosion and Conservation* (Cambridge University Press) 63–85.

Whitmore, T. J., Brenner, M., Engstrom, D. R. and Song Xueliang (1994) 'Accelerated Soil Erosion in Watersheds of Yunnan Province, China', *Journal of Soil and Water Conservation* 49(1), 67–72.

Zhao Songqiao (1986) *Physical Geography of China* (New York: Wiley).

13
Erosion in Deep Gorges: The Leaping Tiger Gorge on the Upper Yangtze

David Watts and Zhou Yue

The Hutiaoxia (Leaping Tiger) Gorge is located in Henduan Mountain region of Yunnan province in the south-west (Map 13.1). This part of the Qinghai–Tibet Plateau in southwest China includes east Tibet, west Sichuan and north-west Yunnan, and is bounded on the west by Burma. It is transitional between this plateau and the lower Yunnan–Guizhou Plateaux (Zhang 1992), as well as the eastern end of the Himalayas (Ives & Messerli, 1990). A number of large rivers cross the region, including the Salween, the Mekong, and the Jinsha (the upper Yangtze). The last runs across the region from the north-west before turning abruptly to the north-east to enter the gorge proper in its middle reaches.

Physical environment of the Gorge

Geology and landforms

The gorge is located on the eastern side of the zone of contact between the Eurasian continent and the South Asian block (Zhang 1992). Its tectonics are extremely active and complex. Rocks are essentially Devonian (Palaeozoic), with some Carboniferous strata and Permian strata and basalts. The exposure of this series arises from the fact that the present Yulong Shan and Haba Shan mountain ranges form a large north–south anticline, the origins of which date back to late Miocene earth movements (Lacassin *et al.* 1996). Mica-schists and marbles are perhaps the most commonly exposed rocks in the anticlines. It is generally understood that the course of the Jinsha river in the gorge is antecedent to the growth of the great anticlinal fold (Ren 1959; Sheng 1965; Lacassin *et al.* 1996), the maximum uplift of which took place after the end of the Pliocene. During and since the Quaternary, the

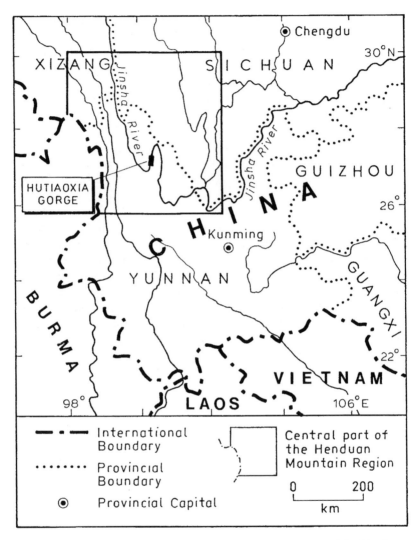

Map 13.1   Location of Hutiaoxia Gorge and the central part of the Henduan Mountain region

Qinghai–Tibet plateau has continued to rise intensively, creating a large difference in attitude between it (average elevation is 5000 metres) and the lower Yunnan-Guizhou plateau (average elevation 2200 metres). This difference allows a substantive headward erosion of all rivers within the region, and further results in a large number of valleys and alpine gorges of different types (Li 1992). In the Jinsha the Gorge cuts through the centre of the Yulong Shan–Haba Shan anticline, with the Yubong Snow Mountain (5569 metres) on its south-east side, and the Haba Snow Mountain to its north-west (5369 metres): since the water surface of the river lies at around 1750 metres, the elevation difference in the gorge amounts to a minimum of over 3600 metres, making it one of the deepest in the world.

The gorge itself has developed into a sharp, V-shaped and asymmetrical form (Figure 13.1 and Map 13.2). The topography on the south-east side is precipitous, most areas being massive cliffs of exposed rock, with the average slope gradient being in excess of 45 degrees. On the north-west side, slopes are slightly more gentle, with a mean slope of around 35 degrees: most areas are covered with talus of different sizes, including landslides, debris flows and alluvial fans. Erosion is an ever-present threat everywhere in the gorge. On a vertical basis, there are however some subtle differences in slope and erosion potential on the north-west side, for traces of valley shoulders at between 2200 and 2800 metres can be found in the middle section. These shoulder traces form an area of relatively gentle slopes, on which gorge residents have built their villages and farm the land. There is consequently a 'valley

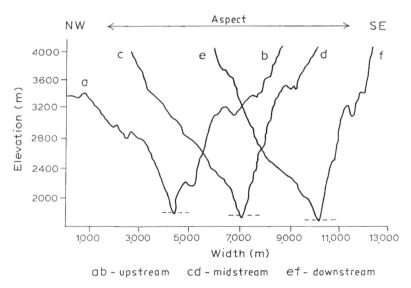

Figure 13.1   Landform of the Hutiaoxia Gorge: cross-sectional view

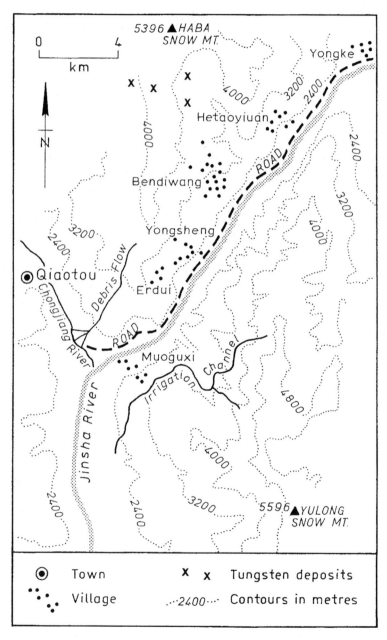

Map 13.2 Contours and anthropological factors in the Hutiaoxia Gorge

within a valley' (Figure 13.1a), and this has considerable significance for the development of soil and vegetation, and the general pattern of human activities.

The entire gorge is roughly 20 kilometres in length, and the river runs between 30 and 60 metres wide, occupying the whole bed of the gorge throughout the year. The vertical drop from end to end of the gorge is *c.* 200 metres.

Climate

Although the actual climatic conditions in the gorge vary considerably from place to place, the overall climate may be classified as subtropical plateau monsoon: it is warm, but has both dry and wet seasons (Yunnan Institute of Geography 1987). During the rainy season (early June to Mid-October), conditions are determined by the south-west monsoon, a damp and warm airstream coming from the Indian Ocean; in the dry season, the weather is controlled by the southern branch of the West Stream, a dry inland airflow originating in tropical and subtropical areas of West Asia and the Middle East.

The rainy season can be divided into three stages. The early stage is high-intensity, when the intensity may reach 33 milimetres in an hour: although the total precipitation in this stage is lower than in the other two, the intensity ensures that a great amount of soil erosion is caused each year. The middle stage produces heavy and frequent rain, in August and September: it results in the greatest amount of rainfall and creates a number of landslides and debris flows annually. The last stage is characterised by lighter but frequent rain. Every year, too, there is a short rainy period in March, which local people call the 'small rainy season'. The dry season usually has fine and dry weather.

Values taken in the decade 1978–88 indicate that the mean annual precipitation is 853.4 milimetres at the upper end of the gorge, and 585.4 milimetres at the lower end: inside the gorge it is somewhere between the two. For instance, in 1993 (our own recordings) the total rainfall was 740 milimetres, with 71 rain days. There is, however, a good deal of variability in annual precipitation, dependent on the strength and duration of the monsoon.

The two sets of high mountains on each side of the gorge serve to obstruct the free passage of both the south-west monsoon and the West Stream, which then concentrate on the gorge. This is therefore windy throughout the year, but especially so in the rainy season, when it is dominated by the south-west wind. The earliest recorded wind data are for 1993, when the monthly mean wind speed during the rainy season was 1.4 to 1.6 metre per second, with a maximum of 8.1. A daily maximum speed of over 6 metres per second was frequently recorded from June to September. As may be expected within the gorge, a series of local climates prevail, about which little is yet known. With such a difference in altitude it is however warmer and drier at river level, and cooler and wetter upslope, especially above 2800 metres.

Soils

The slope materials on both sides of the gorge are affected by gravity and flowing water, and are very much subject to downslope move- ment. The parent materials generally are slope wash and collapsed material, developed from a range of bedrock, which includes marbles, schists and basalts. The soils themselves vary considerably in proper- ties, depth and extent of development, and do not have uniform char- acteristics. Soil depth varies with the nature of the parent materials, angle of slope, and extent of erosion, fertility, however, normally is good for plant growth.

Both zonal and azonal soils are found in the gorge, although down- slope movement usually ensures that none has a complete profile. The zonal soils (Cinnamon Red: Red; Yellow–Brown Earth; Brunisolic) are all widely distributed in the Jinsha river basin (Li 1992). According to the local government, Cinnamon Red Soil is found between 1800 and 1950 metres in the gorge, Red Soil between 1900 and 3000 metres, Yellow–Brown Earth between 2500 and 3000 metres, and Brunisolic Soil between 2500 and 3200 metres: there is, accordingly, a broad vertical differentiation of these major soil types. Because of variations in micro- climate, the red soil group may be differentiated further into Dark Red Soil, and Regosolic Red Soil. The Dark Red Soil is found on relatively gentle slopes, with gradients of 20 to 35 degrees, and an elevation of 2000 to 3000 metres: it develops in a relatively stable environment and is close-textured, with a poor water permeability, relatively poor aera- tion, and a weak acid-to-acid reaction. The Regosolic Red Soil is distrib- uted in the same elevation range, but is more scattered, and found mainly on the steeper slopes and on collapsed material: it contains a large quantity of stones, to a level that is often 50 per cent more than the total soil weight. Both Red Soils have a good fertility status, if they are not severely affected by natural or human processes.

Natural vegetation

The composition of flora in the gorge is very diverse, owing largely to its great vertical range, its location at the meeting point between the two large plateaux and the transition that results. Overall, the gorge is dominated by Chinese–Himalayan elements, with tropical elements in the lowest altitudes, and subtropical elements in the middle ranges of elevation (Yunnan Vegetation Editorial Board 1982). Some species, like *Antiotrema dunnianum*, are endemic to the Jinsa river catchment, and *Nouelia insignis* forest is a unique subtropical community, endemic to the gorge (Chou 1992).

Vegetation pattern is differentiated, predominantly on a vertical basis (Figure 13.2), into six main communities. The lowest (I: 1750–2000 metres) is essentially zerothermic and azonal, suited to the local gorge environment, with its dominant species, *Nouelia insignis* (the only species in this woody genus), forming a very open forest. Somewhat higher (III) is the most conspicuous vegetation community within the gorge (2000–2900 metres), the *Pinnus yunnanensis*, a zonal pine forest that is also widely distributed in south-west China at these altitudes. Between I and III are two related, xerothermic subgroups forming a *Cyclobalanopsis* – oak–pine mix (II. One, a *Cyclobalanopsis* – *Quercus* forest, is part of the widespread, zonal, subtropical evergreen, broad-leaved forest of southwest China; it used to grow commonly in relatively wet and shady gullies in the gorge in the past, but is rare now. The other is a *Cyclobalanopsis* – *Pinus yunnanensis* mixed forest, with an ever smaller distribution area, mainly on relatively even slopes with gradients of 25 to 30 degrees. The edaphically controlled *Nallootus*

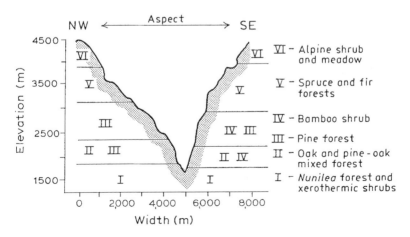

Figure 13.2 Specific vertical distribution of the Hutiaoxia Gorge vegetation

phillipensis shrub community is mixed in with the two *Cyclobalanopsis* communities, mainly on marble talus: it grows densely and serves often as a barrier to rolling stones. Above the talus, *Pinus yunnanensis* forest pine is gradually replaced by spruce *(Picea likiangensis)*. Finally, another edaphic community, dominated by the shrub *Sinarundinaria nitida*, is distributed in a large area, mostly on the shaded south-western bank, and on steep slopes.

Local documentation and oral tradition suggest that natural vegetation was little changed by human impact until the 1940s. Moreover, many of the larger animals including bear, deer and boar were frequently seen. This is much less the case today.

Human impact on the natural environment

Human impact on the gorge environment began in the 1880s, when a group of Naxi people (a national minority based in Yunnan) moved in (Rock 1945). They hunted wild animals, and undertook some cultivation. Although they were joined later by other immigrants from Yunnan, Sichuan and elsewhere, population growth in the gorge was slow, at least until the 1940s (Figure 13.3).

During the early 1940s, a nomadic tribe of Yi people came into the gorge, and burnt forest for farming, or simply for hunting animals. After two or three years, they would move on to other sites, and burn and farm again in a form of shifting cultivation. Then, in the later 1950s and early 1960s, following the national Great Leap Forward (1958–61), some of the more erosion-prone slopes were cultivated, and two big projects (an irrigation channel and a road) were constructed. Not only was forest cut for these projects, but a large amount of soil was excavated, and many engineered slopes produced, all of which in turn created serious soil erosion, and some mass movement. The final phase of economic development took place in the 1970s, when tungsten deposits were found: since then, the area in the vicinity of the main mine has seen seriously affected by digging, timber cutting, and the dumping of waste soil and rock materials.

Today, in the Hutiaoxia Gorge there are 1107 people in 167 families (data from a local government survey in 1994). Most live in the middle and lower sections of the northwest slopes, mainly in three villages: Yanchajiao (elevation 1900 metres), Bendiwan (2600 metres) and Hetaoyuan (2000 metres). Only six families with about 30 people live on the southeast side, since most slopes there are too steep for cultivation. The total area of land farmed in the gorge is 99.13 hectares,

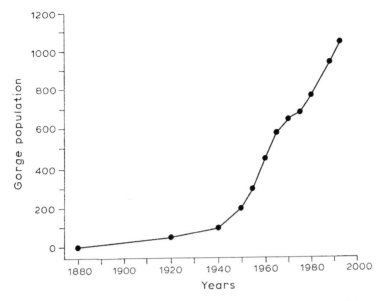

Figure 13.3 Hutiaoxia Gorge population growth (according to statistical data of the local government)

almost all of it below 3500 metres. These cultivated lands are scattered, and the slope gradient ranges in the main from 25 to 30 degrees: the main crops are maize, wheat, potatoes and rice. There were 651 horses and cattle, 3326 goats and 1025 pigs (1994 data, above). The total income in the gorge reaches the equivalent of around £47,000, of which mining accounts for 5.71 percent: the average annual per capita income is around £42.

Vegetation retogression

As a result of these varying human impacts on the gorge environment, the natural vegetation has been partly destroyed, a notable reverse succession has evolved, and some new communities introduced and maintained by man have become prominent (Figure 13.4). Today, the *Cyclobalanopsis – Quercus* forest has nearly disappeared, and the distribution of the *Pinus-Quercus* mixed forest and the pine forest has contracted. The *Nouelia insignis* community now is limited to occasional sites, rather than being the intermittent belt it once was. The upper-slope *Picea likiangensis* forest has been replaced in many parts by a secondary shrub and grass community. In contrast, the areas of

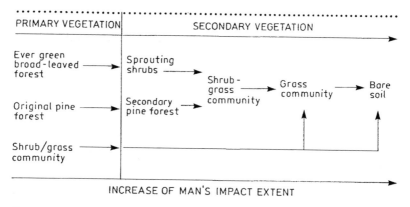

Figure 13.4   Retrogressive succession of vegetation in the Hutiaoxia Gorge

cultivated land, and abandoned or waste land, have expanded, especially in those areas near villages, or with relatively gentle slopes, and much of this expansion has been at the expense of former pine forest (Map 13.3), in the manner indicated in Figure 13.4. The main example of new communities introduced by man into the gorge (other than grassland communities) is that dominated by the shrub *Elsholtzia rugulosa,* which is developed widely on abandoned cultivated land between 1950 and 2700 metres elevation.

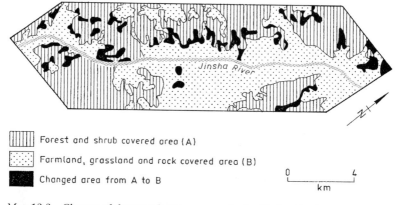

Map 13.3   Change of the pine forest coverage in the Hutiaoxia Gorge over thirty years (1961–1990) (drawn based on 1996 maps and 1990 air photographs)

Accelerated erosion

In recent years, accelerated soil erosion has been a further manifestation of the effects of human impact, being attributed largely to deforestation, cultivation, overgrazing and civil engineering projects, and occurring mostly from farmland, or from badland on steep slopes. According to measurements taken during the rainy season in 1993, the soil loss from experimental plots within the gorge is 29.28 grams per square metre in the pine forest, and 57.93 on bare land, both very high figures. However, soil loss from the grasslands was relatively low, at only 6.95 grams per square metre.

Increased drought

Vegetation retrogression and accelerated erosion also has resulted in changes to the mountain hydrology. In the 1940s, there were 34 brooklets and streams of different sizes running seasonally or year-round (Rock n. d.): today, only 16 still exist, and no more than five run year-round.

Total environmental degradation

Two major levels of environmental degradation can be identified in the gorge (Table 13.1). Level A is a light level, normally confined to vegetation and usually reversible. It develops fairly frequently because vegetation is especially sensitive to human impacts. Level B is at a more serious and fundamental level, usually resulting, at its greatest extent, in unrecoverable destruction of the environment.

Two general processes governing these changes in the environment may be inferred. One is stabilising, in which there is not much human influence present. In this, while geological (natural) erosion occurs, the gorge vegetation grows well, and the soil develops at a faster rate than it erodes. Both vegetation and soil support each other, and the natural environment develops positively. The other is the degrading process, in which human activities are deeply involved. Once the gorge vegetation, the natural protective layer, is disturbed or destroyed, serious accelerated erosion results. This erosion in turn limits plant regrowth, and prevents vegetation redevelopment, which might limit soil loss. The two processes coexist, and the relative dominance of one over the other determines which way the environment changes, positively or negatively. At present, in many parts of the gorge, the negative process is dominant.

Currently, three zones of environmental degradation may be categorised within the gorge, according to the above parameters (Map 13.4).

Table 13.1 Two levels of human inpact on the environment in the Hutiaoxia Gorge

Impact level	Results of impact	Reversibility of impact
Level A (primarily on vegetation alone)	(i) small and temporary changes in species composition, population, growth status of plants	Recoverable
	(ii) obvious and more permanent chanves in the type of vegetation and the natural succession	Conditionally recoverable
	(iii) all vegetation removed	Difficult recovery
Level B (on both soil and vegetation)	(i) natural vegetation partly replaced by secondary or cultivated vegetation; changes in soil properties; heavy accelerated soil erosion	Difficult recovery
	(ii) secondary vegetation heavily destroyed; forest and shrub disappeared	Non-recoverable
	(iii) both soil and vegetation removed; desertification	Non-recoverable

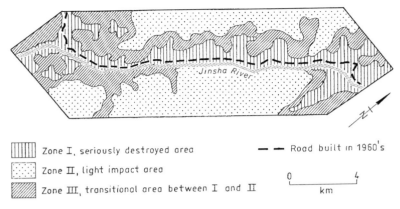

▥ Zone I, seriously destroyed area	— — Road built in 1960's
▦ Zone II, light impact area	0 ⸺⸺ 4
▨ Zone III, transitional area between I and II	km

Map 13.4 Regionalisation of human impact in the Hutiaoxia Gorge

Zone I is the main district of human occupancy, and also an area of serious degradation. Natural forest has been replaced largely by farmland, secondary shrub or grass communities, and abandoned or waste land. Here, retrogressive vegetation succession is most obvious. Zone II is one of light human impact. It is customarily inaccessible owing to its steep slopes or location, being some distance away from settlements. Light human impacts include animal grazing, and forest litter collection for mulching. Zone III is transitional, between the other two, in which activities such as temporary cultivation, tree felling, frequent forest litter collection, and frequent animal grazing, occurs at differing intensities from place to place. The broad-based forest has largely been replaced by mixed forest, and the pine forest, and there is some accelerated erosion.

Environmental treatment and improvement

In response to the gradually deteriorating environment, not only in the gorge but also in the Upper Yangtze catchment as a whole, both central and local governments have set in train a large-scale campaign for environmental treatment and improvement in the Jinsa River watershed. Land use patterns have been adjusted, and forest and other vegetation has been planted, so as to curtail erosion and stop the general environmental degradation. A natural reserve has been established in the Hutiaoxia Gorge. To cope with the further exploitation of water resources and hydrology by the growing population, which may cause even more environmental problems, both governments and academic institutions are undertaking a series of research projects on environmental issues and land use, in order to better make use of available resources in a balanced way, as between necessary development and environment.

In this research, the main concern is with how to protect gorge slopes under the human and environment circumstances that currently prevail. Apart from possible engineering measures, the use of vegetation as a means of controlling soil erosion and stabilising slopes in itself has been attempted as an alternative approach. Over the last few years, research into the effects of the pine (*Pinus yunnanensis*, French) forest on slope protection in the gorge has been conducted by the Yunnan Institute of Geography, with which both authors are associated.

Results show that the pine forest can play a significant role in slope protection, to the extent that soil loss in the forest is 50 per cent less than on non-vegetated land. Some other conclusions are indicated in Table 13.2. Forest canopy will intercept incoming precipitation to mean values of 31 per cent, implying an equivalent reduction of rainfall below the canopy available for erosion and infiltration, which is beneficial to both surface erosion control and slope stabilisation. Raindrop splash is also reduced by 32 per cent, which also further reduces erosion possibilities. The presence of pine roots, especially laterally close to the soil surface, mitigates the potential sliding force of mass movement, and so additionally stabilises the soil.

Conclusions

Under the prevailing circumstances of geology and geomorphology the Hutiaoxia Gorge of the Jinsa River has, potentially, a severly unstable environment. This is particularly easily destroyed, especially by human impact that on flat or gently sloping land would do little damage. Under natural conditions, and even with some natural erosion, the gorge is able to keep its environment in a good state through its self-maintenance patterns of well-established vegetation and soil, and a unique biodiversity. These patterns now face an increasing challenge each year, in the face of population growth and economic demand, and, if not resolved, the challenges can lead to severe environmental degradation.

Table 13.2 Summary of the hydrological and mechanical effects and their significance in the Yunnan pine forest: experimental results from the two sites

	Significance in	
Effects	*Soil erosion control*	*Shallow stabilisation*
Hydrological effect		
1. The canopy intercepts rainfall by about 36 to 37%.	B	B
2. The canopy weakens splash potential of raindrops and reduces splash detachment by a net amount of about 19 to 48%.	B	N
3. The canopy creates leaf drip splash which increases splash detachment during the later rainy stage by 59 to 161%.	A	N
4. Overall, the forest reduces the ultimate soil loss by about 43 to 50%.	B	B
5. Possibly, the root system depletes soil water and then reduces soil moisture	B	B
Mechanical effect		
6. By modelling, the lateral roots increase soil sliding resistance notably at depth of 0 to 60 cm, with the greatest value of 4194 to 4513 N on the set vertical cross-section area at 20 to 40 cm.	B	B
7. By direct testing, the lateral roots exert a tractive resistance in the uppermost soil layer by 421 to 577 N on the set cross-section area, an increase rate of 33 to 38%.	B	B
8. The lateral roots increase in-plane tensile strength of the uppermost soil zone by at least 4.2 to 5.8 kPa.	B	B

B – beneficial effect; A – adverse effect; N – no direct effect.

References

Ives, J. D. and Messerli, B. (1990) *The Himalayan Dilemma: Reconciling Development and Conservation* (London: Routledge).

Lacassin, R., Schauer, U., Leloup, P. H., Arnaud, N., Taponnier, P. Liu, X. H. and Zhang, L. S. (1996) 'Tertiary Deformatroy and Metamorphism Southeast of Tibet: The Folded Tiger Leap Decollement of Northwest Yunnan, China', *Tectonics*, 15, 605–22.

Li, M. S. (1992) 'Land Resources and Their Rational Utilisation in the Dry Valleys', in: R. Z. Zhang (ed.) *The dry valleys of the Hengduan Mountain Region* (Beijing: Science Press) 134–40.

Ren, M. E. (1959) 'Problems of Geomorphology and Capture in Jinshe River Valleys', *Journal of Geography* 25.

Rock, J. F. (1947) *The Ancient Nakhi Kingdom of Southeast China* (no publisher data).

Sheng, Y. Z. (1965) *Geomorphology of the River Valleys in the Upper Reaches of the Yangtse river* (Beijing: Science Press).

Yunnan Institute of Geography (1987) *Yunnan Geography* (Kunming: Yunnan Press of Science and Technology).

Yunnan Vegetation Editorial Board (1982) *Yunnan Vegetation* (Beijing: Science Press).

Zhang, R. A. (1992) *The Dry Valleys of the Hengduian Mountain Region* (Beijing: Science Press).

Zhou, Y. (1992) 'A Newly-Discovered Vegetation Type in the Hutioxia Gorge, China: The *Nouelia insignis* Community', *Global Ecology and Biogeography Letters*, 2, 126–32.

Zhou, Y. and Watts, D. (1997) 'The Traction Effect of Lateral Roots of *Pinus yunnanensis* on Soil Reinforcement: A Direct In-Site Test', *Plant and Soil*, 190, 77–86.

Index